Broken Silence
of the Elite

by

Laushaun Robinson

In loving memory of my grandparents
Beatrice and Herbert Britton

Printed in the United States of America

ISBN: 978-0-615-34966-4

Library of Congress Control Number: 2010925720

Contents

Acknowledgments

I'D FIRST LIKE TO GIVE THANKS TO THE ALMIGHTY CREATOR, BECAUSE WITHOUT Him and His ever-loving grace and patience, life itself wouldn't exist. Thanks, Pastor T. D. Jakes, for your messages from God (I am grateful) and Steve Harvey and his show every morning. Next, I'd like to thank Minister Fred McGRay and Pastor Leroy Henry, and all those who have supported me in the creation of this autobiography. I'd like to give a special thanks to my children; sorry that I didn't include you all in the actual story, but please know that you were there with me the entire time ... every step of the way. I love you! A very special thanks goes to my mother, Barbara Sue, who never stopped believing in me. I am appreciative for all the support you gave me that made this endeavor a reality. Thanks to the greatest rapper in the world, my nephew, Damien Benjamin a.k.a. Show, I believe in you! To my man Alvin "Supreme" Jones, thank you, you were a vital part of the process. I'd like to give another special thanks to my attorney Mr. Robert "Bobby" Smith; I am ever so thankful for all that you have done and continue to do in my favor. You have been very vital to the process that I know without a doubt that this project would be at a standstill; you easily are the greatest of friends and I hope that will never change. Thank you so much Bobby.

Special thanks to the two people who I believe saw something in me worth saving even when I may not have; it is because of you two that I began the process of truly waking up and seeing that my life has a purpose and hope for a future. First, Federal Judge Raymond Jackson; though you sentenced me to prison, I now know that it was a blessing truly in disguise, and one that has afforded me the opportunity to see past all the obstacles that were in my path and that kept me in a mind frame of negativity. Next, there is the prosecutor in my case, Ms. Laura Evaheart, who took it to the wire and saved me from my then destructive self. Thank you both and may the blessings of our Lord be upon us all. I would also like to thank Cindee Brickhouse and Martin a.k.a. "Chuck" Bondmen of the seven cities; thanks for the support. To my second mom, Christine Britton, who has been like a first, thanks for your unconditional love. T-Love, thanks for keeping it 100; I got you. James Sugg, thanks for being a great friend and giving me assistance. Wahida Clark, thank you for providing me the necessary tools to succeed in publishing. To Attorney Coats, thank you for your assistance and legal guidance. John Wilson, thanks so much for your professional and technical expertise. Thank you, Melissa Smith, for being my eyes, I appreciate you for taking a walk in my shoes. Last but not least, thank you, Pamela Hardy, for believing in this project; you're the greatest!

May we be reminded of the Serenity Prayer: God grant me the serenity to except the things I cannot change, the courage to change the things that I can, and the wisdom to know the difference.

Mr. Willie L. Robinson

Prologue

What's up 1st am 100% and I have love for you and your family and after going through this shit a real friend is hard to find and I want waste a person time never again in life. I just did a show for H.B.O that will be on T.V. November 25 and after that the book people will find me you know. I have info about Barry Bond, Marion Jones, Bricks (kilos), Boy (heroin) and so many people but that's in do time. I got you and we will work together but 1st you have to touch 2nd with the best agent and then but you on after what happened to me out there. I pray 1st and think 2nd and then do 3rd so take your time and you will be bless and 9 yrs I should only have 5 yrs do to the cut and out of 5 yrs I will have to do 3 yrs at most and if New York come back and help out I will be free by Aug 2009. My people are very smart and went into protection mode but if I wanted Gonzalez, I could have got him when I was out there. but God is going to handle them. I am out of VA am going to take my time planning where should go and who you should miss with. We are all we got. This is what make real friends.

When you come from bottom to the top but **ATL** is the spot and from then **MIA** and play it real low key just taking care of family only. I have put everything in god hands so I am ready when I get free. I wish you had this plane we you 1st came home but god plane is god plane. I am going to study and over think my every move so I need to sat something up for you when you get home far as money so I am got to start that. Now I am going to put you with a girl I know. Will her man is my dude and he is **100%**. She is **100%** but I will give you the run down on what to do when we get a line. I got to stop my pen game up but it's a time to talk. My goals in my life have improve. I am working on some new land. I will let you know soon so when you get home things will be good **ATL** or **MIA.**

If we stay here, we will be right back in the same place. I am trying to sell my half the club and the boat plus other things. So don't worry but I will never come back here in no one jails but I am trying to get a phone call to you but I am new to this so give me some time and I will make something happen. I am the realest nigga you ever you will see.

Love
Tim

SITTING IN MY prison cell, I struggle to read one of the first letters from Tim Montgomery. I wondered, *How did a man so illiterate graduate from Norfolk State University with an actual degree?* Hmmm, his letter takes me back to what brought us both to prison in the first place …

Before you begin reading about my journey, I want to start by saying that although no one may ever know who I am or even care that I exist, I am going to tell the truth, the whole truth and nothing but the truth! Scandals and secrets will be revealed that many celebrities, athletes, and entertainers don't want you to know about. Secrets including involvements of the BALCO (Bay Area Laboratory Cooperative) scandal, money laundering, and drug trafficking from some of the biggest celebrities; including Olympic Gold Medalists Tim Montgomery and Marion Jones; baseball's great Barry Bonds; my ex-brother-in-law, NFL cornerback Dre Bly; Tony Gonzalez, the manager of the platinum rap artists, The Clipse; and many more.

I was the 'inside man' to many of these celebrities; I have done many illegal and unjust things to make them millions; but when I needed them the most, they were nowhere to be found. I have served a prison sentence of eleven years for my crimes and I have repented for all I have done. Therefore, I have nothing to lose and everything to gain by telling you my story.

I know this book is going to change lives in many ways; lives of the celebrities and all of you, the readers. Every person in this book has a story they want to hide; however, skeletons in their closets will be revealed and people will finally know the truth. These celebrities will be exposed for the unlawful crimes that they have committed. I am "Breaking the Silence of the Elite" … and you will never see these celebrities the same again.

Chapter I

No One Wants to Be the Villain

ONE DAY, JAMAR CAME TO VISIT ME TO CHOP IT UP ABOUT SOME IDEAS THAT he had for a clothing line. Since he was Tim's brother, and Tim and me were just like fam, we trusted each other to discuss ideas for future business ventures. After we had been talking a while, our conversation diverted to his brother, Tim Montgomery, and his relationship with the once Gold Medalist sprinter, Marion Jones.

"How is Tim coming along after all that has taken place?," I asked, but received a cold stare instead.

"He's finding it very hard not being in his son Monte's life!"

"Why is that?" I asked out of concern. I didn't understand … if you do the crime, then you have to do the time. He knew what he was getting himself into and the consequences that could have prevailed.

As he sat up in the small plastic chair, getting comfortable, he looked me straight in the eye and said, "You know about Marion having to go to prison over the $5 million check scam, right?"

"Yeah, who hasn't heard?" I knew that thanks to Tim's testimony, Marion would actually be doing some hard time behind bars.

"Well you also know that she had to return her gold medals too then, right?"

"Yeah, but what does that have to do with Tim not seeing his son?" I asked.

"Marion is pissed. She has hard feelings towards my brother because of how everything went down. So she ain't trying to let Tim see Monte. "

"She can't just disown Tim and deprive him from being a part of his son's life, can she," saying it more as a statement, than a question.

"Well that's what she's doing. She's trying to save her face and redeem her status by continuing to deceive the public."

Looking at him in confusion, I asked, "How's that? All she did was inform the public that she never knowingly used steroids. What's wrong with that?" I didn't understand how she was trying to save face.

"C'mon now Shaun, you know I used to live with Tim and Marion in North Carolina. We used to train under the same coach."

"Okay—and your point is what? What does that have to do with her lying?" I asked, still not understanding what he was trying to say. After staring at me for a few seconds longer than I could handle, he walked over to me, got so close to my face that I almost couldn't breathe and in a low, deep, vicious tone he said, "NO ONE WANTS TO BE THE VILLAIN!"

Then things took a turn; he started the Q&A games on me. "Did you watch the Oprah show that Marion did once she was released from prison? She was telling her side of the story, which was a bunch of bull if you ask me, and she even had the nerve to totally disown my brother. Can you believe it, Shaun? She even has Monte calling her husband, 'daddy'." I shook my head and told him I never saw the show, but I was sure I could find it on YouTube. I was very interested to hear what she had to say about the whole situation … How she felt about going to prison behind her involvement in the $5 million check scam … I also wanted to know about the BALCO scandal and the athletes that were being accused of using the steroids.

Jamar continued to speak; he was so livid; it took everything in me to calm him down. "All she said on the show was that she didn't do it. She completely bypassed the whole subject on national television. She just sat up there and lied to all her fans. She was sitting on stage acting like she was the victim, when in fact, they all knowingly cheated when they got involved with BALCO, because everyone wanted to be the best."

After standing there with a frustrated look on his face, he then continued, "When you looked at the photos of her and Tim at the house, could you not see the damn difference?" I could see a hell of a difference between the photos of her then versus now. In the pictures they had tremendous muscle mass, but I had assumed that the weight gain had just come from the proper weight training, diet, and protein intake. I thought that's how everyone got "buff" these days.

As I sat there quietly for a few seconds taking it all in, Jamar continued to enlighten me on the many celebrities that were involved with the BALCO scandal. Some were the industry's highest respected artists and managers. I was shocked at the behind the scenes "underworld" of illegal activities that went on with the elite. When he told me that Tony Gonzales, manager of the platinum rap artists "The Clipse", was indicted for conspiracy to distribute cocaine, tons of marijuana, and money laundering, I was floored. Especially since Tony Gonzales and Tim Montgomery were business partners in a lucrative nightclub called Encore Night Club. Tim's testimony was the reason for Gonzales' indictment in a $10 million conspiracy.

As I headed back to my cell, I thought about all the friends and associates I knew who were indicted or convicted of charges. A long time associate Pernell Peace, a.k.a. "P Funk", and NFL superstar

Michael Vick were also indicted for playing a major role in an underground pit bull fighting ring. This was right after a federal government indictment of kingpin drug lord "Willo" for distributing hundreds of kilos in the Tidewater, Virginia area. After raids in several homes of Willo, the government found video evidence of the dog-fighting ring, which clearly implicated Pernell torturing numerous dogs on Vick's property.

Trying to save himself, Willo informed the Feds of his association with Pernell and the heavy ties to Michael Vick. Searching for a super siege indictment, Vick was forced to stand up and accept his role and responsibility in the illegal ring. Being as loyal as he could, Pernell tried holding ground and protecting Vick's career, until all fingers were pointing to him. Feeling like he was backed into the corner, Pernell had to "rat" out Vick; or so it seemed to the public, when all in all, Willo tore the operation to shreds for a lesser charge.

Man, so many people are being taken down by being wrapped up in this underworld shit. I then looked at myself in the reflection of the glass window in my door, and said aloud, "Taken out of the game, just like me."

"No one wants to be the villain!" I remembered Jamar saying to me while we were engaged in a deep conversation. Out of everything that he said to me during his visit, that statement is what stuck in my head and will probably stay there forever.

Chapter 2

My Dream Is to Be Just Like Uncle

AT NORFOLK GENERAL, A 3LBS 8OZ BABY BOY WAS BORN TO BARBARA Robinson and Willie Britton. Because I was not given a name, the hospital called me "Baby Unknown." Addicted to heroin and premature, I had to be kept in an incubator for the first four months of my life. It wasn't until the fifth month that I was in the hospital that my father finally took me home to be with my mom and my five siblings.

Growing up, I was the darkest of six children. My father was a heroin addict and abusive towards my mother. As a result, I always received the backlash of his abuse. Resembling my father, my mother always reminded me of how much she hated me and how she could not stand the sight of me. Even though my mother said these things, she was still my momma and I loved her unconditionally. However her harsh treatment of me, she taught me at an early age in my childhood how to fend for myself by making a way out of no way.

I lived in the projects of Diggs Park in Norfolk, Virginia. There, I was a student at a middle school where I was placed in a special education class because I was classified as Learning Disabled (LD). Although I was classified as LD, I did not let it hinder me from excelling in school. I did well in all my subjects, but my favorite subject was math. I loved to add, subtract, multiply and divide; I had an uncanny ability to manipulate numbers and quickly, I began to figure out ways to use my skills for my benefit.

In my neighborhood, there were numerous candy stores where I could buy gum and candy for little of nothing and double my profit. Calculating what I could get from the kids at school, I started to get my hustle on. So before the little yellow bus would come pick me up in front of the house to go to school, I would steal coins from my mother's purse and buy a bunch of candy from the corner store. When I got to school I sold it to the kids and made my money. Throughout the year, kids would do anything to get their hands on what I had. They would buy it at double price; give away their lunches and even place-advanced orders for the next day. They would stop at nothing to get the candy that I sold them, and I would stop at nothing to get my money. Although my mother nicknamed me 'Bookie', the kids at school nicknamed me 'Candyman'.

I would save up my money and place it under my mattress; when I finally had enough stashed away, I would run out and buy the best jeans or sneakers that money could buy. However, the hustle did not last as long as I planned—my teacher called home to inform my mother of my 'candy business'. When I got home, my mother interrogated me, "How in the world did you get the money to buy the candy in the first place, Bookie?" After I confessed everything, my mother whooped my ass for stealing from her purse and selling the candy at school. It's clear to say, my 'candy' hustle stopped immediately.

After my teacher killed that hustle, I started going to neighborhood grocery stores to help customers take and load their groceries to their cars. Staying until almost dark, I would wait until I saw someone with several grocery bags. I would approach them with,

"Hello, Ma'am or Sir, would you like for me to help you with your groceries?" For as many that would say yes, and for the few that would say no, I would always tell them in a sweet, innocent voice, "You don't have to give me anything for it." Even though I would tell them this, they would still give me a coin as a tip anyway.

Soon I learned that the first of the month was the best time to hit up the grocery store. I made the most money helping people with their groceries at this time of the month because everyone had gotten his or her welfare checks or social security checks, so money was plentiful. For the slow days, I would bring home no less than $5, but on days around the first, I would pull in $50 or more. Just like I did when I was selling candy at school, I would put the money underneath my mattress and save it all to buy the latest fashions and clothes.

During Christmas, I would always buy my own gifts since my mother always used the same excuse when it came around, "I'll buy you a bike or some toys during the first of January when I get my next check, okay Bookie?" Therefore, I had to make sure I had my own. I never bothered to spend my money on toys, because I was never into things like that. Why? I was never introduced to toys—so it just really didn't even matter to me. Although I was never into things like that, the few times that I did try to ride one of my brothers' bikes or play with the race car tracks, someone would run and tell my mother and I would hear her yell, "Bookie, give him that damn bike back."

Growing up as a child, no one ever taught me anything. I always taught myself. Instead of bringing my homework home, I would do it at school as fast as I could so that I could hit the grocery stores up when school let out. Every night I would come home, my mother would ask, "Where have you been all damn day and where is your homework?" Of course, I always had an excuse. "I was at my friend's house and we did our homework together, momma." I would tell her, knowing she would never check behind me since my teachers never called home and complained about my grades.

One day while cleaning up my room, my mother found almost $100 under my mattress. Coming in the house as happy as can be, my happiness was interrupted with her standing at the door with my bag of money and a barrage of questions. Unable to explain how I got so much money, I had to tell the truth. Crying, I told her that I was helping people at the grocery store. I then laid it on thick by explaining to my mother that she gave me no choice but to do it because she never bought me anything. Right when I thought my story would work, I got the shit smacked out of me and landed on the floor. Trying her best to continue whooping my ass, my oldest brother stepped in to save me. "Don't hit him anymore, momma! I'm sick of you treating him like this." Furious, she tried to swing on him, but he grabbed her arm before she could land a punch. Unable to contain her rage, my mom ran into the kitchen, grabbed a knife, and told us, "Get the hell out of my house!" Trying to calm our mother down, my brother walked over to her and before we knew it, she swung the knife and stabbed him deep in the shoulder.

Scared for his life, I ran to the next-door neighbor's house to ask them to call the police. "Please ... I need an ambulance to help save my brother, he's been stabbed and he's bleeding really badly." When the ambulance finally arrived, the police were already there caring for his wounds. After putting my brother in the ambulance and sending him off to the hospital, the police handcuffed my mother and put her in the police car. The officers finished taking the evidence out of our house and before they took my mother off to jail, they introduced a social worker to us. Everything seemed to be happening in a fast forward mode. I was overwhelmed—my mom was being hauled away by the police for stabbing my brother—and now social services. What are they going to do with us? Then before I even knew what was happening, my question was answered—social services was taking us into custody.

While my brother was in the hospital for several days with a stab wound just a few inches away from a main artery, my dad's sister saved us from the system by letting us stay with her. My aunt took custody of us, because the court deemed my mother as an unfit parent and sentenced her to one year in jail. For the next two years, our aunt was our foster care guardian and we were officially properties of the state. I adjusted to living with her quickly, especially since her husband was a major drug dealer who I admired.

His name was Ricky and I got the opportunity to ride with him everywhere he went. I remember when I used to ask if I could go with him I would use the 'puppy dog face' to emphasize how bad I wanted to hang with him. And it worked every time! He would tell me, "Boy, your aunt's gonna kill me if she finds out I'm taking you with me."

If it was one thing I couldn't stand, it was sitting around the house watching television; I would do any and all chores that needed to be done to keep busy. If the grass needed to be cut, I did it. If the cars needed to be washed, I washed them. I volunteered to do everything and in return, Uncle Ricky would give me money and take me shopping all the time.

I can remember one day when my uncle came to pick me up after school. When I walked out of the school doors, I noticed a big white Cadillac parked right in front. As I walked further down the walkway, I noticed all the kids admiring the big white wall tires and I heard many of them say, "That's the kind of car I want when I get big." Boy was his car clean; you would have thought no other car existed in the parking lot the way the kids were starin'.

As I walked up to the car, he got out to greet me. I loved my uncle because he was always so clean. Uncle Ricky was wearing his red silk shirt, a black three-piece suit with a matching pair of Stacy Adams. His neck was adorned with a few gold chains and he wore a couple of rings on his fingers. The final addition to his ensemble was his jui-ceee 'Ready for the World' Jerry Curl hanging down. Everyone thought that I looked more like his son than his nephew, which to me, was a compliment.

I walked up to him and curiously asked, "Uncle Ricky, where are we finna' go? Are you gonna take me home?"

"Yeah, I came to take you home. I'm here to pick up my favorite nephew," he said as he gave me a handshake. I felt like I was on top of the world.

While pulling out of the school parking lot, I felt a sense of security come over me. I thought to myself, *Uncle Ricky makes me feel secure; he was being the father figure that I'd never had in my life.* Riding home with the radio blasting Earth, Wind and Fire, my mind went into a daze. I started thinking of my mom . . . *I would love to see her.* It had been a year since I'd seen her face and just the thought of her not being present brought tears to my eyes. Then I started to think about my life and how it was when I grew up. Things were tough. And at that moment I had a revelation ... *No more tough times for me—for my mom—for nobody in my family. I want to be—no I'm gonna be just like Uncle Ricky. I'm gonna buy my mom a big house and a nice car.*

From that day forward I was determined to do what I had to do, to make my vision come true. I started asking Uncle Ricky questions about the game so I could follow in his footsteps. However, every time I asked him a question, he would always say, "You don't wanna be like Uncle Ricky, Bookie. Uncle Ricky breaks the law." I didn't care what laws he broke, he was ballin', and I wanted to be ballin' just like him. Even though he would respond the way he did, I still asked him numerous questions that a child my age shouldn't have been concerned with; and although I didn't expect him to, he was always brutally honest with me.

I can recall one day when we were riding together. I noticed he had a big Ziploc bag and many brown envelopes in it. We made several stops and with each stop, he would take out several envelopes and hand them to his friends. In return, they would hand him a wad of cash. I was so curious about how he did his business, but I figured I'd reserve my questions for another time. Instead, I just sat there and observed him while he counted his money before placing it into his pockets. As we drove up and down Church Street, people would wave at Uncle Ricky as if he was a celebrity. I was so amazed at the power that he had around town. When we drove through, he would either blow his horn at people or pull over to the side of the road and do some quick business.

After Uncle Ricky was finished handling his business, he would take me shopping. He would always buy me the newest Nikes or Calvin Klein jeans that were out. He always kept me looking nice! I could always depend on my uncle; every day after school like clockwork, he would be there to pick me up. My relationship with him boosted my self-esteem. I felt like he wasn't just my uncle, he was my pops. He always told me to be the best at whatever I did and I took that to heart.

I continued to do well in school and always stayed fly. Fly to the point that I was considered the best-dressed kid in middle school. Not only that, I was also considered the most popular kid in school. However, I knew the only reason why everyone wanted to hang around me was because they thought my pops was rich. Kids thought by hanging with me that they could benefit and get a piece of the pie.

After a year had passed, it was time for Moms to get out of jail. The day of her release, my uncle had taken us all to pick her up. We were so excited to see her as we rode in the car. While on the ride to pick her up, he informed us that although we all loved our mom and respected her, we were welcomed to stay with him and my aunt. Before my uncle could even get the sentence out of his mouth good, I was the first one to blurt out, "I wanna stay with you, Uncle Ricky." Everyone looked at me, as if I was crazy. I felt awkward until he turned around, looked at me, and said, "You're my little man. My home is always your home, always." I smiled both externally and internally as he kept talking to the others.

When we arrived, I saw so many police cars around the building that it started to make me nervous, not for me, but for my uncle. However, before we exited the car, he placed his ziploc bags in the glove compartment and safely locked it. After twenty minutes of sitting in the lobby, I finally saw my mother exit the elevator. Before the door could open completely, I heard her scream, "Oh my God, my kids!"

As we all ran over to our mom, we started hugging and kissing her all over; telling her how much we loved and missed her. After we all finally calmed down, my uncle walked over to her, kissed her, and said, "Welcome home, Barbara!"

"Thank you for watching my kids, Ricky." It reminded me of a tearjerker scene in a movie; all the emotions were definitely there.

As we walked back to the car, I noticed that my mom had gained a lot of weight while locked up. Even her hair had gotten longer. As we rode in the car, I noticed that we weren't going in the direction of my aunt's house. Soon we were pulling in front of some new brick apartments. Uncle Ricky turned off the engine and told us to come inside. As we walked in, I was confused on where we were headed. I thought that maybe it would be another drop, but I knew that he wouldn't do a drop with everyone in the car. As he pulled out a set of keys, he handed them to my mom and said, "Barbara, this is for you and the kids." She was so touched that she immediately started crying, which was understandable considering she had no idea where she was gonna live with us kids. The apartment was fully furnished, including food in the refrigerator. I was happy for Moms because all of our possessions were stolen after the police took her to jail a year earlier. Everything was great! My mother and siblings had a place to call home.

As we sat there, reminiscing about the good ol' days and catching up on old times, I heard Uncle Ricky say, "Barbara, I gotta run but I'll bring their clothes over tomorrow." I almost tripped over my own foot jumping up and letting it be known that I was going with Uncle Ricky.

"Is it okay if Bookie goes with me?"

My mom looked at me and asked, "Boy, don't you wanna spend time with your mama?" For as bad as I wanted to spend time with her, I wanted to spend time with Uncle Ricky too. I was confused because I felt torn between the two and didn't know what to do.

I looked at my uncle and then back at my mother and said, "Yes momma. I wanna spend time with you."

Looking at me, I could tell that Uncle Ricky understood my pain. "I'll see you tomorrow. Bookie, pick your head up and tell your mom how well you've been doing in school and what your plans are when you get big." I knew that was his way of getting my spirits back up and I was thankful for that. I smiled and gave him five as he exited the house.

For the next few hours, we sat in the dining room and started telling Mom about everything that took place over the past year that she was gone. Starting to get hungry, she headed to the kitchen to fix one of her famous home cooked meals that we all missed so much. Mom called us to the table and my mouth began to water looking at the fried chicken, collard greens, mashed potatoes, and homemade rolls. I sat down in the chair and thought … *We are a family again.* While my mom blessed the food, she thanked God for sheltering us while she was gone and giving her a chance to reunite with her family again. After saying amen, we dug into our delicious meal and continued to talk about our school accomplishments and how well taken care of we were by Uncle Ricky.

The next morning, Uncle Ricky surprised us with clothes for school. As he placed the boxes down, he yelled for us to hurry and get dressed so he could drop us off at school.

My eyes widened knowing that he had kept his word about coming back to get me. After getting dressed, our mom kissed us one by one as we exited the house and got into Uncle Ricky's car. Since I was the closest to Uncle Ricky and felt we had a special bond, I yelled quickly, "I'm riding shotgun." To my surprise, no one disagreed. I guess it was obvious about the bond Ricky and I shared. After he dropped my brother and sister off at their school, we had a talk about me living with them. He told me that my aunt had no disagreements with me staying with them as long as I continued to excel in school and complete my chores. Doing those things weren't a problem, because I knew that Uncle Ricky would compensate me for my hard work.

As he dropped me off at school, he gave me $5 for lunch money and I jumped out of the car. Before I walked too far away, I turned around, looked at him, and asked, "Ricky, are you going to pick me up today?"

"I'm gonna pick you up everyday, son," he said as he smiled and drove away. Hearing him say that made my day. I had always felt that he was more my father than he was my uncle, so when I heard him say that he confirmed my feelings. I made it official, from that day on, when someone asked if Uncle Ricky was my father, I would proudly respond, "Yeah, that's my dad."

From then on, I continued to live with my aunt and uncle, which really opened my eyes to the lifestyle of the streets. I watched every action that my uncle made during his daily routines. I noticed him bagging up weed in the bedroom and counting his money. I watched him without being noticed, but a few times I got caught. When that happened, I would hear him say, "Bookie, go outside and play." That made me mad at first, but I knew he was doing it for my own good. When I went outside, I had no intentions to actually play games; I would go and wipe down Uncle Ricky's Cadillac. I'd pretend it was mine, saying to myself, *one day I'm gonna have a Caddi like my uncle!* But as usual, in the middle of my fantasy I would be interrupted. He'd say, "Bookie, I need to make a run. You can finish wiping down the car when I get back." I didn't mind the interruption, because I wanted to go wherever Uncle Ricky did. No matter where it was he was going, I wanted to be right by his side. Before he could even get the words completely out of his mouth, I'd say, "Can I go Uncle Ricky?" Then I'd put on my infamous 'puppy dog face', which worked on him every time.

Uncle Ricky's response was always the same, "Jump in, son" and from there, we would ride out. While making his stops, people would ask who I was, and Uncle Ricky would say, "This is my son, Bookie;" because I was 'his son', people would cater to me hand

and foot. I remember many people coming up to me and saying, "Boy, you gonna' be rich just like yo' daddy, ain't you," then they'd hand me money for no reason whatsoever. I never questioned why they were handing me money; I'd just politely put it in my pocket, smile, and say thank you.

As time went on, our daily routine consisted of Uncle Ricky picking me up from school, making runs to drop off packages, and getting his money from whoever owed him. Our routine became second nature to me after a while and I grew used to the schedule. After making our daily runs, we would then go home and he would hand me all his one-dollar bills and tell me to save them for a rainy day. And of course, after every run, he would make me promise to never tell my aunt that I had been riding around town with him so she wouldn't get upset. I understood that this was 'grown man business' and was determined to keep my mouth shut. Not having kids of his own, I believe Uncle Ricky took to me; therefore, he made sure I was always taken care of.

While Uncle Ricky counted his money, I would sit down with him and we would talk. He would always tell me to make sure I watched what he was doing, because one day he was going to help me become rich so I could buy my mom a house. I felt like he was telling me, "This is what I am preparing you for," but I kept them thoughts to myself. I held on to every one of my uncle's words, I kept them close to my heart and I promised myself that one day I would be just like Uncle Ricky ... or better.

Chapter 3

Ghetto Celebrity

In high school, I began to feel the peer pressure to sell weed ... Having a big time drug dealer as a father, many times, my friends would try to convince me to steal out of his stash so they could have some free smoke. Some even offered to buy it from me. Although the money was tempting, I wasn't going to steal from him; plus I knew that if I asked him, I would get a 'hell no', so I made it very clear that I wasn't getting involved in stealing no weed from my uncle. Many people called me a punk for being scared to steal from my dad, but I knew I didn't have to steal from him. He would give me any and everything I wanted ... Well, almost anything. Plus I had money stashed away with all the one-dollar bills he gave me, so I could buy weed if I wanted, too.

Since money was always on my mind instead of hanging out and smoking weed, I started to seriously consider getting into the game. With all the kids partying, smoking and having sex, I had my own audience ready to get what I had access to ... I knew this could be my chance for a come up. However, I had to convince Uncle Ricky that this was something I was ready to do. I thought long and hard about when and how to approach him, but I wasn't sure it would happen—from that point on, I would no longer stress myself out thinking about getting in the game.

One Friday, our school was having an end of the year dance that I wanted to go to; and since I had never been to a dance or any other school functions before, I really wanted to go. I just needed to ask Uncle Ricky for his permission to attend. I thought to myself, *it's the last day of school, Uncle has to say yes!* The school bell rang and I proceeded to get my stuff together and head out to the parking lot. As I was walking, I was thinking, *I will ask Uncle if I have permission to go to the dance and if he could drop me off and pick me up at school when it's over at 11 o'clock.* As I got to the car a surge of confidence overcame me; I knew I could convince him to let me go to the dance, because I was so responsible.

"How was your day today, Bookie?"

"My day was good … I'm glad today is Friday," I told him, opening an avenue to ask about the dance.

"Because you know it's the last day of school, which is always good," I paused for a minute, but he could tell I had something else to say.

"And … I know that's not all you gotta say, Bookie." Damn, he knew me like a book.

"How you know that, Uncle Ricky?"

"Boy I've been around you all your life. I know you like the back of my hand. Now tell me what's on your mind," he said with a light chuckle. I figured since the mood was as light as it was, I could go in for the kill.

"Well we have this dance at school tonight that starts at 6 and ends at 11. I really wanna go to it Uncle Ricky. Can I please?"

"Bookie, you know me and your aunt are responsible for you. If anything happens to you, I don't know what I would do," he said with one of the most serious looks I'd ever seen on his face as he glared off into space.

"Ain't nothin' gonna happen to me. It's only a school dance. What could happen?" Then I started to think, *what could really go down? The party would be chaperoned by teachers so couldn't too much happen, right?*

"It's not you I'm worried about. It's those nappy-headed friends of yours that will be there. I know what they do Bookie, I'm not stupid now." I had an idea of what he was talking about, but I wasn't going to admit it … at least not right now when I'm trying to go to this dance.

"Alright, if you don't want me to go then I'll just stay at home tonight," I said with a pitiful look on my face. I knew he had a soft spot for me, so I played it to my advantage.

After a few minutes of looking at me, he took a deep breath and said, "I'll tell you what. Since you wanna go to this school dance, I'll let you go under one condition and one condition only." Oh shit, I was worried about what the condition was. He had never given me a condition to do anything.

"Alright, what's that," I said with a little hesitation in my voice.

He looked at me for a few minutes, which started to make me a worried as hell. "I'd like to come with you to the dance, if you don't mind." Hell yeah he could come. All my friends looked up to my uncle... They wanted to be just like him! Smiling, I thought, *I would be the coolest person in the world if Uncle Ricky came to the dance with me.*

"That's a deal!" I said with a wide ass smile on my face. Even though I was okay with him coming, he still wanted to explain why he wanted to come to the dance. He said, "I just want to make sure that you're safe, Bookie."

"Uncle Ricky, it's a dance. What could happen?"

He said, "I am concerned with you experimenting with stuff."

"What do you mean by that, Uncle Ricky?"

"You know, sex, drugs, hell everything that goes with being a teenager. I just don't want you to mess up your life, Bookie."

"I ain't gonna do nothing stupid or anything like that," I said, and then he asked me questions that shock the hell out of me.

"So you wouldn't get any weed from the guys that have been begging you to get it from me? You wouldn't sneak in my stash and steal a little to be the cool kid on the block?"

My eyes got so big. *He knew about that? Damn, I'm happy I didn't go in his stash. I would be in a messed up situation right now.* Playing it cool, I asked, "What are you talking about, Uncle?"

"C'mon Bookie, I'm no fool. You must not remember who I am. Hell, I sell weed to these kids' parents. They know I'm selling, which means they know you have access to it." My uncle was serious; he was talking to me like a man and not just a son. I listened intently as I took in everything that he was saying to me. After he finished, I sat in silence, as we headed the rest of the way home to get ready for the big dance.

That night I had experienced many things for the first time. It was my first official dance and I was so excited. It was also the first time my uncle would be around all my friends, and I couldn't wait to see how they were going to react when Uncle Ricky walked into the dance with me.

While in the shower, I heard my uncle go into my room and then I heard the door shut. I wondered what he was doing, so I got out the shower, grabbed a towel and wrapped it around my waist. Curious, I walked quickly to my room and opened the door. To my surprise, I saw a brand new British Knights sweat suit and matching sneakers sitting on my bed.

"Thanks Uncle Ricky," I screamed from the top of my lungs with exhilaration. I knew he probably didn't hear me though, because he had gotten into the shower.

After getting dressed and admiring myself numerous times in the mirror, I headed downstairs where my aunt was cleaning.

"Where the hell are you going all dressed up like that?"

"A school dance," I told her, looking fresh as can be.

"Who said you could go to a dance?" she asked skeptically as she looked me over.

"Uncle Ricky," I said.

"Really, Bookie," she said with disbelief in her voice.

"Yes, Auntie," I replied. After assuring her that Uncle Ricky said I could go, I knew there wouldn't be any more questions asked, because he was the man of the house and what he says, goes.

"Make sure you don't get in any trouble," she said.

"Oh I won't. Uncle Ricky is going with me." Her mouth flew open so wide; it was like she'd just seen a ghost or something. She stormed straight to the bedroom where he was and opened the door to find him putting on a British Knights sweat suit too.

"Why the hell are you going to a kid's dance?" she asked with her hands on her hips. You could tell that Uncle Ricky was caught off guard, because he almost fell on the bed when she walked into the room screaming.

"Baby, why are you acting like this? The boy asked me if he could go to the school dance, and I told him that he could if I went with him. I'm not going to embarrass him or anything. I just want to see the crowd he's going to be around. I just want to make sure he's safe. You know how these teenagers are these days," he said as he continued to get dressed. My aunt was so mad, I thought that fire was going to come out of her ears as she stormed back into the living room and continued to clean.

As my uncle came walking out of his bedroom, he was looking as fresh as I was. To tell the truth, we looked like we could have almost passed as the Doublemint twins. The only difference was the colors of our sweat suits and sneakers. Mine was black and red and his was black and white with a Kango hat to cover his Jeri curl. My uncle asked me if I was ready to leave and I gave him a head nod for yes. We said good-bye to my aunt, my uncle then grabbed his keys and we headed out the door.

Right before pulling off, he reached over me and went into the glove box of the car. He grabbed a package of weed and said, "I forgot to deliver this earlier, after I'd picked you up from school. We were so busy talking about the dance … " I thought we were going to make a quick stop before the dance, but instead, he took the package inside the house. A few seconds later, he came back to the car talking to himself like a crazy man. When he entered back into the car, he turned to me and said, "Boy you making me lose money today. You know today is Friday." I didn't know what to say, because I didn't know what Friday money meant versus Monday or Tuesday money. I kind of felt bad that he missed out on his money; but at the same time, I felt good knowing that he put his money to the side to make sure his 'son' was safe at his first school dance. That alone told me how much my uncle loved me.

When we got to the school around 7, the parking lot was jam-packed with people going to the dance. There were kids either walking into the dance or parents dropping their kids off at the door. My uncle found a parking space right in the front. He flicked on his blinker and then rolled his Cadillac right into the space, which just happened to be near the front door. I felt like a king. As we got to the entrance of the gym, the lady at the door said, "That will be $4 each, please." Uncle Ricky pulled out his money clip and paid the fee to get in. When we were about to start walking into the dance, one of my teachers who was collecting money stopped us to speak.

"Hi Willie, how are you?" At school, my teachers and peers called me by my first name.

"I'm doing fine, Mrs. Wilcox," I replied. "Oh—and by the way, this is my father, Ricky." I introduced them as they shook hands.

"Pleased to meet you sir, I am so glad you came with your son. Most parents don't even bother to come and enjoy school functions with their children." She continued to tell him how great of a student I was and finished the conversation with, "I hope you enjoy the dance," and then we strutted off.

We made our way to the refreshment stand and bought two orange Nehi drinks. I was about to take a sip of my drink, when I notice two of my classmates heading over my way.

"What's up Willie," they said.

"What's up y'all? Hey, this is my pops." They both then introduced themselves to Uncle Ricky.

"Y'all are looking really fresh sportin' those British Knights suits," they said, sweatin' us.

Then one of my homeboys turned to me and said, "Damn Willie, your pops is cool as hell man." As we stood there talking for a while, I smelled the aroma of weed and noticed their eyes were bloodshot red. Hoping my uncle didn't notice, I complimented them on their Troop sweat suits and then suggested we go near the DJ. While walking over to find a place next to the DJ stand, we watched everyone doing the 'wop' and the 'snake' to Run DMC's "King of Rock."

Getting into the groove of the music, I became aware of some fly young ladies headed in our direction. One of them approached one of my friends and whispered something in his ear. Then all of a sudden my friend turned to me and out of the clear blue sky asked, "Hey Willie, you get high man?"

"Nah dawg, my pops won't allow no shit like that." I quickly responded. Now he has never seen me do anything like that, so why would he ask me now that I'm here at the dance with Uncle Ricky. Blowing off what just happened, I started to dance around and have a good time with my friends, while I watched my uncle sit back and drink his Nehi.

I was having a great time dancing and having fun with my peeps. But before I even realized it, the DJ was announcing that the last dance was approaching, as I heard Keith Sweat's "Make it Last Forever", beginning to blast out of the speakers. Ready to get my groove on, I grabbed this girl named Nicole who was dancing with her girls next to my friends and I; but she started to pull away from me.

"Where are you going?"

"I don't know how to slow dance."

"Of course you do, everyone knows how to slow dance," I told her as she looked at me with her bashful, beautiful eyes. Instead of trying to convince her to dance, I grabbed her hand, pulled her closer to me, and whispered in her ear, "Just follow my lead."

She wasn't as bad as I had expected. I'd put my arms around her waist and she repeated my motion. We both two-stepped the last dance away, gazing into each other's eyes. Through the middle of the song, I noticed that my penis started to grow on her thigh and I started to freak, hoping she wouldn't get upset. But to my surprise, she moved closer and started grooving with me in the same motion. When the song was coming to an end, our lips got closer and closer until we were passionately kissing. After about a minute or so, she revealed a confession to me that both shocked and excited me …

"I have had a crush on you forever."

"I'm feeling you too girl," I said, making sure she understood what I meant by feeling her. After the song ended, I asked her if I could walk her outside. She told me she would love for me to, so we walked hand in hand as I led her and her girls to the parking lot. Before she got into the car, she went into her purse, wrote down her phone number, and told me to call her tomorrow … To call Nicole was a request that I was more than happy to oblige. Receiving one last hug, I gladly said goodnight to her mother and the rest of the girls and proceeded to my uncle's car.

My uncle was patiently waiting for me in the car. When I got inside the car, I said, "Thank you Uncle Ricky for bringing me to the dance. I had a blast."

Uncle Ricky looked at me smiling from ear to ear and then said, "Yeah, I had fun too. I saw the girl you were dancing with. She was cute."

"Yeah she was, wasn't she?" She was better than cute. She was fine.

"I saw you two kissing on the dance floor, you little mack you. Do you like her?"

"Yeah, I like her a lot. I'm gonna call her tomorrow," I told him.

"You ain't ready for no lady yet, boy," he said laughing. I then started to tell him about my friends talking to me about getting high during the dance.

"Yea, I smelled the weed on them when they came close to us," he said, then in a serious tone he asked, "Bookie, you ain't never tried to smoke weed before, have you?"

I knew he was gonna ask me that question, but I was proud to tell him, "No, I never have Uncle Ricky. I'm on a natural high."

"What kind of natural high are you on?" he asked chuckling.

"A natural high of motivation … I wanna get money like you. I wanna be able to buy my momma a house and get a Cadillac just like yours."

Keeping quiet for a second, he dropped something on me that I did not expect. "Son, this game ain't for everyone and I don't want it to have to be an option for you. That's why I give you everything you want. I want you to do well in school. I want you to be an athlete or a doctor or something. You need to be something greater than just a drug dealer."

"I feel where you are coming from Uncle Ricky, but I don't like sports or anything like that. I want to be like you. What's wrong with that?"

Breathing a heavy sigh, he responded, "Okay. I'm not gonna force you to live a life you don't want to. You have to make your own decisions as a man, but I want you to remember this. You can talk to me about any and everything, okay. Do you understand me, Bookie?" he asked looking me dead in the eye.

"I know…that's why I'm telling you now that I wanna sell weed like you. I've even been saving all the money you've been giving me to start up."

"So you still got every dollar that I've ever given you."

"Yeah, I still got every single one."

"Why haven't you used any of the money?"

"Why should I spend it, you give me everything that I want. If I need anything, you give it to me. I don't want this to sound selfish, but why spend my money when I can get it from you." I hoped he understood where I was coming from. I didn't mean it in a negative way, but if I can stack my money and still get what I want out of life, why not.

"I understand what you're saying son," was all he said as we sat in the car listening to the O'Jay's 8 track, "Money Money." As we pulled into the driveway, Uncle Ricky turned off the ignition, looked at me, and said, "Okay son, if this is what you really wanna do, then I'll teach you everything I know. But if I ever hear your mother or aunt finding out that you're getting your weed from me, then that's the end of it. You understand me; because if they ever find out and come to me about it, I'll deny it."

"I understand Uncle Ricky."

"So from now on, I'm not giving you anymore money. I'm not buying you anymore clothes or anything. What I'm gonna do is show you how to make and save money in this game." After the conversation ended, we were home, so I exited the car and headed into the house with butterflies in my stomach.

When the next morning came, I was tired as hell. I couldn't sleep worth anything. All night I tossed and turned while dreaming of the conversation I had with my uncle the night before. When I wasn't dreaming about that, I was dreaming about Nicole, the girl I met at the dance and how I was gonna make her my girl. Man, I wanted her so badly. Lying in the bed, I thought about her and wondered what type of girl she was. I wanted to get to know her better; I needed to call her. I rolled over, grabbed my pants, and pulled her number out of my pocket. Picking up the phone, I dialed her number and the phone began to ring. When someone picked up on the second ring, I started to get butterflies in my stomach as I heard a sleepy voice say, "Hello."

"Uh—hello, may I speak to Nicole?" I asked, scared as shit.

"This is she."

"Are you still sleeping?"

"Oh—oh no, I was just getting up right now," she said, although I knew she was lying. I could tell that she really wanted to talk to me and didn't want me to get off the phone. As we talked on the phone, she told me how much she enjoyed my company the night before and would love for us to go to the movies and see the "Crush." I had heard about that movie, everyone said it was a good, so I was down to go to see it.

"Okay, we can do that. I'll get my dad to drop us off at the mall if that's cool with you."

"Well, you don't have to worry about your dad taking us. I got my driver's permit and I can get my parents' car if you want me to come get you." Hell yeah, I wanted to ride with her. Why wouldn't I want to?

"That's cool. What time do you wanna meet up then?"

"I'm looking at the newspaper right now and there's a five o'clock showing. Wanna go to the five o'clock movie?" I agreed and gave her the directions to the house. After telling me that she wanted me to call her before she'd come over, we hung up the phone and I was floating on cloud 9. I couldn't wait for my date with Nicole.

Jumping in the shower before breakfast, I heard someone calling my name but couldn't make out who it was. After turning off the water, I heard Uncle Ricky yelling for me, so I jumped out of the steaming water and walked out the bathroom to find out where he was calling me from. I walked toward my bedroom and saw him standing there with a paper bag in his hand.

"Is that for me?"

"That shouldn't be the question, the question should be, 'Are you ready for this?'"

"Hell yeah I'm ready!" After listening intently to him, finding out the ins and outs of the drug game, he let me know that he'd already bagged the weed up in separate bags for me and said he wasn't going to charge me for the pound of weed that he was giving me. Uncle Ricky then explained that each bag was an ounce, and was worth $100 a piece. Being good at math, I had already begun to break down pounds to ounces so I knew that there was 16 ounces in a pound. Multiplying that by a hundred, I said, "That's $1600, Uncle Ricky."

"I'm happy to know that you can add!" he said sarcastically, but I knew he was impressed with my skills. He also told me that he would charge me $1000 for each pound that I bought from him, so my profit would be $600 a pound.

He asked, "Can you handle that?"

"Yeah, I can handle it." As he got up to walk out of the room, I reached under my mattress and stopped him. "Hold on Uncle Ricky. I think I got $1000 on me right now."

I reached underneath my mattress and pulled out all the rubber bands I had, each rubber band equaling $50. Uncle Ricky looked at me and said, "What the hell am I supposed to do with all these ones? I never liked counting them, that's why I always gave them to you," he smiled and chuckled.

"Okay, then I'll take them to a bank and cash them in, then when I'm finished selling this, I'll give you $2000 for a supply. How about that?" I asked as he gave me a high five.

"Look son; listen to what I'm saying. Don't let anybody know what you're doing, especially since you're doing business with me. Be smart and I will show you everything you need to know in this game. You hear me?"

"Yes Sir, I understand."

He then asked me if I knew how to drive. As much as I wish I did, I wanted to lie and say 'yes', but I couldn't; I've never even tried it.

"Alright Bookie, I'm gonna sign you up for a driver's course and after you pass it and get your permit, we'll go get you a car."

I was so excited that I gave him another five and a light hug, thanking him. After leaving the room, I got an empty shoebox, put the weed in it, and put the box in the farthest part of my closet so my aunt couldn't smell it.

I looked at the clock and realized it was time for me to get ready for my date with Nicole. Wanting to look good, I started to think about what I was gonna wear. Shit, I had to be fly if I was going to be with the finest girl in school. I decided to wear my blue and orange Patrick Ewing sneakers with the matching sweat suit. Smiling at myself in the mirror, I reached for my Polo cologne that was sitting on top of my dresser and sprayed it on my neck. I was finally ready, now it was time for me to call Nicole and make sure she was fixin' to leave to pick me up.

The phone rang four times before she answered it and said, "Boy, I thought you forgot about me and our date. I was just getting ready to call your ass."

"Nah cutie, I would never stand you up," I told her. After a little small talk, she told me she would be there to pick me up in twenty minutes. Getting ready to meet her outside, I grabbed $100 for the movie tickets and some refreshments. I knew that would be more than enough to do whatever we planned that night.

Exiting the house, my aunt got one look at me and said, "Where are you going, looking and smelling all good?"

"I have a movie date with my NEW friend, Nicole."

"Oh hold on. I know you ain't going on any date with a girl and not introduce me to her?" she said snapping her fingers.

Laughing, I said, "She's on her way right now, when she gets here, I'll have her come in and I will introduce you to her."

"How is she getting here?"

"She's driving her parents' car," I told her with a huge grin on my face. My aunt just smiled and headed into the room where my uncle was bagging his weed. The weed was so strong that you could smell it in the living room. I didn't want Nicole smelling it when she came in to meet my aunt and uncle, so I quickly lit incense to kill the smell.

Within ten minutes of sitting on the porch, Nicole pulled into the driveway. To my surprise, she was pushing a black Fleetwood Cadillac. I couldn't believe it. She had the speakers blasting Slick Rick's "The Ruler." I walked up to the car, helped her out and greeted her with a big warm hug, she said, "Ooh Willie, you smell so good."

We then made eye contact and kissed each other passionately. After our embrace, I invited her inside to meet my aunt and uncle.

"Baby, we gotta hurry up so we won't be late for the movies."

"It'll only take a second, I promise." Heading inside the house, I saw my aunt and uncle sitting in the living room.

"Uncle Ricky, Auntie. This is Nicole. Nicole, these are my parents," I told her in a proud voice.

"Nice to meet you Nicole," they said in unison.

"She's a very pretty girl—don't you hurt my son," Auntie said with a smile, as she shook Nicole's hand.

"All I want to do is love him … that's if he allows me to."

"I heard that girl!" Auntie replied.

"Well, umm— … we gotta get going," I said, as I started to turn and begin to pull Nicole towards the front door.

"Ya'll enjoy yourselves and drive safely," my aunt and uncle said, walking behind us to the door.

Once we got comfortable in the car, Nicole turned to me and asked, "Hey Willie, why do you call your parents Uncle and Auntie?"

"Well they're more like my parents by obligation. They're really my aunt and uncle. I choose to call them my parents because they treat me like their son."

"If you don't mind me asking, where are your parents?" she asked. It was something I never really talked about, but I felt comfortable with Nicole so I told her what was up.

"My mom lives in Chesapeake with my other brothers and sisters and my dad was never around."

"I understand," was all she said and we changed the subject to how much fun we had at the dance last night and how neither of us wanted it to end. Then she threw me for a loop by changing the conversation.

"Willie, do you have a girlfriend?" she asked shyly.

Surprised in a good way, I said, "I thought you were my girlfriend," looking into her eyes and smiling.

"You so crazy Willie—are you for real?" she asked seriously.

"Why, you don't like what I said?"

"No, I love it," she said smiling. "So from here on out, am I your sweetheart?" she asked. I replied by stroking her hair and telling her, "As long as you don't cheat on me," and I meant every word of it.

"I don't get down like that. I've never even been in a relationship with a boy."

Her confession shocked me. As pretty as she was, I knew guys were lined up to get with her. "You ain't ever had a boyfriend, why not?"

"My parents won't let me," she said as she told me how strict her parents were. She couldn't even give her phone number out to guys.

"So why did they let me call then?" I asked, hoping that I was really that special to her.

"Oh, I told them about you last night when they drove me home from the dance. They think you are respectful. In fact, my mom thinks you are a handsome young man and a nice gentleman for walking me and my girls to the car last night."

"So I guess it's official now … You and me, we're connected, huh?"

"Yeah, I guess we are, as long as you don't hurt me either Willie … It goes both ways." I could never hurt Nicole. Even though we were just getting to know each other, I felt like she was my soul mate. My feelings were kind of deep for her, which made me not want to do anything to jeopardize our relationship.

Riding down the road, we continued to listen to Slick Rick's song, "Teenage Love." She turned the music up loud as she swayed her head side to side, saying, "This is my song." Pulling into the parking lot of the mall, we noticed the line was long as hell. Everyone was waiting to see the new movie.

Waiting in line, I was so surprised when she put her hand into mine as we stood there like a couple who'd been dating for months and not just a day. Standing there, I noticed that many couples were dressed alike. Most of them were all over each other, kissing and hugging like they would never see each other again. At the front of the line, I noticed my cousin Scoot and some friends from school buying their tickets. Being the slick guy I am, I grabbed Nicole and led her to the front of the line.

"What up, cuz? Let me and my girl get behind ya'll so we won't have to wait in that long ass line, man," I asked Scoot, giving him and the guys from school dap.

"No doubt ... Jump in," Scoot replied.

While buying our tickets and heading into the theatre, I noticed that Nicole was wrinkling her nose, but didn't know why. I assumed she had allergies until we got inside alone and she whispered, "Your cousin smells like weed."

"Yeah, I noticed too. That's his thing," I told her.

"Do you do that too, Willie?" she asked. At first, I didn't know if I wanted to say yeah to sound cool or just tell her the truth. After a few seconds of debating with myself, I decided to tell her what I told everyone, "Nah, I don't do that stuff. My parents would kill me."

She grabbed my hand tightly, looked at me, smiled, and said, "That's why I like you, Willie. You're not like your friends ... you're different."

Because my cousin hooked us up in line, we decided to wait on him and friends at the concession stand. Man, they were loud as hell, laughing at absolutely nothing. All I could do was just shake my head. When they began to take too long, I gave my cousin an inpatient look. He nodded his head to tell me okay, while he was ordering his food. I couldn't believe it! These mutha fucka's were buying so much food; they could feed an entire damn army. I knew at that point they were high as a kite, especially when they walked toward us and I saw their bloodshot eyes. After they said they were ready, we finally made our way to the top row in the theatre. Reaching out to grab Nicole's arm, I stopped her a few seats away from them.

"Don't you want to sit next to your cousin?" she asked.

"Nah, I don't even wanna be associated with them right now. They're acting crazy," I told her as we spaced ourselves about three seats from them.

The movie started and Nicole laid her head on my shoulder. As the movie went on, she began to rub my leg. I wanted to kiss her so bad, but I didn't want to mess up and make the first move. However, that changed when we happened to make eye contact. I decided that there was no better time to make a move, so I gave it all I had. I drew in close and slowly began to kiss her lips. As our lips began to part and I gently moved my tongue into her mouth, I got bold and started to feel on her breast. Although I thought she would stop me, to my surprise, she let me keep going. I was in heaven—until she started coughing and choking out of the blue.

"Are you okay?" I asked her concerned. She shook her head no and pointed to where my cousin was sitting. I looked over to where she was pointing, and saw my cousin and his friends blowing smoke from their nose and mouths as they giggled and passed the cigar around amongst each other. I was curious about what they had in the cigar … I'd never seen anything like that before, and I wanted to know what it was.

"Hey man, what are you smokin' in that cigar?"

"Man you ain't never seen one of these before? It's called a blunt—wanna hit it?"

"Nah man, I'm straight," I told him as I headed back to Nicole, but he stopped me before I got back to her.

"I see you're handling your business over there …" Right when I was about to answer him, I noticed security heading our way.

"Hey cuz, I think you've been spotted smokin'," I said pointing at the fat security guard as he searched for someone. Right when we looked up, the security guard made eye contact with my cousin and I knew he had an idea of where the smoke was coming from. Plus, it didn't help that the smoke was heavy in our area. I went and sat back in my seat and told everybody to chill out and focus on the movie, but next thing you know, the damn security guard posted himself up against the wall for the rest of the movie. You talking about some nervous dudes … They were sweating like they had just run a 26-mile marathon. It was comedy.

When the movie was over, we quickly headed to the exit to beat the crowd. Seeing that everyone else had the same thought, I held Nicole's hand tightly so that she wouldn't get lost in the shuffle.

As we got ready to leave, once outside, I gave my boys a five and my cousin some dap. Once he was close enough, I whispered, "Hey cuz, when you get the chance, I need to talk to you about some business."

"What's up, cuz? What kinda business?" he asked. I knew he was interested about what I was talking about.

"Just say it's something we can make a lot of money off of," I told him as I tried to walk away. He quickly grabbed me and asked, "Where are you going now?"

"Well I'm going to chill with Nicole for a minute, but when I get to the house, I'll give you a call."

"Aight cuz, I'll be home no later than 11 p.m., make sure I get that phone call," he said as we dapped again and said goodbye.

We got into Nicole parents' car and exited the parking lot; then I turned to her and asked, "Are you hungry, Sweetie?"

"I can stand a bite of something," she said smiling. "Do you like Wendy's?"

"Girl yeah, I love their Bacon Double Cheeseburger and fries," I told her. I was getting hungry just thinking about it.

"Are you serious? I love it too. That is my favorite burger. I can eat them all day," she said giggling as we headed to the nearest Wendy's restaurant.

As we entered their parking lot, I couldn't wait to get inside so that we could talk more privately. After placing our order, which was the same down to the drink, we sat down and enjoyed our meal. We were having a great time until she stated, "Willie, I'd like to introduce you to my parents before I drop you off back home. Do you mind?"

Of course I mind. I didn't want to meet her parents now. I wasn't prepared. I thought this would come later. Now I know she met my parents—but—but it's different when you meet a girl's parents. Meeting a girl's parents is serious and I didn't know if I was ready for that.

"Do—you—think—your pops will have a problem meeting me?" I stuttered, hoping that it would change her mind.

"I already told him about you silly—you're so crazy. My mom spoke highly of you to him. I think he'll love to meet you, but I gotta tell you something." Damn, how she said it, that 'something' did not sound good …

"What's that?"

"I'm his only daughter—so—he's kinda—well—he's very protective of me. So expect a lecture from him, okay?"

Whew, I was almost shitting bricks before she said that. I didn't know what to expect to hear. "That's it … aw girl, I understand. You're just a daddy's girl!"

"So what if I'm Daddy's girl. I'm not a baby," she said as she playfully punched me in the arm as we finished our meal and headed to her parents' house.

Pulling into her community in Chesterfield Heights, I noticed all the houses turned into huge two-story fenced homes. I mean, I've seen some pretty big houses, but these were some BIG houses. As we pulled into the driveway, I saw another Cadillac that matched the one she was driving except it was the extended version.

"Whose car is that?" I asked. It was clean as hell.

"Oh, that's my dad's car. Every year he buys my mom and him a new Caddy. He bought this one for her as a Christmas present." I was amazed. Who had that type of money to buy a new car … and a Cadillac at that?

"Is your pops rich or something?"

"Let's just say he takes very good care of his family," she said smiling while waving me to come inside to meet her parents.

Making our way to the front entrance, her mother opened the door with a gigantic smile plastered on her face. "Hello Willie. Pleased to officially meet you, welcome to our home. Come in—are you hungry? Please have some dinner," she said as we shook each other's hand.

"Mom, we just had Wendy's. We're not hungry," Nicole said, kissing her mother on the cheek. "By the way, where's daddy at?"

"Oh, he's in the backyard feeding the dogs. He'll be in to meet Willie in just a few seconds."

While sitting in the living room, I heard the back door open and close; I knew it was the decisive moment. Even though I thought I would be nervous as hell, I actually wasn't. I was calm. I heard her dad turn on a water faucet in the kitchen; he must've needed to wash his hands from feeding the dogs. Before he entered the room, I made sure I looked presentable enough to introduce myself.

"Daddy, this is Willie. We go to school together and he treated me to the movies," Nicole said smiling as her father entered the room.

"Pleased to meet you," was all he said, as he looked me up and down while shaking my hand.

"Would you like something cold to drink or some sort of dessert?" Nicole's mom asked to break the silence in the room.

"No thank you ma'am. I'm fine," I told her sitting there nervously. You could feel the elephant in the room and I didn't know what to do.

"Well, Nicole and I will leave you two to talk for a little while," Nicole's mom said as she grabbed Nicole's hand and they headed to the dining room. As Nicole was being escorted out of the room, she looked back at me and gave me thumbs up to ensure me that everything was okay.

"So son, how is your attendance at school?"

"It's great. I only missed one day of school in the last three years because I had a bad cold. Other than that, I have perfect attendance," I said feeling confident inside.

"And how are your grades?"

"They are great, sir. I have all A's and B's. My parents don't play when it comes to school." Our conversation went on with him telling me that I was the only guy that has ever come over and that Nicole normally wasn't allowed to date. He told me the only reason I was allowed to be the first … and hopefully last in my eyes, was because of how much of a gentleman I was last night. He actually gave me his blessing to date his daughter. Now who said chivalry was dead!

As he continued explaining the importance of being a gentleman to his daughter, Nicole interrupted our conversation when she returned to the room.

"Dad, are you lecturing Willie?"

"No baby, I'm not lecturing him. I think Willie is a great young man," he said as he hugged his daughter. Score one for the good guy was all I could think as I sat there making sure I controlled my breathing so I didn't look so nervous.

"I knew you would approve," Nicole said with a huge grin on her face.

"It was a pleasure to meet you Willie, make sure you take care of my baby girl," he said as he shook my hand once more.

"Yes sir, I will take care of your daughter."

After sitting and getting acquainted with her family a little longer, I told Nicole it was time for me to be heading home. Plus, I didn't want her to be on the road alone too late. She headed to the dining room and told her parents that she was taking me home and would return soon.

I heard her dad say, "Nicole, don't worry about it. I'll give him a ride home. I have to make a run across town anyway."

What? Oh lord, somebody please pray for me.

"Willie, do you mind if 'Pops' takes you home or do you want your princess to take her prince home?" Nicole asked. I could tell she wanted to take me home badly, but I wasn't going to tell her father no.

"No, I'm cool with your pops taking me," I told her, as we walked from the dining room to the living room. Right before her father came to get me, I managed to steal a hug and a quick kiss from her and I told her, "I'll call you once I get home, okay."

"Okay boo," she said with a sheepish smile and a slight look of disappointment on her face.

Grabbing his briefcase and keys, her father gave Nicole and his wife a kiss on the lips and told them he would return soon. We then exited the house and got inside of his Caddy. When he started the car, Master Flash's "Jungle Sometimes" came on and I wanted to jam to it, but just casually bobbed my head. As he drove he asked me where I lived.

"Campo Stella on Melon Street," I responded.

"Really, my best friend stays on Melon Street. Do you know a guy named Ricky that lives there?"

"That's my pops!" I said proudly.

"Man, it's a small world. Ain't that some shit—boy you are family."

"Yeah we are family; because I'm gonna marry Nicole."

That smile quickly left his face, then he turned to me and said, "Hold on now boy, you're moving too fast. I said y'all could date, not get married. I'm her husband until she moves from under my roof and pays her own bills."

"I know it sounds pretty sudden, but I'm planning to marry her, sir."

"And where do you work?" he asked, skeptical of my future.

"Well, my dad's gonna buy me a house," I told him. I couldn't let it be known that I was selling drugs.

He smiled with the mention of Pops. "Ricky is my right hand man. I hope he's home now."

When we pulled into the driveway, my uncle's Caddy was already parked. When we entered the house, my aunt and uncle were in their bedroom, so I went to knock on their bedroom door to let my uncle know that Nicole's father was in the living room. When I was about to knock on the door, I heard the headboard of the bed hitting the wall and my aunt moaning. I started contemplating whether I should knock on the door or not, when all of a sudden Nicole's father saved the day.

"Ricky, get your ass up, man." Nicole's father yelled through the house.

"Who the hell is that?" my uncle yelled.

"It's Ollie, man! Get your ass up!"

"Aw shit, man. What's up! Give me a minute to slip some clothes on. I'll be in there in a second." While waiting on my father in the living room, Ollie began to tell me how close he was to him.

"Wow, I didn't know that Ricky and Laverne had any kids?"

"Well ... actually sir, I'm not biologically theirs. I call him my dad, because he's been like a father to me for so many years."

"I understand. I can relate because my pops didn't raise me either. I didn't have a father figure around so the streets taught me everything I know, so I understand how you could embrace Ricky as your pops, he's a good man. He's—he's one of my best friends that I grew up on the streets with."

In the middle of our conversation, Uncle Ricky walked out in his silk robe and house shoes, Ollie looked his direction and said, "Man, your son is family. I was just sitting here telling him that we go way back."

Uncle replied, "That's my boy. He's gonna fall into position too, because I taught him well."

Ollie was surprised of the revelation he just heard. "Man, you gotta let that boy enjoy his life before introducing him to the streets. That's what we're out there for so that our family won't have to struggle and throw brick in the penitentiary."

"Man, my son is next in line so you better get used to seeing him, because I'm falling back. I've been running the streets for over twenty years ... I'm tired, man. Ollie, I've been paying lawyers to throw cases and some more shit. My rabbit foot is just worn out. This is the man you will see when you're ready to get more. In fact, Bookie, go upstairs and get that bag from your closet." I couldn't help but look at both men's expressions as I got up. I could tell Nicole's father didn't approve of me doing illegal activity at such a young age. Not to mention that I was dating his daughter.

"Bookie, what you slow poking for? Is that how you gonna move when I send you to deliver?" Uncle Ricky asked, looking at me with fire in his eyes.

"No—no sir," I stuttered and picked up the pace to retrieve the bag.

Coming back downstairs, I heard my uncle and Nicole's father talking about me being next in charge. When I walked back to the room, my uncle introduced me to Ollie like I'd never been in the room less than three minutes before.

"Ollie, this is my son Bookie. Bookie, this is one of my three partners that you'll do business with when I'm done." We both shook hands, then Uncle Ricky told me to give Ollie the weed. When I lifted the bag, Ollie swallowed and extended one hand to grab it and the other to embrace me. As he pulled me closer, he whispered, "Bookie, whatever you do, please don't let my daughter know we're doing business together. She'll lose a lot of respect for her pops. Know what I mean—can you promise me that?"

I stared him straight in the eyes and said, "No problem, Ollie." Then out of nowhere, we heard, "Now, when the hell am I gonna get my $1,600?"

"Man, have you ever had any problems getting your money, Ricky?"

"See the shit I have to go through with these dudes, Bookie?"

"That's my new father-in-law so I'll make sure he stays straight," I told them, making sure they knew I was serious.

"Now Bookie, don't you be a shrewd businessman like your daddy. You hear me." Ollie said jokingly.

"He can't help it. It's in the bloodline," Uncle Ricky said as they laughed.

"Bookie, when you come over to our house tomorrow, I'll give you the money then, okay?" Ollie said as he gave Uncle Ricky and me a handshake while securing the pound of weed in his jacket. He said goodbye and headed out the door.

Right when Ollie left, my aunt came storming out of the bed-room mad as hell.

"Ricky, I know you ain't got that boy selling that shit." Before my uncle could even come up with a story, she said, "I heard the whole conversation, asshole."

Standing there defending my uncle, I said, "Don't be mad at Uncle Ricky, Auntie. You all have been good to me—and—and I'm not a little kid anymore. It's time for me to make my own money, Aunt Laverne."

"The hell you ain't, BOY!" She made sure she emphasized the word boy to make sure I heard it loud and clear.

"Laverne, stop all that damn yelling! Hell, Bookie's gonna do what he wants to do anyway … with or without me. I might as well show him the right way so he won't end up like his friends … or anyone else for that matter. You know kids his age are doing shit worse than this. When we went to the school dance, every last one of them damn kids were high as hell. At least he's not doing the shit."

After sitting there silently for a few moments, she responded and said, "I see I have no say so in this matter. It's apparent that what I have to say don't mean shit, so I'm gonna stay out of it. But I want both of ya'll to know this, if Barbara Sue finds out about this shit, I ain't got shit to do with it." Then she turned directly to me and said, "Bookie, if your ass gets into trouble, don't you come calling this house. I ain't getting you out of nobody's detention center. You hear me?" she said, looking at me angrily. I told her I understood and I had no plans to be in anyone's detention center, because I had Uncle's guidance and he wouldn't steer me wrong.

She looked at me and then looked at Uncle Ricky, spun around on her heels and walked back into the bedroom and slammed the door. Uncle Ricky looked at me and said, "Well, I'll be hearing her mouth all damn night. Don't worry though, I run this house—everything will be alright."

I smiled and sat down on the couch and said, "Uncle Ricky, I wanna learn how to drive so I can get to where I'm going when I need to. Everybody I know has learner permits but me."

"Didn't we already talk about this Bookie? You know I got your back. My partner has a driving class that I'm gonna enroll you into. This guy owes me a lot of favors anyways, so I know he'll take you in. Once you go through the class and learn the rules of the road you will get your permit. Plus, I can't risk you getting pulled over with a bunch of weed on you. So in the meantime, until you get your permit, we gonna go out tomorrow and buy you a scooter so you can get around. How's that sound, Bookie?"

"It sounds cool."

He extended his hand in the air to give me a five and said, "Now let me go in here and calm her ass down. I'll talk to you in the morning and we will go over everything, okay?"

"Okay Uncle Ricky."

Walking upstairs, I thought about everything that took place. I couldn't believe that I was going to be selling weed to my girlfriend's dad. On top of that, my aunt even knew about it. Damn. I started laughing to myself.

Lying in the bed, I wondered what my profit would be for every pound of weed I sold. I knew my uncle was selling it for $1,600, but I didn't know what he was paying for it. He was probably making a killing. I stared at my ceiling for a while, going over the day's events and then—*shit, I had forgot to call Scoot.* I picked up the phone and quickly dialed his number, and then I wondered if this was a good move. My uncle told me to only deal with the people that he dealt with and my cousin wasn't one of them. My cousin answered the phone on the second ring.

"What's up, cuz?" he said, sounding high as hell.

"I told you I'd call you tonight, cuz."

"Hell, I've been waiting about two hours for you to call. I'm supposed to be at Loo Loo's house … You making me miss some loving."

"Now I'm not supposed to tell anyone this, but since you're family and about making a dollar, I wanted to know what you're paying for your weed."

"Hell, too damn much. I'm paying $150 for an ounce of weed."

"Come holla at me tomorrow and we can fix that problem."

"Shit, why wait until tomorrow. I'm out now! I was gonna holla at Jo Jo tomorrow and cop some from him."

"Cuz, just hold on to your money … I promise, it's gonna be worth it. I'll holla at you tomorrow. Okay?"

"Alright cuz, just don't be playing games come tomorrow. I'm gonna be looking for you."

"Cuz, we gonna be rich. Just hold your money. That's all I'm telling you." After we said our goodbyes, I laid back, closed my eyes, and fell into a deep sleep. The day was long, but promising and starting tomorrow, I was going to be a ghetto celebrity just like Uncle Ricky.

Chapter 4

The New Captain

W<small>HEN</small> I <small>AWOKE THE NEXT MORNING,</small> I <small>HEARD THE BIRDS CHIRPING AND SAW</small> the sun beaming through my bedroom window; I could tell it was gonna be a great day. With everything that had taken place, the weekend had gone by so fast. The dance was cool on Friday, and Lord knows I enjoyed myself with Nicole at the movies on Saturday; but the big event that really topped off my whole entire weekend, was the episode that occurred last night between Ollie and Uncle Ricky. That was a trip, but not as much as a trip seeing my sweet Aunt Laverne yelling at Uncle and me. Damn she was pissed. I hoped she was in a better mood, because I did not want to face the wrath again.

Getting ready for my usual Sunday breakfast, I could hear my aunt speaking to Uncle Ricky in the kitchen. It seemed like she was over her attitude from the night before. Uncle Ricky must have finished handling his business from when Ollie and I had interrupted him.

Cautiously, I walked in the kitchen and placed myself at the table. I was surprised when my aunt gave me a big smile and said, "Good morning, baby."

"Good morning Auntie and Uncle Ricky," I said smiling. I thought to myself, I don't know what kind of power Uncle has in him, but he has made Auntie do a 360 in the attitude department.

"Are you hungry Bookie?" Uncle Ricky asked, as he smiled at me and gave me a sly wink. Giving him a nod, I hurried to fill my plate with bacon, scrambled eggs, buttered toast, and grits. Hurrying to sit down, because a brother was hungry; I jumped into my plate like it was nobody's business, then Uncle Ricky looked at me and said, "Tomorrow, we'll go and enroll you into your driving class for your learner's permit, okay."

"Cool," I said.

After I had responded to Uncle, I noticed Aunt Laverne was quickly fixing her plate. When she was finished she walked towards the door and said, "Excuse me from the kitchen men, but I don't want to hear your plans or conversations," and walked out swiftly trying to keep Uncle Ricky from smacking her ass, but had no such luck.

"I love you, Verne."

"Yeah, yeah, I love you too Ricky," was all she said as she walked into the bedroom and closed the door behind her.

I was excited because now it was time to get down to business. As we sat and ate breakfast, he began to explain to me how I profited from each pound of weed I sold.

"Bookie, you give me a thousand and you pocket six hundred per pound. Every two months, my men and I move about 100 pounds ..."

I started calculating the numbers Uncle Ricky was throwing at me. Okay so that's six ... a thousand ... a hundred pounds ... a big smile came across my face and I said, "Uncle Ricky, that's $6,000 every two months."

"What ... is that not enough for you? You don't think you can buy your mom a house with that type of money coming in," he said jokingly.

"Nah, that ain't what I'm saying ... I'm just making sure I'm adding my money up right." In a couple of years I knew I could buy her a house and then some. Man, I couldn't wait to get started making my money.

"See that's why I want you on my team, Bookie. You hella good with them numbers AND you have paid attention to everything that I've told you." I thanked him for trusting in me—for seeing my skills, and continued to listen to him while he said, "I'm proud of you for saving all that money I gave you. You know, most kids would have run out and spent the money before it could have even got in their pockets good. I knew you were about the almighty dollar since you were a little boy selling candy at school and helping people at the grocery store. That told me a lot about you."

I smiled remembering those days … Yeah, I was getting my hustle on as a little boy. Uncle Ricky went on to tell me how those years were my best years, because it taught me responsibility and how to fend for myself and protect my mom.

"Since our first man-to-man talk … You know, when you told me you wanted to buy your mom a BIG house. I knew I would be the one to show you the road to riches and wealth, but there's a flip side to this entire thing, Bookie. There's a lot to learn about the streets—rule number one is you gotta learn and know the law. The law will tear you down." Uncle Ricky started breaking stuff down, taking everything he said in; I learned that although I was still underage, I was still old enough to be charged as an adult, depending on the crime. He told me that I could get sent to this joint called Bo Mount or do time upstate. Continuing to school me on the streets of hard knocks, Uncle ended the conversation by asking me, "Bookie, are you willing to sacrifice your freedom to help yourself and your mom to a better living?"

I understood my newfound profession came with great risk and said, "This is the choice I'm making, so I must reap whatever consequences that comes with making this choice—good and bad."

"I trust and believe in you, son. I know you can get the job done," Uncle Ricky said as he looked me dead in the eyes and gave me a big bear hug. As I looked away from him, he stopped me dead in my tracks.

"Hey Bookie." "What's up Uncle Ricky?" I said as I turned his way.

"Son, whenever you speak to a man, always look at him in his eyes. The eyes will never lie. They'll speak something totally different from the words that come out of his mouth … Those eyes will help you win every battle that you encounter. Do you understand what I'm saying about reading eyes and body language?"

"Yes sir. My mom helped me hone that skill at an early age. I knew when she was mad, sad or getting ready to whip my butt … and I tell you, being able to read her helped me know when to run before she got her switch."

Uncle Ricky chuckled loudly, grabbed me by the shoulders and said, "Well it's the same thing dealing with the streets. Knowing when to attack, knowing when someone is being honest, or the worst … knowing a liar. Because remember, if they tell you one lie, they'll continue to lie to you over and over, so the best thing to do is cut the relationship off when you've recognized the first lie. It may cause you to lose money, or it may even hurt a little. But son, in the long run you'll appreciate your judgment and make even more successful moves in life."

Losing myself in deep thought, I wondered what the game would really be like. My thoughts were interrupted by a loud bang on the kitchen table, as my uncle asked, "Now, is this the life that you choose to live?"

Looking directly in his eyes, I responded, "I'm not going to stop until I get my mom her home." I meant every word that came from my mouth and I knew Uncle Ricky believed me. With every fiber in my body, I wasn't going to stop until I was on top of the world.

After cleaning the kitchen a little bit, Uncle Ricky had to make a few runs and I was going with him. Walking out the door, he yelled to Aunt Laverne, "Baby, if anybody calls take a message and let them know that I made a run to the store and I'll be back within two hours."

Aunt Laverne said in a sarcastic tone, "I know your two-hour runs Ricky, but I'll tell whoever calls what you said." I laughed inside, because I knew we was gonna be gone well over four or more hours and we wasn't gonna see the inside of no store. And it seemed like Aunt Laverne knew it too.

Once outside, we jumped in the Caddy and headed onto the interstate. As we rode, we made a detour, but I didn't know why.

"Where are we going Uncle Ricky?"

"I want to take you to my stash house and show you everything."

Uncle Ricky pulled his car up into a driveway and I began looking around the neighborhood. There were kids playing outside next door—it appeared to be a middle class neighborhood. We exited the car and entered the house. I noticed that it was set up just like the house that he had for my mom when she got out of jail. Looking around, I saw there were bars on the windows from the inside of the house. My uncle was smart because the bars weren't noticeable and it kept the house from looking suspicious. I followed my uncle down a hallway to a door that led to the basement. Once in the back of the basement, he lifted a rug, which covered a safe in the floor.

"Bookie, I'm going to let you place my money in this safe when you're finished with everything, and if you choose to, you can place yours in there as well, there's enough room," he said as he shut the safe and handed me the combination to it. Heading upstairs, we reached the master bedroom and walked into the closet. Once inside, Uncle Ricky reached for the ceiling and pulled down a ladder that leads to the attic.

"Come on up," he demanded as I made my way up the ladder. Once in the attic, I could smell the weed. Walking towards the back of the attic, I saw boxes and boxes of weed already bagged up in pounds. I knew my eyes probably looked like a deer caught in headlights, because I had never seen that many drugs before in my life.

Uncle Ricky began to explain how he received his shipments and said, "The weed is stashed inside of furniture, and the furniture is then sent to various spots through U-Haul."

That's how he got all that furniture for the apartment he'd let my mom move in.

"From here on out, we're not bagging anything up in ounces. We are just going to give my lieutenants a pound at a time. Son, NEVER do you EVER bring anyone to this house and always take different routes when you're coming here. I doubt that you'll need a gun, but I keep a .38 special on the shelf with a full box of bullets next to it. That's for your protection if you ever feel that you need it. Have you ever used a gun before?"

"Yeah, a pellet gun," I responded, not realizing how ignorant I sounded.

"Well this ain't no pellet gun, but you do the same motions as you did with your pellet gun. Run, aim and shoot. Hold it with two hands now, because it'll kick a little bit and make sure you prepare yourself for the noise … and whatever you do, don't hold it too close to your face. Now that I have shown you everything, Bookie; do you think you're ready to take over the whole operation?" Deep down I knew I was ready to take over … I was just happy that he entrusted me to be his successor to this empire, instead of someone else.

"Yes I am. Thanks for believing in me, Uncle Ricky," I answered. I promised myself that I wouldn't let him down either.

"You're the captain of the ship now," he said, giving me a high five, right before we left the attic to make our way to the car.

When we got in the car, Uncle Ricky handed me a double set of keys and said, "Make sure you lock both locks every time you leave the house."

"I'll protect the house with my life," I told him meaning it. Back on the interstate, he told me he would introduce me to the other lieutenants on his team. They were brothers who lived in the same house and made their order at the same time. After a ten-minute ride, we pulled up to a house that had two huge Rottweilers circling the backyard. Exiting the car, I kept my eyes on the vicious animals as they barked and jumped high on the fence; I thought they would eventually jump over. Two seconds later, a head looked out the window to see about the commotion. Opening the door laughing, one of the brothers said, "Ricky, why didn't you call and let me know you were coming over?"

"Man that ain't going to stop them dogs from barking," my uncle replied while giving the guy daps before walking into the house.

"Where's Rollo? I want you all to meet the new captain." As the bigger guy called everyone in the room, my uncle continued talking, "Fat Mike, this is my new captain. Bookie, this is Fat Mike, one of the brothers that you'll be dealing with. Rollo, bring your ass downstairs man!"

"Give me a second. I'm taking a shit!" I heard someone strain fully yelling from the back of the house.

"That dude has been shitting all day. I don't know what's wrong with him," one guy said as we laughed at Rollo's expense.

"Fill me in on the laugh so I can laugh too," Rollo said as he came downstairs fixing his belt, wondering what was so funny.

"We were laughing at your loose bowels ass. Man, I heard you had the shits all day," Uncle Ricky said as we burst out laughing again, getting comfortable in the living room. "This is my son Bookie and he'll be handling the business from here on out," Ricky informed them with a proud smile.

"I didn't know you had a son. Where the hell has he been?" Fat Mike said, interrupting Uncle Ricky.

"This is Willie and Barbara's son. He's been under my wing for the last year and a half—so like I said this is my son, Bookie. When ya'll need some weed, he'll be the one handling the business because I'm relaxing now." Extending their hands out to embrace me, I could tell they didn't expect to hear such news by the flabbergasted looks on their faces.

"So what's your pager number?" Rollo asked. That was an answer that I didn't have.

Uncle Ricky quickly interjected and said, "He'll use the same number that I have since I just got this number a month ago." He also let them know that everything would remain the same unless I felt the need to change the routine. Thinking we were ready to go, I was about to get out of my seat until I heard Ricky say, "So fellas, can I pick up my bread while I'm here?"

"We knew there was something else that you had come over for, because you never come out on Sundays," said Fat Mike.

"Come on gentleman; let's make a good first impression for ya'll new captain." Uncle Ricky said as they headed to the back of the house to retrieve the money.

When returning, they both had rubber band stacks of $1,000 a piece. Each person handed Uncle Ricky four stacks of money apiece, then they said, "We're out and we was going to call you tomorrow.

"We have some business to take care of in the morning, so Bookie will see ya'll tomorrow after five p.m. to hook you up."

"Fellas, I'm looking forward to joining the team and making us all some money," I said as we shook hands agreeing to meet with them tomorrow.

"Hey Bookie, just don't be a hard ass like your pops. All he knows is pay me," Rollo said as we all laughed and said our goodbyes.

"Ricky there's something that I'd like to ask your opinion on," I said as we exited the house and headed back to the car.

"What's that, son?" he said, looking at the road ahead. I then went on to ask his opinion on letting my cousin in on the operation and tried convincing him on how my cousin knew everyone in the younger crowd. My uncle kept his eyes on the road, but quickly glanced at me and said, "How do you feel about him moving pounds of weed? Do you think he is ready for such big responsibilities?"

"I think he can hold his own. Besides, he's already selling weed. It's just his connection is charging him an outrageous price."

"Son, it's your call. You're the captain now, but I respect you for asking me for my permission before actually involving him in the operation." While we continued driving, my uncle's pager started beeping repeatedly. Looking at the pager and reading the number aloud, he said, "Damn, didn't we tell Ollie that you would see him today when you go to visit Nicole?"

"I guess the money is burning his pockets."

"From this point on, this is your pager. I'm out of the game. Welcome aboard Captain," he said as he threw the pager into my lap.

Later that afternoon, I called my cousin to speak with him concerning the new plan that was about to go down and how Uncle had made me captain of the entire operation. As I dialed his number, the pager went off again. While the phone rang, I checked the pager to see who was calling. I noticed Ollie was calling again. I better call this dude after I finish speaking with my cousin.

While I was in thought, my cousin picked up the phone. "What's up, cuz?"

"Man, I've been waiting all day for you to call," my cousin said sounding antsy.

"Relax man … I've been with Uncle Ricky all day taking care of business."

"Cuz, are you bullshitting me or what man?"

"That's why I'm calling you now, to let you know that it's on pimpin'! We're getting ready to get this paper dawg!"

"So what's the number on the ounces?"

I laughed, "Man, ain't no ounces popping off … It's a pound or better."

"Cuz, are you for real? So what's the number on them pounds big timer?" he asked excitedly.

I told him, "Since you're family and if you're going to move them, I could give you each pound for $1,400 under the condition that you bring cash money and you do not let anyone know who you're getting it from."

"Cuz, I got a grand now, but give me a few hours and I'll have the other four hundred."

Should I trust him, is he responsible?

"Hello?" he said after hearing silence for a few moments too long.

"I'm still here, cuz. Ain't no problem—but remember—this is between us."

"Fam, I got you. So when can I get that?"

"You can come over later tonight. I have to make a run first, but I'll call you once I'm back at the crib."

"Cuz, thanks for the lookout. I'm fenna be rich!"

"I'll call you once I'm back in, so lay at the crib for the call." I hung up the phone with him, and called Ollie back; he was blowing up my pager like he was a crack head looking for a hit.

"Damn Bookie, you getting like your uncle already. I've been calling for several hours now."

"We got tied up handling some business. I'm gonna get my uncle to bring it over, that way I can spend some time with Nicole and I'll have her bring me home later."

"I'll be here for the rest of the day. I don't have any plans." When I was getting ready to hang up the phone, Ollie suddenly stated, "Bookie, I want you to remember—my daughter knows nothing about you and I."

"You got my word Ollie," and then I hung up the phone. I headed back downstairs and informed my uncle that we had to go back to the stash house immediately for a pound for my cousin.

"Boy, we're going to get you a scooter tomorrow, first thing in the morning and I'm taking you to see my friend to get you enrolled in that class, so you can learn how to drive and get your license quick. Let's roll, so we can get this day over with."

"Uncle Ricky, after we drop off the pound to my cousin, don't forget Ollie has been calling all day. I just spoke with him not too long ago and told him that we'll be over shortly … Yeah, when we get there, I'm gonna stay and have Nicole bring me home later. Is that cool?" I told him as we headed to the stash house.

"No problem, but I'm not pulling up at your aunt's house doing no business with Scoot. I don't care if she knows what he's doing. I'll drop you off around the corner and wait for you."

"That'll work. I'll run in and make it quick."

Pulling up to the driveway, Uncle Ricky said, "Go ahead and grab that for your cousin, you have the keys."

The inside of the house was dark as hell since there weren't any lights on in the house. Feeling alongside the walls for a light switch, I turned on the lights and made my way to the attic to grab a pound of weed. Grabbing a pound, I felt my pager go off again. It was Ollie. I wonder if he's calling to say that he's ready for another one. Just to be on the safe side, I followed my instincts and grabbed another pound of weed. I saw a book bag my uncle kept laying next to the boxes; grabbing it, I packed the weed inside and then made my way back downstairs.

"Did you lock both locks?" My uncle asked as I entered the car.

"I'm on point; I remembered what you told me. By the way, I brought another pound for Ollie because he had paged me again while I was in the house."

"That was smart thinking, he's probably finished with the one he grabbed yesterday." Making our way to my cousin's house, I grabbed the bag and stuck the pound inside my pants and pulled out my shirt to hide the bulge.

"I'll be right back."

"Stick and move, Bookie."

When I walked up to my cousin's house, he was on the front porch talking on the phone. "I'll call you right back, I got some business to take care of." Once he hung up the phone, we dapped and he asked, "Damn cuz, how'd you get here?"

"Ricky parked around the corner; he didn't want your mom seeing him."

"Shit, man I'm grown now. I take care of myself," he said as we walked inside the house and went into his room. Once he shut the door, I pulled the pound of weed from underneath my shirt and placed it on the dresser.

"Damn cuz, I thought you were runnin' game," he said with his eyes as big as golf balls.

"Man, we're getting ready to be rich. I just need you to be safe … Let's lock this game down and buy our moms houses."

"I'll have the four hundred for you by tomorrow," he said while placing the grand in my hand. Grabbing a pen and paper, I wrote down my pager number. "This is my pager number. Call me when you're ready," I told him as I left the house.

"Was your aunt there?" Uncle Ricky said as I got back inside the car.

"I don't think so. Her car wasn't in the driveway."

"So, was everything straight?"

"Yeah, everything went well. I don't need this money on me around Nicole. She'll start asking questions." I said as I handed him the $1000 that I just received and then we made our way to Nicole's house.

We pulled up to Nicole's house and Uncle Ricky said, "I'll handle this one. You just go and enjoy your time with your girlfriend and I'll have Ollie come outside to the car. That way Nicole won't know or see anything … I'll see you later. Oh Bookie, remember you have to go get that scooter tomorrow and enroll in driving school so don't be out late tonight, alright?"

I wasn't planning to be late … I was making money and nothing was gonna stop me.

Chapter 5

Here Today, Gone Tomorrow

FOUR YEARS HAD FLOWN BY AND A LOT HAD CHANGED. MY TEAM AND I WERE makin' that paper. The lieutenants, including my cousin, were makin' moves by having several regions of Virginia on lock. Scoot was moving 50 pounds, Ollie was moving 20 pounds and the brothers, Rollo and Fat Mike were moving 30 pounds. Business was good and there was nothing for me to complain about.

Not only was business poppin', but my relationship with Nicole was poppin' too. We both had fallen in love and decided to move in together to this cozy little place in Virginia Beach. There was nothing I wouldn't do for that girl, I loved her so; but like any relationship, we would have our ups and downs. Our ups ... well we were inseparable, but our downs were mostly about us not having sex. Nicole was trying not to give it up. She would always tell me, "Bookie, I want to wait until I'm married." That shit made me frustrated at times, because I found it extremely difficult not being able to make love to the girl I loved and lived with. But because I loved her, I respected her wishes. Until one day out of the blue, Lil' Mama caught me off guard.

"Hmmm, what smells so good? Baby, what are you cookin' for your man?" I asked, aroused by the aroma.

"It's your favorite, steak and potatoes and chocolate cake for dessert."

"That's what I'm talking about. I'm hungry as all get out."

"Baby, do me a favor. Would you please go upstairs and run a bubble bath? Oh and make sure you light the candles." I didn't even bother to say yes, my ass ran up stairs to the bathroom and began to run the water and squeeze soap into the tub. By the time the tub was ready and I had lit the candles, Nicole had come upstairs with our food on a tray.

"Baby, what are you doing?" I asked. She told me that she wanted us to have dinner in the tub and that she thought it would be romantic. She turned around and I asked, "Where are you going?" She told me she had forgotten the glasses for the wine and would be right back.

Waiting for her to come back, she yelled, "Baby, go on ahead and get undressed and start dinner in the tub."

She didn't have to tell a brotha twice, I was undressed and in the tub in a flash. The water felt good, I grabbed the tray and started eating my food. *Damn, Nicole really outdid herself.* As soon as that thought came to my mind, Nicole walked in flaunting her birthday suit. Admiring every inch of her body, I began smiling. She gave me a look that said, "Are you gonna help me in?" Snapping out of my trance, I put down the tray, stood up and helped her into the tub. In the tub, Nicole laid back on me and I began to caress her neck and shoulders; then slowly I brought my hands around and began to rub her breast. I knew she was feelin' what I was doing, because she began to moan. All of a sudden, my manhood started to rise and Nicole wrapped her hand around it and started to stroke it up and down.

"I love you baby," I told her, trying to control my breathing.

"I—I love you too," she responded, stammering her words.

I grabbed Nicole gently and stood her up over me with her nicely shaved vagina staring me right in the face. I spread her legs and then the lips of her vagina, and started to slowly tickle her clitoris with my tongue. Before I knew it, her body started to tremble and a tidal wave of juices began to flow from her vagina into my mouth. She screamed, "Shit, my legs are going to give out." I assured her I wouldn't let her fall as she climaxed.

We made our way from the tub to the room and continued our game of foreplay. No longer able to wait to enter her, I took my manhood and slowly entered inside Nicole. "Damn, baby you're so wet," I said, as I moved in a motion that Nicole followed. We moaned and groaned, while our bodies intertwined, until we both exploded into ecstasy together.

The next day I went to my uncle's house to meet with him about some business. When I got to the house, my Aunt Laverne answered the door with tears in her eyes, shouting, "They got Ricky—they—they took him, Bookie."

"What? Who—what—what are you talking about? Who got Uncle Ricky?" I shouted, barely able to get the words out of my mouth.

"The Feds took him this morning."

I couldn't believe it, I had to get my head straight and figure out what the hell happened. All of a sudden the phone rang; it was Uncle Ricky. Aunt Laverne talked to him quickly, and then handed me the phone. Uncle Ricky told me to clear the stash house and to inform the team that the game was over. After talking to uncle, I told auntie that uncle would be fine, and I gave her a hug and kiss and jumped into my Z28 and took off.

While I was driving to the stash house, all kind of things ran through my mind. *Dang, while I was getting deeper and deeper into the marijuana game, Uncle Ricky introduced Virginia to cocaine ... and he was getting rich doing it. He was making money hand over fist ... We both were making money ... Now it's all over. Damn, I need to tell the boys ...*

I arrived at the stash house and got all the money out of there quickly before it was raided. I did just what uncle told me to do, 'get every red penny out of that house …' but that wasn't all I got. There were kilos of cocaine aka 'white girl' that I found and although I didn't know a lot about 'white girl', I planned to someway make some money off of it. After I left the stash house, I telephoned each of the lieutenants and explained to them everything that happened. The person that took it the hardest was Ollie; he could not believe it.

"Bookie, tell your pops if there's anything he needs, I mean anything, I got him. Tell him we'll take care of Laverne too—just—just tell him not to ever hesitate to call, you hear me?" he said, stumbling over his words in a deep depressing tone.

"I'll tell him Ollie, thanks."

The next day, I went to the jail with my uncle's lawyer and saw Uncle Ricky. While there, I got to spend some one-on-one time with him. During the visit, he said something to me that I thought I would never hear my uncle say; he told me that although I was making a killing dealing drugs, I needed to make my money legally.

"You need to get out of this business and do something that can provide for your family without you having to give up your soul, Bookie. I don't want to see what happened to me, happen to you. You understand me?"

I understood what he was telling me, and even though I was doing my thing in the drug game, I decided it would probably be a good idea to use some of my money for an investment and I think I knew just what would bring the money in … and well. "Yes sir, I understand and I think I know what I'm gonna do …" I replied.

"By the way, I found five bricks of cocaine in the stash house, what you want me to do with them?" I said in a whisper.

"Each kilo is valued at 24K a piece, sell them all to Rollo. Once you sell them, take that money and start your business," he said in low, but stern tone.

When I'd returned home from visiting my uncle, I still had some unfinished business to take care of. I needed to store my money and the kilos of cocaine in a safe place. Uncle Ricky always told me to never keep anything where I laid my head or frequented, that kept the police off my front porch and thieves away. While pondering where to stash my stuff, my grandparents' place finally popped in my head. My grandparents were good Christian folks, who'd always pray for me and on occasion would ask, "Bookie, when you comin' to church with us?"

I'd always responded with, "Uh, one day soon." They'd say okay and continued to love me just like grandparents love their grandbabies.

When I got to Granny and Granddad's house, I told them I had some valuables I wanted to store in their closet. They were hesitant at first, but then they agreed to let me keep my safe in their closet. Of course, I didn't tell them about the drugs, I felt bad for omitting that information, but they'd kill me if they knew that shit was in their house. Besides, I wasn't gonna have it there very long … I was gonna flip that shit with the quickness.

When I got home, I called my cousin to update him on Uncle Ricky and to see if he wanted in on that 'white girl'; plus I wanted to tell him about my entrepreneurial venture that I was about to start.

When I called Scoot, I began by updating him on Uncle Ricky's status; after, I started telling him what Uncle suggested I do. "Man, I'm gonna be a legitimate entrepreneur. I got a plan," I said with excitement in my voice.

"What you gonna do? You ain't got no damn degree or nothin' like that. You really wanna start a business?" he asked sarcastically, but I knew he was interested in hearing me out.

"Yeah man, that's what Uncle told me to do and I'm cool with doin' it. He don't want me to end up like him."

"I hear ya, cuz. But, what kinda business you gonna open with no diploma?"

"I'm gonna open a car wash," I told him with so much confidence, it was pouring out of my skin.

"What you know about a car wash, cuz?"

"It's a car wash, it ain't rocket science. If I don't know anything else, I know this. Everyone wanna floss in their ride and ain't dudes out here looking for no females with no dirty ass car." After telling him that, I could tell he understood where I was coming from.

"Aight, I feel ya there—where you gonna open it? Have you thought of any places?"

"Not really man, but I kinda got an idea in mind." I told him about the SPUBS gas station being for sale right across from Norfolk State University on Brambleton Avenue. I knew the dollar signs were dancing around in his eyes like they were in mine.

"Cuz, you a genius."

"I know, cuz, and just think about it. Dudes already gonna wanna be clean in their ride, but with it being across the street from the college, they are really gonna come over because they are gonna wanna show off for all the females." I knew the way men thought when it came to women, especially when it came to getting some pussy. Dudes would floss in their cars that took them all day to clean, sporting their new outfits they just bought from the mall the day before, hoping that a female would check them out. Women basically think the same way too; I've seen many females go to car washes in their skimpy little outfits looking for brothers to hound them. No matter how you looked at it, I was gonna have a gold mine.

"So what you gonna do about all the weed you been selling?" my cousin asked. I knew what he was leading up to. He wanted to take over where I left off and I planned to let him, but I wanted to put him onto something that would make him more money than weed could any day.

"I'm gonna put you on, but I got something better than weed, cuz."

"Man, are you crazy? What could be better than weed?"

"That white girl," I told him. Cocaine was taking off in our community and I had a few kilos that I wanted to get off my hands.

"I ain't never even thought about selling cocaine, but I know it's a lot of money in it. Can you hook me up?"

As I told him about the kilos I had that were worth twenty-four thousand on the streets, I knew his wheels were turning … I had him. After he agreed to sell them, I explained that I would give him two kilos the next day for forty grand and he would be able to flip it. Although I knew there was a lot of money to be made in the drug game, I had bigger and better fish to fry and my oil was just starting to sizzle.

Before we got off the phone, we agreed to meet the next day at a pancake house restaurant's parking lot. Right after talking to my cousin, I called Rollo and told him about the kilos and set a meeting time and place for the next day too. After I got off the phone with him, I laid across the couch and before I even knew it, I was fast asleep.

The next morning, I woke up early 'cause I had some runnin' around to do before I met with my cousin and then with Rollo later that day. I decided to use Nicole's Honda Accord that her father got her for graduation to transport everything from my grandparents' house. Once I got to my grandparents' house, I briefly spoke and went straight upstairs to get the trash bag of kilos and money in the back of the closet. I stuffed the money in a duffle bag to the point that it wouldn't zip anymore. I looked at my safe and made a mental note to buy one that was more secure than the one I had; the last thing I needed was for my grandparents to start snooping around and 'accidentally' find the stash of money, which would then result in an onslaught of questions from them that I did not need. My grandparents weren't any fools, I knew it wouldn't take long for them to put two and two together and figure out that their precious little grandson was a drug dealer.

When I went downstairs, I tried to fly by them, but somehow I knew my fly-by was not going to work. "Bye, I'll see you later." I said trying to fly to the front door before they could respond.

"Hold on baby, where you going? You ain't never just run in and out of here without sitting with us for a while. Come have a seat and talk to us." Damn, this really wasn't the time for me to talk to them. I had a lot of business I had to handle.

"Grandma, I ain't got time. I gotta go."

"Bookie, what you mean you ain't got time? You always got time for your grandparents. What's more important than us right now?" my grandfather said. And although at that very moment, I did have something a lot more important to do, I wasn't going to tell them that.

"I know ain't nothing more important than ya'll, but I'm opening a car wash and I gotta meet with the owner to give him this money before he sells it to someone else," I said as I tapped the garbage bags.

"Are you sure that's money in that bag, Bookie? It doesn't look like its money, it got a funny shape," my grandfather said as we both looked at the bag of kilos I had in my hand. I didn't know what to say to him, but I had to think fast.

"Yeah, Grandpa, it's all money. I just got it stuffed in there funny." I knew my grandfather wasn't stupid by far, but I hoped he would believe me ... at least this time.

"Well bring it over here so we can rearrange it. It just doesn't look right to me." I knew that couldn't happen. When he looked in the bag, I would never hear the end of it. So I had to come up with a lie ... and fast.

"Grandpa, I really need to get out of here. I was supposed to meet with him over an hour ago, but once I realized I didn't have the money, I had to fly over here and get it. This is my one opportunity to start this car wash and I don't wanna blow it. This could be my big break to really make something of myself," I told him, trying to put the guilt trip on him, hoping it would make him decide to let me leave without any more questions ... And what do you know, to my surprise, it actually worked.

"Let Bookie go. He got some business to take care of. I'm proud of you Bookie. I can't wait to see that car wash when you get it up and running," my grandmother said as she stopped my grandfather from harassing me long enough for me to get out the door and run for the hills. My grandma was my lifesaver that day and I thanked her repeatedly in my mind ... Thank you Grandma, thank you—thank you!

Later that day, I had two stops I had to make. First I had to meet Rollo to give him the kilos my uncle promised and after dropping them off, I'd proceeded to meet my cousin at IHOP. I was in a rush 'cause my grandparents kept me longer than expected, so when I was headed to Rollo's house, which was just five minutes away from the restaurant, I called and told him to have the money ready in a duffle.

"Aight, I'll have it ready. Uh—but listen, you have to meet me outside, because my brother is still here."

"No problem, I'll be there in a minute."

When I got there, I seen Rollo in his old school Cadillac and I started to laugh to myself. It's funny how these cats always try to be like Uncle Ricky, imitating his style with the cars, clothes, and everything else. When I got into the car, I handed Rollo the duffle bag so he could get a peek to make sure everything was legit.

"Damn this stuff is strong man. What's up with that?"

"Man, when I went to get it from the stash house, it was a hole in the bag. All of them were like that."

"That's alright man, I can fix it." I checked in the duffle bag to make sure the money was in place.

"Yeah man, it's all there. It's all $100 bills in stacks of thousands. You can count it if you'd like." I knew he wouldn't cross me or short me in any way, so I took his word for it. When I went to grab the duffle bag and got ready to exit the car, he quickly stopped me.

"Hey man, I need that duffle bag, that's how I transport everything." Dang, he was making this harder for me, but I understood where he was coming from so I left everything to make his life easier.

"Man who do I call if I need more? Do I call you or is this just a one shot deal."

"It's a one shot deal, but if I get a hold of anything else, I will let you know ... alright."

"That's a bet," he said as I exited the car, put the bag in the trunk and quickly headed to IHOP to meet my cousin.

When I get to the restaurant, I see my cousin trying to hook up with the waitress. He was mackin' really hard too, it look like he was trying to get her phone number. When I sat down at the booth, the waitress smiled from ear to ear as she introduced herself and asked me what I wanted to drink.

"I'll take a cappuccino please," I said with my picture perfect smile, and then she turned and walked off.

When the waitress was a good distance away from us, I looked at my cousin eye-to-eye and then blurted out, "Man, we gotta make this quick. We can't just be sitting here all day, while we got that stuff in the car. I don't want anything to happen to it."

"Stop being so paranoid, Shaun. Ain't nothing gonna happen."

"Cuz, I'm being serious. Either you come on now—or—or I'm gonna dump the rest of this on Rollo." He could tell I was as serious as a heart attack and I didn't have time to play around with him.

"C'mon cuz, you messing up my game ... You see I'm trying to get some of them goodies tonight," he said smiling while looking towards the waitress. He then turned and saw the look on my face and his expression changed quickly.

"Aight cuz, I got the forty G's in my trunk outside for you."

"Okay, I'll pull to the side of your car and place the two kilos in your trunk and just get my money and roll," I told him as I got up and headed to the parking lot. Even though we were leaving, my cousin quickly wrote down his number on a napkin and dropped a hundred dollar tip for the waitress. Once outside, we both went our separate ways to our cars.

Luckily there was an empty space next to my cousin's car. While rolling up into the space, I saw that he already had his trunk popped open. Happy he was prepared; I hurried out of my car, grabbed the kilos, concealed them under my shirt, and headed to the trunk of his car.

"Cuz, what the hell is wrong with you? Why you ain't got them in a bag or something? You wanna get caught, don't you?"

"Nah man, my other bag is filled, so I had to roll like this fam—I had no choice," I told him while dumping the bags in his trunk under some old clothes and grabbed the duffle bag of money. Before I headed back to my car, I told him that I would holla at him after I had secured the money and talked to the owner about leasing the gas station.

"That's a bet! Be safe, cuz," he said as we high fived each other and went our separate ways.

After I left my cousin, I immediately headed to the gas station so I could get the contact number for the owner off the sign posted in the lot. Approaching the lot, I noticed that a lot of college students were coming and going across the Brambleton Avenue intersection right where the gas station sat on the corner.

As I got closer into the lot, I then noticed a work truck parked on the side of the building and two older men pulling a ladder off the back of the truck. I prayed that no one had already bought the building, but I was definitely going to find out by asking. I parked my car, got out and walked towards the two men and said,

"Excuse me gentlemen, do you know who owns this vacant lot?"

"Oh, good morning son, how are you doing today?" the older man said as he smiled at me.

"I'll be better if you tell me that this lot is still for sale. I would love to buy it!"

"Well, nice to meet you. My name is George McCadden and I'm the proud owner of this lot. You said you might be interested in buying it—huh. Well let's talk," he said extending his hand to me, as I gladly shook it.

"Yes sir, my uncle left me a very fine inheritance with the specific instructions to open a lucrative business that would not only help me and my family, but the community as well. I think this would be a great place for a car wash and detail shop."

"I see—so this is your first business you are trying to open?"

"Yes sir."

"Well son, I would be more than happy to leave here with a signed four year contract and have you the proud owner of this new car wash, but I want you to understand that with this contract come stipulations that are to be met. My main concern is that no type of illegal activities is done on this property ... You understand. Also, there is no loitering over here as well. I am very respected by the president of that fine university over there and I want to keep it that way. Oh and by the way, I'm not sure how much of an inheritance you received, but I will need a five thousand dollar deposit to secure the lot. Are you able to abide by these rules son?" the man asked me while staring me in the eyes.

"Yes sir. I sure can."

"Well son, looks like you are about to be the proud owner of that car wash that you've been dreaming of. Let me just go and get the contract out of my briefcase so we can do the necessary steps to make this legal ... and once you pay your deposit, I'll have the keys and lease contract ready for you. All you will have to do then is just go to City Hall and get your business license. How does that sound?"

"That sounds great Mr. McCadden ... Thank you for this great opportunity."

"Oh that reminds me son. I never caught your first and last name."

"Please excuse me for not properly introducing myself. My name is Willie Laushaun Robinson, but I'd rather be called Laushaun."

"I will honor that, Laushaun," he said smiling.

"I just want to let you know, Mr. McCadden, that this is a new beginning for my family and me."

"That's wonderful."

"Oh by the way, we can finish this paperwork today, Mr. McCadden. I came prepared in hopes of getting this business."

"I like a man who's prepared, Mr. Robinson. Step into my office so we can go over all the paperwork and I can verify the deposit that you brought with you today."

"Yes sir, just let me get the money out of my car and I will meet you in your office in just a second." I responded in an exhilarating tone, feeling great knowing that I was about to have my own business.

Once he went into the office, I headed to my car and pulled out one of the ten thousand dollar stacks from the duffle bag. After I got the money out of the car, I literally ran to the office. When I got there, Mr. McCadden was sitting in his office chair behind his wooden desk. I sat down in the chair on the opposite side of the desk and he placed the contract in front of me … I read over it briefly. Being satisfied with what I read, I signed the contract and counted out the money; placing it on the table in five stacks of a thousand dollars apiece.

Mr. McCadden took the money, reached for his large key ring and found the set of keys that went to the old gas station and handed them to me. "Congratulations Lashaun! I wish you well on becoming a young black entrepreneur," he said while shaking my hand.

"Thank you sir," I said, ready to run out the door so I could start taking care of business.

"By the way, there's a small leak in the roof, but I'll have it fixed by today."

"Sounds good, sir," I said and then walked out of the office. I began walking around the lot … and then I stood in front of the gas station and smiled, visualizing what my car wash was going to look like. Man, I'm going to make this the best car wash in town. I could see exactly how I wanted everything to look. It felt so real. I couldn't wait until it was up and going.

Driving downtown to City Hall, I was anxious … butterflies were dancing in my stomach … I'm gonna get my business license! Uncle Ricky is gonna be so proud of me … Shoot, I'm proud of me. While filing my paperwork, I had to come up with a name and after a lot of consideration; I decided to name the car wash 'State Auto'. Why? Because it was located right across the street from the university, and I wanted people to think it was associated with the school ... Personally, I thought it was an excellent marketing strategy that would bring me in lots of business. I finished filling everything out, handed the woman my paperwork, paid the fee and before I could blink my eyes twice, I had the license in my hands. Walking out of City Hall with the biggest cheese on my face, I couldn't stop looking at the business license that said I was the owner of 'State Auto Car Wash'. My next stop was to Office Max so I could buy all the supplies I needed to get my business started.

Over two hours and five thousand dollars later, I had shopped at various stores; I had a pressure washer, paint, 2 safes, and all the other materials I needed to successfully open State Auto. After making all my purchases, I had the things I couldn't carry out the door delivered to the car wash. Once we got to the car wash and the delivery folks finished unloading everything, I decided to make a much-needed run to put one of the safes I purchased at my grandparents' house. Putting a safe in the backseat of my car, I headed to their house so I could secure the money that was in the trunk of the car, as well as the money that was in the closet.

When I made it to their house, I was so excited I almost forgot to grab the business license so I could show it to them. I was so happy to be able to truly show my grandparents that I started my own business. Plus, I was even happier that my business would keep them from being suspicious of any 'other' activities that I was involved in.

"What in the world is that, baby?" my grandparents asked as I walked in the house with the safe covering the upper half of my body.

"I got some good news ... Just let me take this upstairs first," I told them, heading upstairs to drop off the heavy safe. When I got to their room, I placed the safe in the closet and quickly ran back outside to my car to get the gym bags from the trunk. Dripping with sweat, I finally got the bags inside the house and sat them down inside the living room.

"Look, I got the lot I told you about—here's my business license!" I said so excited and out of breath, I could barely get it out.

"Hallelujah! Thank you Jesus!" They both shouted with glee and smiled, reading the business license. Coming towards me with their arms extended, they gave me the tightest hugs that I'd ever received in my life. It was one of the greatest feelings in the world.

"Baby we are so proud of you! I tell you what … Sunday you should come to church with us, so you can thank the Lord for His blessings and give to His Kingdom by tithing. Bookie, without the Lord, nothing is possible. Please come."

"I'll make sure I'm there first thing Sunday morning, Grandma, Grandpa—I promise." I replied and reached down to pick up the bags so I could take them upstairs.

Now that I had everything in order—the lot, the business license, and the kilos off my hands, I finally was able to sit down and actually count the money that I had. I counted each stack of money located in the bags and inside the closet. The grand total, even after spending the ten thousand dollars to get the car wash set up, was $440,000. Man, all those years of selling weed, I stacked my paper—the money Uncle Ricky gave me—I can take care of the family—I can buy Moms a house. I proudly placed my money in the safe, locked it and headed downstairs.

"What on God's earth have you been doing up there to be sweating like that?" my grandparents asked me when I got downstairs with my shirt sticking to my body and drenched in sweat.

"Grandma, I was placing the safe in the closet and putting Granddaddy's shoes back in order, it was a lot of work," I said in a light tone, smiling, hoping to keep them from asking any more questions.

My grandma looked at me and said, "Well baby, sit down, and take a break."

"Okay, just for a little while because I want to go home, take a cold shower, and rest." I sat down on the couch, closed my eyes and said, "Mr. Robinson, you're officially a business owner."

Chapter 6

Everything Goes Down at the Car Wash

It had been a year since the car wash had opened and I had money coming in from everywhere. I had contracts with Norfolk State, Norfolk Police Department, Ford Motor Company, and TRT Transit; but being the entrepreneur that I was, I knew there was more money to be made so I didn't stop there. I had a mobile truck that went to various car lots and other destinations to wash and detail vehicles by appointment. There was nothing that State Auto Car Wash couldn't do.

I contributed to the community by bringing jobs; I hired a twelve-man crew that consisted of people who were unemployed and needed a steady job. The men who worked for me were dedicated; they would work almost 12 hours a day, seven days a week.

They were loyal and never complained and for that, they were compensated tremendously.

Even on the days that it rained, we were still bringing in a lot of dough. On average, we would wash and detail over two hundred cars and trucks a day with prices ranging from ten to twelve dollars; the prices were based on the size of the customer's vehicle.

The car wash was truly a blessing. It allowed me to take care of my mom, Uncle Ricky, Aunt Laverne … and, uh … Nicole. Nicole, Nicole, Nicole! Where do I begin with this …? Well, we eventually had a daughter together. We named her Sade, my little jewel. Soon after, our relationship became distant. By no means was it because of my daughter; it was Nicole's resistance to being a productive citizen. Nicole didn't want to work, go to school … her ass didn't want to do shit. She was SPOILED—used to having every damn thing. I tried to deal with it, but after some time I became very frustrated by her attitude towards work, and I began to resent her. Finally it got to the point that I fell out of love with her and when that happened, I knew it was time for me to go … so I moved out of the house. Even though I was no longer in love with Nicole, I still had love for her. Since the girl refused to work—monthly, I paid all of her bills. After I left, the only time I'd ever see her was when I picked up my daughter to stay with me on the weekends.

***

ONE DAY AT the car wash, I ran into Cindy, an old junior high sweetheart of mine. I was sitting in my office, when this BMW that rolled up in front of the car wash caught my attention. I couldn't help but look at the 18" BBS chrome rims and hear the bangin' sound system that was out of this world. When I seen the owner of this tight ass ride, step out of the car, I couldn't believe who it was … *Oh shit, that's Cindy.* I jumped out of my seat and swiftly made my way outside to personally greet her, and to make sure that she knew that her car would be handled with care. When I got about arms length from where she was standing, she removed her glasses; I could see that she had been crying by how red her eyes were and the low tone in her voice.

"Hey Sweetie, what's wrong?" I asked concerned, while hugging her. I wasn't sure what hurt her so bad to make her cry, but I wanted to comfort her in any way possible.

"I'm okay," she sniffed as she avoided eye contact with me. "I just need to get my car detailed for the funeral tomorrow. Can you do that for me?" I didn't know what funeral she was referring to, but whomever it was that had passed away, I knew it was tearing her apart.

"If you don't mind me asking, who passed away?"

"My child's father was killed at his barbershop on Park Place the other day," she said as she put her sunglasses back on to keep the tears from falling.

"Are you talking about Lil' Tom, who is also called Chad?" I replied in shock.

"Yes—my—my son doesn't have a father now," she stuttered as tears fell from her face like a waterfall. I embraced and tried to console her; I couldn't help but feel bad about her loss.

"Cindy, Lil' Tom was a great guy. If you don't mind, I'd like to attend the funeral to pay my last respects to him."

"Sure, I'm okay with that."

To give us some privacy, I escorted her to my office so we could further chat. We started talking about the good ole days and what our lives had become. She told me how she was the owner of a beauty salon right next to Lil' Tom's barbershop and that she was really doing well for herself. I gave her kudos, and then told her that I was the owner of State Auto and would always ensure that she received the best service when she brought her car through.

"By the way, whose car is that you're driving? It's pretty tight," I said to her while chuckling, trying to lighten up the mood.

"It's my car, Lil' Tom bought it for me for our wedding last year. The beauty salon was a wedding gift too."

"Damn Ma, you had it where he was spendin' paper like that," I said jokingly, in hopes to bring a smile on her face.

"I can't front, he made sure we were taken care of. He bought me a three-bedroom house in Chesapeake and his people in New York are making sure we don't need for anything. My son has a savings account that will set him for life and he has his college tuition paid for already. He can go to whatever school he wants to. I guess he made sure we would be okay in case something ever happened to him. It's the possible negative consequence of living the lifestyle of a drug dealer."

With a little hesitation in my voice, I asked, "So do you know who killed him and why they did it?"

"It's a long story, but he's locked up now. I guess it's better for him to be in jail than out here on the streets because he would be getting carried by six versus being judged by twelve. He'll have to answer to God now," she said as she looked down to the floor to keep from giving me eye contact.

Our conversation was cut short when one of my employees brought her keys into my office and handed them to her. When she went to get up, she reached into her purse to pay me for the wash.

"Don't worry about it Cindy. It's on me. Just make sure you tell all your friends about the car wash and the great services we provide," I told her, pushing her money-filled hands back towards her.

She put her money back into her purse, pulled out a handful of her business cards to her salon and sat them on the desk and said, "You're still a gentleman I see. Well can you do me a favor? Can you put these on your bulletin boards so people will know about the salon? Oh yeah, give me a few of your cards as well and I will return the favor." I did what she asked and handed her about 30 business cards before she headed towards the door.

"So I'll see you at the funeral tomorrow?" I asked her, making sure she knew that I would be there for her.

"Okay, I'll see you there. The funeral will be at First Baptist Church at noon. The repast will be at my house after … I'll see you tomorrow," she said, giving me a hug while we said our goodbyes.

It was an infamous Friday and business had topped the charts; two hundred and fifty cars had been washed and we couldn't even close shop until after 8 p.m. Part-in-due to it being a pay day for folks and people wanted to make sure their rides were clean for the weekend. Also, on Fridays I gave a discount to the college students and senior citizens, which made up for more than half of our clientele. My crew and I got to know the regular clientele pretty good; especially those that took advantage of the Friday specials.

There's this one guy in particular that would come to get his Land Cruiser cleaned every other day. I noticed his plates were from South Carolina, so since we were in the VA, I figured he was probably a student at Norfolk State. But what student rolled like that? Another thing that I paid attention to was every time he came to the car wash, he would have a whole entourage of his homeboys with him; he or his boys weren't ever disruptive or anything … they were cool. As a matter of fact, my men started giving this guy special treatment … Whenever he got his car detailed, he would leave a twenty-dollar tip to whoever did the job, so in return he always got hooked up when he came to get his car cleaned. As soon as he'd drive up, one of my men would provide him immediate service by moving his car to the front of the line; because this guy frequently patronized my business, I did not mind the special treatment that my guys were giving him. Actually, I encouraged it.

Although we always engaged in small talk, this guy and I never formally introduced ourselves, so one day I made it a point to show a little Virginia hospitality.

"Fam, we've been shaking hands for while now, but never formally introduced ourselves …

"Hey, my name is Tim, Tim Montgomery," he said as we shook hands.

"What's up Tim? My name is Laushaun … Ay dawg let me ask you a question. I know you go to the university across the way, so how in the hell can you afford such an expensive car?" I asked him, not in a disrespectful way, I just wanted to know what was up with him.

"I am a professional track and field athlete. I'm just going to Norfolk State so I can get my degree," he replied.

"Damn, so that's how you're eating huh." I didn't know a lot about track and field, but I could tell he was doing big things.

"Yeah dog, just wait, one day I'm going to break the world records in the Olympics and make millions. Just wait and see."

"Really? I didn't realize there was that type of money in track and field." I knew that baseball, basketball, and football players were getting paid like crazy, but I never knew they paid track stars millions.

"Yeah, if you're good at what you're doing." His car was just getting finished; I handed him his keys and we dapped each other and headed our separate ways. From that day on, we started a friendship that was closer than most blood brothers were.

The day of the funeral had arrived and I had to mentally prepare myself for what was ahead. When I got to First Baptist Church the parking lot was packed, it was almost unbelievable all the people that was there to pay their respects to Lil' Tom. When I walked into the sanctuary there was standing room only; but I was able to find a spot in the back that nobody else had spotted. I looked around and noticed most of the older guys were dressed in black suits, while the younger crowd wore black t-shirts with Tom's picture on the front. I continued looking around, and finally I spotted Cindy. She was holding her son on her lap, listening to the Pastor's message. When it was time to view Tom's body, I watched Cindy as she walked up to the casket with her son. I could tell that she was trying to be strong for herself and her son, but when her son began to call out for his dad, she broke down. I felt so bad for the both of them and wanted to run to embrace them both, but couldn't get to them. Eventually, a tall dark skinned dude gently grabbed Cindy's son and walked him outside. Having enough of the eye-filled tears and whaling of pain, I got up to leave. Plus, I couldn't bring myself to look at Tom in the casket; I wanted to remember him as the dude I last saw at the club … celebrating and dancing.

When I walked out of the church, I saw the dude that took Cindy's son, holding and calming him outside. I walked towards him and acknowledged his presence by saying, 'what's up', and then began to talk to Lil' Tom.

"Hey Lil' Tom, I'm a friend of your daddy's and he asked for me to give you this money so you can get yourself some new toys." I put the money in his little hands, and he managed to give a smile of gratitude. "My name is Laushaun, but your daddy called me Bookie, and since you're Lil' Tom, you can call me Bookie too." He smiled at me again and then placed his head on the dude's shoulder. I turned around and when I was about to walk off, I heard this thick New York accent say,

"Yo, thank you for embracing him. Real recognizes real. My name is Boo-Bee. You gonna be at the repast, son?" he said, extending his hand out to shake mine.

"Nah, I didn't plan to, besides, I think I've had enough sorrow for one day."

He looked me straight in the eyes and in the sincerest tone said, "Yo, I'd appreciate if you come … not for me, but for Tom." When he put it like that, I had to go.

"Aight man, I'll be there. I got some business to take care of, but I'll be right over afterwards." I gave him another handshake … jumped in my car and headed to the car wash.

After I handled my business at the shop, I quickly headed to the repast at Cindy's house. When I got there Cindy greeted me with a hug and began introducing me to friends and family. After I did my rounds, I decided to sit down and give Lil' Tom my attention, for I thought he needed it the most, because he now was fatherless. While I was interacting with him and bringing smiles to his face, Boo-Bee walked up to me and said,

"Yo, Shaun, let me holla at you … I wanna introduce you to some peeps."

"Oh—okay. Excuse me little man, I'll be right back, alright," I told Lil' Tom, hoping that he wouldn't get disappointed.

"Play with Marde, Lil' Tom … Shaun will come back to play with you." Marde was the son of one of the men that I was about to meet … I followed Boo-Bee to a private area, where I was introduced to two gentlemen.

"Yo Shaun, this is Peter and Unique … They're brothers." I extended my hand to shake each of their hands.

Both men said simultaneously, "What up god? What's the science?"

I immediately recognized that these men were 'Five Percenters' and I did not want to disrespect them so I responded, "Peace god." We then shook hands and from there, we hit it off like old friends catching up.

I learned that Tom's friends were in the entertainment industry—and they were doing some big things here in Virginia. While we continued to converse, we all learned that we had a lot of things in common—the drug game being number one.

"Hey, I'm no longer in the game though. After the man that taught me everything I know got locked-up, I promised him and myself that I'd legitimately make my money … It's been over a year and my business has been holdin' me and my family up—we don't want for nuffin'. We eattin' … know what I mean."

"Yo, we respect that god," Unique said, speaking for the group. As we got deeper into our conversation, the ringing of Unique's cell phone interrupted us. Excusing his self, he answered and began speaking in his native language, Patois, which sounded like broken English to me. He was sitting right next to me so I couldn't help but get my ear hustle on. I listened as he told the person he was talking to, to set an important appointment for noon the next day because his plane was leaving early that morning and it would give him ample time to return from New York and prepare for his meeting.

When he got off the phone, he told his brother and friend, Boo-Bee about a video shoot that was taking place the next day. Then

Unique turned to me and asked a question I didn't expect. "Yo god, you wanna roll with us to New York for the video shoot for my new album that's about to drop?"

Although it was a generous offer, I had to decline. "Man, I would, but I gotta run my car wash. Plus, I ain't messin' with any airplane. They call it the friendly skies, but they just don't seem all that friendly to me. Know what I mean."

"Are you serious? What do you got against flying? You'll love the flight, I promise. Plus a man's got to get away sometimes. You got to get a breather, if nothing else, just get away and regroup. That's how men become rich, god! Have you ever been to New York?"

I hadn't even been out of Virginia period. Funny, I never even thought about it until he asked me.

"Nah man, I haven't. I've been too busy grinding and getting my business off the ground."

"You should come with us Lo-co. You like fam now and we gonna take care of you just like you family," Boo-Bee interrupted.

I thought about every possible scenario that would keep me here ... and wondered if everything would run smoothly without me. I wondered who would run the shop in my absence. Would everything still go as smoothly as it would have if I was present; I wondered if my grandparents would get worried if they didn't see or hear from me for a few days. I thought about my daughter that Nicole and I had, I wondered if she would be disappointed that I didn't come to get her like I did every weekend for our time together. I wondered what my uncle would think if he knew I went to New York ... Would he think I was doing some illegal activities and become disappointed in me?

"So you rollin' or what, fam?" Unique shouted, while my mind was bombarded with so many thoughts.

"Yeah, I'm down for the ride. I just gotta make sure everything is in order before we go," I said quickly.

"Laushaun, I like you dawg. You ain't like these other cats out here who just answers a question without thinking about it. You strategize your thoughts and moves before you give your final answer. I can see whoever taught you, taught you well," Boo-Bee exclaimed.

"Yeah, my uncle took me under his wing early, instilling all his wisdom, game, and love in me, so being thoughtful about what I do is like second nature … It's a natural ability for me to plan and strategize," I said smiling, silently thanking Uncle Ricky for everything he taught me.

"Aight playboy, be at the airport at eight o'clock sharp tomorrow morning. That's what time our plane leaves. Make sure you get a lot of sleep tonight cuz it's gonna be party time once we hit the Big Apple," Boo-Bee said while they gave me their phone numbers.

"I'll call and find out how much my ticket is so I can go get it first thing in the morning," I told them. I didn't know how long we were staying, so I planned to buy an open flight so I could stay through the whole video shoot.

"No god, no paper is needed. This one's on me. All you need with you is an open mind and an open heart. Oh, and get some rest, New York never sleeps so you gotta be on point," Unique said smiling at me. After we said our goodbyes, I headed over to see Lil' Tom and to tell Cindy that I was heading to New York with Unique, Boo-Bee and Peter.

"Make sure you call me when you get back," she said smiling as I kissed her on the cheek and gave her son Lil' Tom a hug.

"You know you'll be one of the first ones I call when I get back … I promise."

"And don't be messin' with none of them nasty girls while you're up there. I know how Unique rolls, trust me," she said laughing, although I knew she was serious.

"Of course not …" I told her as I left to head to the shop. While in the car, I called my grandparents to let them know that I would be headed out on a business trip the next day, and that my mother would be there to take care of them if they needed anything.

"Good luck baby. Stay safe. I'll be praying for you," Grandma said before hanging up the phone.

I then called my mom to let her know what was going on … I asked her to please make sure my grandparents were okay, and asked if she did not mind opening and closing the car wash for the next few days. My mom gladly agreed; I knew that if no one else had my back, my mother did. Next person on my contact list was Aunt Laverne. I called her and let her know that I was going to New York to find products at a discounted price for the car wash and to see about possibly expanding the business. That way, if she talked to Uncle while I was gone, he would know that everything was legit. After making several more phone calls to make sure everything was straight for the next few days, I prepared myself for my trip to the Big Apple.

Chapter 7

Big City of Dreams

THE NEXT MORNING I WAS SO TIRED I DIDN'T KNOW WHAT TO DO. I TOSSED and turned all night because I couldn't help but think about the plane ride. Every time I fell asleep I would dream that the plane turned into the Challenger, the space shuttle that blew up in the 80's with that teacher on it. Feeling indescribably uneasy, I decided to talk to God … "Lord, I know I don't come to You as much as I should, but I'm coming to You today to ask You to please make sure that this plane ride is safe in Your hands. Please take away my fear of flying and give me peace of mind. In Jesus' name I pray, Amen."

After the prayer, I felt calm and the images of the Challenger blowing up went away… I knew that the Lord would see me through this trip. I packed my suitcase and grabbed five thousand dollars for spending money. Even though Unique said he had me, I just wasn't the type of person to go anywhere without any money. You just never know what could happen and plus, if I found something that I wanted to buy for me or my family, I didn't have to rely on someone else to buy it for me. I wasn't that type of man.

When I arrived at the airport, I parked my car in the garage. When I walked into the airport, I noticed everyone was waiting on me with their luggage and tickets in hand.

"So where are we headed dawg?" I asked Unique, sitting my bag down next to them.

"Let's go on to gate six and get comfortable before it's time to load the plane. If we get there early enough, we can get a few shots of liquor in us before take-off."

To get something to drink, boy hearing that was like music to my ears. Lord, I know I prayed to You earlier, but a drink could help calm me too.

We loaded the plane, and got seated in first class. While we were getting comfortable, I realized we were directly behind the pilot's cockpit.

"Welcome aboard sir, can I offer you a cocktail?" The stewardess asked each of us.

"Yes, four double shots of Remy Martin for me and my boys," Unique said, pointing his finger at each of us, showing the stewardess where to deliver the drinks.

The plane made its way to the runway to prepare for take-off and all of a sudden, the space shuttle images flooded my mind. I quickly closed my eyes and asked God to please take the images away and to keep me—us safe. When I opened my eyes, I could feel the plane climbing; as we got thousands of feet into the friendly sky, my stomach felt queasy. I didn't know if I had to vomit or shit. At one time, I thought I had to do both. After we reached a certain altitude, the captain gave the green light for people to move about. I was glad, because that meant I was going to get my drink. When I finally got it, I drank my alcohol so fast that before I knew it, my cup was empty.

Now that we were leveled in the sky, I finally tuned into what Unique was saying. He was talking about his plans for the video shoot. He told me that all of his people were flying in from various states to handle business and for me not to talk to anybody about my business affairs.

"Unique, what business affairs are you talking about? What's the big deal about my car wash? It's not like it's a secret ... In fact, I thought it would be great advertisement for my business," I said very confused.

"I'll explain what I'm talking about when we get to New York."

What is this dude talking about? I didn't know what his plans were for me coming to New York, but I had a funny feeling that it had nothing to do with my car wash.

While I finally started to enjoy the rest of our forty-five minute flight, Unique told me some information that didn't really surprise me. He explained to me about an operation he had going with his brother and Tom for the last four years in Virginia.

"Yo, Shaun, don't get me wrong, I know everyone likes to be called one thing or another, but I just don't feel comfortable calling you by your government name. Do you got a nickname or something?" Unique said, changing the subject.

"Yeah, my friends call me Bookie, but since I started my business, I try to keep it professional by going by Laushaun especially since I ain't involved in the streets no more," I told him, hoping to reiterate to him that I wasn't doing anything illegal anymore. I was legit now.

"Well, we gonna call you Bookie from now on. I like that name, it's street," he said as he told Peter and Boo-Bee that I wasn't to be called Laushaun anymore.

"Hell, I'm happy we're calling him something else. That's easier for me to pronounce anyway. You know my English ain't that good," Boo-Bee responded.

I noticed that Peter really didn't say much of anything. He seemed to be the laid-back guy of the crew. Other than introducing himself, I hadn't heard him say anything if he wasn't talking on his cell phone.

Once we landed, I felt a sigh of relief; I quickly got my stuff and exited the plane. While we walked down the terminal, suddenly, my stomach started doing summersaults; drinking all that alcohol on an empty stomach wasn't such a good idea.

"Yo, I gotta hit the restroom," I told them as I ran towards the first restroom I could find. It seemed like the closer I approached my destination, the more and more could I feel the vomit come up as my mouth started to water. No sooner than I made it to the toilet, my insides exploded through my mouth, leaving a nasty ass aftertaste. After I rinsed my mouth out and washed my face, I saw the three waiting on me.

I walked outside of the bathroom feeling a million times better, although I really needed something to eat. They all looked at me with smirks on their faces and then Boo-Bee handed me a Tropicana orange juice.

"Here Bookie, drink this. This should settle your stomach until we get a chance to get a bite to eat."

"Thanks man," I said as I took a quick swig of the juice. "Yo, you mind if we go on and get a bite to eat before we leave here? I'm on empty," I said as I rubbed my stomach while it growled and churned.

"Yeah, that's cool," Unique said as we walked to the food court and ordered hoagies.

"How may I help you, sir?" the lady politely asked, waiting to take my order.

I stared at the menu for a second and then responded, "Yeah, can I get a ham and cheese hoagie?" Man was my mouth watering at the thought of sinking my teeth into that sandwich.

"Nah god, ain't no pork jumping off up in here," Unique blurted out loudly, stopping the lady from ringing up my order.

"Fam, I ain't a Five Percenter … I represent the Dirty South and we love us some pork now," I said, looking at him in disbelief. Wondering how this nigga was just going to order for me.

"I feel ya god, but you reppin' Five while you're with us," he said confidently, and directed the lady to change my order to a turkey and cheese sandwich like theirs. At that very moment, I knew I wasn't just hanging around any old dudes; they were dudes that were all about exercising power and control.

"It's all good," I said to Unique while I smiled at the lady to assure her I was okay with the turkey sandwich. Being well aware that it wasn't the time to see who had the biggest dick, because my ass was no longer in my own backyard. I stayed cool and shook it off … Besides, I was too damn hungry.

After we ate, we made our way to the parking garage where Unique left his MPV. As I entered the vehicle, I was pretty amazed how it looked. Everything was customized from the sound system to the plush leather seats. While getting comfortable, I felt the back seats move.

"Hey Unique, what's going on with these seats man?"

"What you mean, you ain't never been in backseats that rise before?"

"Nah, I ain't, but that's tight as hell man," I said as I laughed. This dude was the real deal.

"Yo Bookie, do me a favor. Reach in that box and grab them three heaters in there for me."

"What box?" I asked, confused on what he was referring to.

"Look under your seat, playboy." I looked down and the seat that I thought was reclining for my luxury was actual a secret compartment for his guns. I bent over and felt inside the open space, and pulled out three Glock 9 mm with infrared beams attached to them.

"Ay playboy, you in the Big Apple now. It's a whole different ballgame here, my man. I'll get yours when we get to the studio, aight." Unique shouted over the blasting music. I didn't even reply back to him, I just looked at him and smiled.

While we rode through New York, the skyscrapers and the constant traffic took me aback. Man, I had never seen traffic so crazy. It was bumper to bumper everywhere; no matter what corner we turned people were cursing and blowing their horns at each other. And Unique fit right in with all those crazy drivers, dipping in and out of traffic without hesitation, while he puffed on a perfectly rolled blunt in his mouth.

When we got to his residence, I tripped out when I saw the barbwire surrounding the place and the guard posted at the front gate.

"What's going on," Unique said as he drove by.

"Everything is great, Unique," the guard said as he waved at the car and let us into the residence. When we headed towards the building, we entered into a lobby full of elevators.

"Yo, Bookie-boy and I are going to freshen up a bit. We'll meet you in the studio in an hour or so," Unique told Peter and Boo-Bee before we got into one of the elevators in the lobby.

"All ya'll livin' here?" I asked.

"No doubt, when I told you we were tight and kept in close range, I wasn't joking. We all live on different floors."

When we got to our designated floor, I saw Unique unlock the door that was directly on the other side of the elevator doors. We literally stepped from the elevator right into his condo. Damn … now that was living large.

The condo was laced … Everything in there was money green Italian leather and there were photos of him and his crew everywhere. I walked deeper into the living room and saw a beautiful caramel colored lady sitting on the couch. Unique walked up to her, sat between her legs and began reading various numbers, while she started massaging his shoulders as if she was trained.

"Yo Bookie, what size you wear god?" he asked. I told him my size, while I continued looking around the condo.

"For real, we're the same size! Yo, go to the room and find you something to wear," he said while sitting back while the girl still massaged his body.

What's wrong with the Polo I got on? I asked myself, shrugged my shoulders and made my way to his room. I walked into the room and entered the enormous walk-in closet. I couldn't believe what was in front of my eyes; there were so many boxes of sneakers and clothes to choose from. I began looking at the stuff and noticed that every item in the closet was brand new with the tags still intact.

Damn, I wonder how it feels to not have to wear shit twice, I said to myself as I grabbed some Guess shorts, a white tank top and a pair of white shell toed shoes that matched.

After picking out my outfit, I jumped in the shower. However, about ten minutes into it, I heard Unique yelling, "Yo Bookie Boy, come on. We ain't got all day."

Damn, I'm not used to taking five and ten minute showers. "Aight, I'm comin'," I yelled. Once I dried off and threw on my clothes, I quickly walked down the spiraling stairs and the smell of weed filled my nostrils. When I walked into the bedroom, I saw Unique from a million angles. He had mirrors everywhere, including the ceiling. Then I noticed that the bed he was sitting on was moving in a slow circular motion.

"Now you look like a New Yorker," Unique said as he went to hand me the blunt.

"Nah, I'm good dawg," I told him. I wasn't the type of person to just smoke weed on a regular basis and I knew them, but not like that.

"C'mon Bookie, smoke a little and get your head right for the video shoot," he said, as I was feeling the pressure to take a hit.

I took a small pull of the blunt to keep him quiet; it almost took the life out of me, that's how strong it was. I started coughing and choking for over five minutes while trying to catch my breath.

"Man, you can't go smoking this shit like that. This is Chocolate. You can't go disrespecting it like that; this shit will put you on your back in a heartbeat," Unique said, laughing at me choking. Right after he said that, the room started spinning and everything was going in slow motion. I didn't know what was going on. What was weird was even though I felt like this, my alertness was still on point.

"Let's go get ready for this video shoot," Unique said as he grabbed the blunt from my hand and jumped to his feet like a ninja.

When we got to the parking lot, I noticed we were headed to a BMW just like Cindy's. If it weren't for the color, I would have thought she'd followed me to New York.

"Jump in, playboy," he said as he hit the alarm.

After getting in, he started pressing a million buttons around the dashboard and underneath the glove compartment was a secret door, and when the secret door opened, he handed me a Glock 9 mm.

"Put this in the box over there, Bookie-boy," Unique stated.

Headed to the studio on the Major Deegan Expressway, Unique then hit a button on the air conditioner controller and I heard a low, slow paced beeping noise. I didn't know what it was and didn't think anything of it until it started to get louder. Then I noticed the police car ahead of us, and the closer we got to the officer, the louder the sound was.

"Man, what the hell was that?" I asked him as we passed the police car.

"Man, it's a radar detector. It lets you know when the police are checking the speed limit and stuff."

"Damn, I'm gonna have to get one of those when I get back to the V.A."

When we pulled up to the studio, I couldn't tell if it was a video shoot or a circus, everyone was running around like chickens with their heads cut off. People were either rehearsing their parts to the song or popping Moet bottles and smoking weed while listening to the latest New York anthem. While we sat waiting for the director to prepare the first setting for the video, I noticed everyone and anyone was coming over and speaking to Unique. He even had the police working for him, making sure no one came into the video shoot that weren't supposed to be there. When the shoot got started, I noticed a fleet of cars pulling up all with 'Unique' personalized tags on each car. Before I knew it, Unique grabbed a mic and started doing the hook of his song.

"A Yo, Aight," he screamed in the mic. On cue, the crowd responded.

"Mecca Audio," they said. At first, I didn't know why they were screaming it, but learned that it was the name of the production company.

I was amazed how everyone was acting as they poured champagne on one another. Next thing I knew, Unique grabbed me and brought me in camera view while he started singing the hook again. It seemed the high I got from the blunt was rising in me and I started bouncing to the beat of the song as Unique and the hype man kept the crowd hyped.

After that part of the video was over, we packed up and moved from Brooklyn to Manhattan and finished the video shoot at Jones Beach. There were so many jet skies out there I didn't know which way to turn to keep my eye on all them. I thought Unique was going to get him a rented jet too, but to my surprise, he had an eight-passenger speedboat but it was only him, me and six sexy women in it. We were the highlight of the video. Once the video was finally finished, Unique announced to everyone that the party wasn't over and that they were all headed to his club, Club 2000 for the after party later that night.

Before we went to get ready for the party that night, we headed to a Jamaican restaurant to get a bite to eat. Since I'd never had any kind of Caribbean food before, I decided to just follow Unique's lead and order the same thing he had.

"So Bookie-boy, you feeling New York or what?" he asked me, and then shoveled more food in his mouth.

"Yeah, I'm feeling it hard. You almost gonna make me wanna leave the V.A. and move down here," I told him. I hadn't had this much fun in a long time.

"It ain't over either, playboy. After we finish this ox tail and rice, we gonna head over to the mall and buy it up. You ready for that?"

"Hell yeah, I'm ready," I told him with a huge smile on my face.

When we were done, we got into his 500 Benz and headed downtown Manhattan for some action. While driving, he started lighting up another blunt and was getting high as a kite. Damn, he smokes weed all damn day, but I guess he got it like that.

When we got to the mall, we headed straight to the store and spent five grand on two Versace outfits like it was nothing. I thought we were balling in Virginia, but it was nothing like this. It was like we were living life for today and it was, fuck tomorrow because we'll ball 'til we fall.

After getting our shopping on, we went to another one of Unique's cribs to get dressed. I noticed that this house was decorated in a similar taste with the Italian leather and many photos everywhere. The only difference in houses was that all the photos read Mecca Audio.

"Yo, I'm about to be out. Meet me at the front of the club in twenty minutes, aight," he said to his crew as he called each one and gave them the same message.

When we finally got to the club, Unique looked at me with a serious look and said, "Bookie, no matter what, I want you to make sure you stay on my heels. When I move, you move okay. People are grimy, so you got to stay on point," and then he grabbed his 9 mm and put it in the small of his back.

We exited the Benz and his crew followed suit, and got out of their European cars that were parked at the front entrance. Everyone was dressed to impress, I didn't know if we were dressed for a club or a damn runway show.

Once we got to the entrance of the club, the security let us in without any questions asked. That shit amazed me because in Virginia that wouldn't have happened; everyone was going to get searched before they entered any club.

"Aw shit, Mecca Audio in the mother fuckin' house," the DJ announced as we entered the club. There were so many women shouting Unique's name, I thought at any minute panties were gonna start flying in the air. As the crowd went wild, Unique made his way to the stage, grabbed the mic, began chanting the New York anthem and jumped in the crowd of women.

As he finished the song, he went over to a crowd of ladies that had been staring at him all night.

"What's up ladies, ya'll ready to leave this party and finish this with daddy?" They all smiled as we headed to the back door to avoid the crowd. When we got outside, he told his crew that he would catch up with them tomorrow. Unique and I jumped in the Benz, while the ladies got into the customized van that Boo-Bee and Peter were driving and we headed to the Presidential Suite at the Waldorf Hotel.

"Let's get naked and fuck," Unique said loudly as we entered the suite.

Being so amazed about the suite, I was the last person to get naked. I couldn't believe he came so prepared. He had a ton of champagne in the wine box and eight boxes of condoms. Before I knew it, it was a big orgy going on. Women were eating each other like they were eating caviar, while we were hitting them from behind. Rubbers after rubbers were constantly being used until there were no more left. When we finished, my manhood was so sore and tender; I could barely hold it to go pee without it hurting.

The night ended and the sun rose, and we had to head out to go handle some business. All the women were passed out in bed, catching up on some much-needed sleep, so we didn't bother waking them up to say goodbye. Before leaving the room, Unique left two thousand dollars on the stand to show his appreciation for all their hard work.

"Yo, I'll catch up with ya'll later, I gotta head to the studio and check on the fellas," Unique told Peter and Boo-Bee, before we made our way to the vehicles.

"Aight dog, we'll holla at cha," Peter said as Unique and I rolled out.

We started our day off with a fresh blunt and to be honest, I was looking forward to it. When I was about to pass the blunt over to Unique, a phone call from the video producer interrupted the rotation.

"Aight … that will work, I'll check for you in about an hour mon," he said with excitement as he hung up the phone.

"Bookie-boy, the producers said that video is hot. It's already making noise in the N.Y. dawg. I'm bout to make a legal million

Bookie, ya hear me!" Unique said smiling. I could tell he was feeling himself hard and I understood where he was coming from.

"Hell, Im'ma have to open a Swiss account."

"How do you open one of those anyway, dawg?" I asked.

"Don't worry about it, playboy, I'll put you on game with that. Just roll with me and you'll be straight," he said as we headed to the studio. When we got there, his whole crew was already waiting for him to listen to the tracks they had prepared.

Unique listened to everyone's music. I could tell that these guys thought he was their messiah and was going to lead them to the promise land.

"That shit is hot ya'll. Let's put Mecca Audio on the map with this shit," Unique said to his crew while he took another pull of the blunt and got out of his seat. "Time to roll Bookie-boy, we gotta head to RCA to check out the video."

"That's a bet," I said as we headed towards the entrance. This dude was really doing his thing ... I've never seen anyone work so hard to promote their own shit.

When we got to RCA, the director met us and led us to the film room. We watched the video, and I was amazed how he took all those small scenes and put them all together to make the video. He had us looking like major celebrities and I couldn't believe how damn good I looked on camera.

"Your single is starting a huge buzz in New York and I want to know if our staff can buy the copyrights to it. We're willing to pay you a half a million dollars for the record," the director said, hitting his hand firmly on the desk. I could tell that he thought he had Unique sold. However, his expression changed quickly.

"Half a million dollars ... Are you serious? That's chump change to me. You gotta come at me better than that," Unique responded immediately, appalled by the director's offer.

"I think that would be a great gain for you, Unique. You can start an empire with that type of money," the producer said, trying to convince him to take the deal.

"Man you must not know who I am. I ain't settling for no half ticket. I'm already selling over 200,000 copies my damn self. You think you can throw that little money over to me and I'm supposed to run out of here happy with it. Man, we are killing it here in New York and we're ready to move down south with this shit. Come hard or don't come at all. Give me a mil' or it ain't no deal," he said, snapping his words at him like a viper ready to go in for the kill.

I could tell that the director wasn't prepared to hear that speech. His voice began to slightly quiver as he began to speak, "Now—now Unique, let's be realistic now. It's not a full album. It's just a single. We don't plan to pay that type of money for a single. A half a mil' is a lot of money to be passing up. I'll let you sit and think about this and if you change your mind, the offer is still on the table. My boss is even willing to give you points on the record sales for this single."

Unique just looked at the man as if he was smaller than fly and told him, "Just give me my video and we can roll out," as he firmly placed several stacks of money on the table while giving him eye contact. Unique grabbed the video and we left RCA.

We headed to downtown Brooklyn to meet Boo-Bee and Peter for lunch. I was glad because I hadn't eaten all day and I was starving.

"So how you enjoying New York, Bookie?" Boo-Bee asked me as we got ready to order our food.

"New York is gonna be my second home. Man, shit moves so much faster here than it does in the V.A.," I said, with conviction in my voice. I had planned to come back to New York every chance I got.

"So how did it go with RCA? Was the video hot or what?" Peter asked Unique right before he took a bite of his food. Unique told him about the bullshit offer that RCA gave him and how he turned the deal down.

"Yo Bookie, can you push this CD down in the V.A.? Being right across from the college, I know it will be banging at your shop, playboy," Boo-Bee said, throwing his hands in the air.

"Yeah, I'm down."

"It'll put some bread on the table for you, and I know you're down for some eating."

"I'm always down for some good eating as long as I can see the end of the road if you know what I mean," I told them hoping they caught my drift.

"Bookie be on point, yo … That's why I fucks with this playboy," Unique said.

After we finished eating, Unique told me he was going to take me to 'Momma's' house. First he called her to okay our visit; I could tell he was talking to someone that he respected. He didn't curse not one time and even finished the conversation with, "God Bless."

On the way to Momma's house, Unique told me that he liked how I handled my business. He explained that taking me to Momma's house would allow her to bless me and keep any harm from coming my way.

"Bookie-boy, da blessin' will protect you from da law and your enemies, but da best part of da blessin' is it will grant you riches. Dat whut it dun for me and gon do for you," Unique said with his Jamaican accent sounding a little heavier than usual.

I didn't know much about what he was talking about, but I was willing to try it, because if that is what got him to where he was, then it must have worked. When we got to Momma's house, I was on edge. I had never experienced anything like this before.

"Mon, you gotta relax. Ain't nuthin' to be worried about, she's family." He then told me that she was from Jamaica, the same native as he, and that she was a hundred and two years old.

"I owe my life to her. For the last ten years she's been protecting me from the mean streets of New York. I don't think I would even be here if it wasn't for her."

When she welcomed us in, I stared at her for a while because she didn't look her age at all. Other than the dark gray hair that rolled down her back in a neat ponytail, there were no signs of her being any older than her mid fifties. She hardly had a wrinkle in her skin and moved like she was in her thirties.

"Hi Unique, I'm so glad you came by. I have some great news for you," she told him as she hugged him tightly. They seemed so close I would have thought that it was his mother for real.

"It's always great to hear good news from you Momma."

She then turned my way and smiled, "I see you brought along a new friend this time. What is your name?"

"Laushaun, but Unique prefers to call me by my nickname, Bookie."

"Bookie, I like that." She laughed as she led us to the meditation room to see what the spirits were bringing our way.

"The energy in here is so strong. I feel wealth is involved and it's God's will for me to speak it into existence." When we entered the meditation room, I almost fainted at the sight of a ten-foot cobra snake that swirled in a glass cage and the various animal skulls that stared straight at me.

When she sat down, she did something that I'd never thought I would see. She started speaking in tongues. At first, I thought she was speaking to us, until I heard the snake hissing back to her as he raised his head. Once she told us to have a seat and get relaxed, I noticed that the snake had stopped hissing and was now lying as flat as a pancake. She then started chanting a prayer while rubbing her hands on unusual scented oil.

She stopped praying, opened her eyes and said, "The spirits are godly and Laushaun is a great asset."

I knew this was real, because Unique hadn't said anything to her about me. *But what did all of it mean?*

"Welcome to the team, playboy. If Momma says you're an asset to the team then I'm grateful to have you by our side."

"What's going on Unique? Is this some kind of voodoo or something?"

"Nah, it is only protection for me and my fam. Before anyone can enter our circle, we have Momma check them out—everyone can't be trusted. You know what I mean."

"Laushaun, I see you are the sole provider for your family. Everyone depends on you to clear all their financial debts," Momma said, looking my way.

"My family is my life and I work hard to make sure they have everything they need."

"The Lord will continue to bless and support your family. Come here, I have something just for you. Here take this," she said as she handed me a bottle of oil. "Use this oil every day after taking a bath before leaving your house."

"What is it? What will it do?" I asked, not understanding the oil's purpose.

"It will give you more wisdom and will help you understand your role in life. It will also help protect you from evil and those who try to do you harm. Make sure you keep this in your possessions at all times. And when you feel in danger, just rub the bag and the spirits will protect you from evil," she said as I looked at the small pouch-like sack that the oil was in.

I felt a chill run through my body like electricity as I grabbed the items from her and put them in my pocket. "Thank you," I said. Then she turned to Unique.

"I see that the demons are trying to take a magnificent project from you by offering you pennies for what it's worth."

"Momma, I'm not letting them devils take anything from me. As long as I promote my own label, they can't have anything I worked hard for.

"Don't worry; the Spirit will lead you to wealth. As long as I'm around, I will make sure that your legacy lives on," she said to him as we stood.

Unique then gave her a hug and several kisses on the cheek while reaching into his pocket and handing her a stack of bills.

"I'll be praying for you over your journey that you're about to travel," she said as she took his gift.

I then paid my respects to Momma and gave her a hug as we left and headed to Boo-Bee's shop.

While we drove down the road, Unique told me all about Momma and how she saved his life by protecting him from evil. He told me the reason he called his production company Mecca Audio was because of her. He said that he wanted to give the younger generation an opportunity to come up and Mecca Audio was the way to do it. When we pulled up to the shop, we saw Boo-Bee on the phone. I looked up over him and noticed a sign that said, "Caribbean Flava."

His shop was located right in the middle of Brooklyn's ghetto Crown Heights. Boo-Bee was speaking in Spanish to whoever was on the other end ...

"No puedo, porque yo soy..." I heard him saying, while I walked by into the lobby admiring all the products he provided for his customers.

"Bookie-boy, this is where I got my shit done to my cars. They do it all, rims, music, stash boxes, and interior. They give you anything and everything that you need for you to get your ride tricked out."

"That's what's up."

"So when you're ready to floss in the V.A. let us know and we'll hook you up."

"Man the Overlord is riding my ass about the shipment that just arrived," Boo-Bee said once he got off the phone.

"What's up papi, are you ready to get busy or what? We've been riding low for so long and our guys in Panama are riding me so hard, I had no choice but to take the shipment," Boo-Bee said while he was throwing his hands around in the air, apparently frustrated.

"I'm with you and all dawg, but this record label has been taking up all my time. Plus since Tom died, I ain't been feeling the same ... You know shit is hot as hell in the V.A.," Unique replied, hoping that Boo-Bee would understand the pressure he's been under.

"Man I feel you and all, but we can't let Tom's death stop us from making this money. Man, you're turning down millions. We have families to take care of ... and now that we got Bookie, we can get him to step up and help us move these bricks."

"What you think Bookie-boy? Can you handle pushing a hundred bricks or what, playboy?" Unique asked.

"Man I gotta be honest with you. I don't know anything about that part of the game. In fact, my cousin is the one that's pushing them thangs for twenty-four grand a piece," I said, while thinking … *What the hell am I about to get myself into?*

"Man, just undercut his price. I'll tell you what. We'll sell them to you for thirteen a piece and you turn around and sell them to him for twenty. Hell, you'll make seven grand off of them bitches and ain't gotta even do a lot of work, because with prices like that, they'll be flying out of your hands like fireworks," Boo-Bee said, still flinging his hands all over the place.

"I don't know, dog."

"Man, just think about it. You'll make seven hundred thousand dollars off of this shipment alone."

"Man, where the hell will I keep that kind of weight? I ain't got no stash houses or nothing like that. That's too much for me," I said, getting kind of hyped up.

"This is what we will do then. I'll send you ten bricks a week. That's forty bricks a month. That way we can play it safe, okay." I didn't know if that was the right thing to do, getting back in the drug game, but that was a lot of money to make in a short period of time. Unique then told me that he would have a driver bring it down to V.A. and all I had to do was get the car and secure the bricks. Once I get the bricks out, just put the hundred and thirty grand back inside the car and park it back where I found it. Then a driver will just bring it back to New York and it will keep both of us from driving with all that on us.

"So are you in or what, Bookie?" Unique asked me. All I could think about was Uncle Ricky and how I would be letting him down by taking this deal.

"Damn dawg, I didn't think the decision was that hard. What are you thinking about?" Boo-Bee said impatiently, waiting for my response. I didn't know if I was making the right decision, but I had mouths to feed … my daughter needed to go to college.

"Everything's good. I—I'm in. I got a family to take care of and I gotta send my daughter to college."

"Welcome to the family, Bookie," they both said as they congratulated me with high fives. They told me that I would take the first flight out of New York to head back to Norfolk and by the time I got there, the van would already be waiting for me with the work in it. Unique then explained to me that he would have Cindy pick me up in one of Tom's cars, because all of his cars had stash boxes in them. He strongly recommended that I should buy one of the cars from Cindy since she had no use for them anymore. They were just sitting in her yard with car covers on them. I might as well put them to use. Then I could take the drugs around town without having to be paranoid about getting caught. Everything was final. I had committed myself to a new family, a new game, and a whole new way of life.

Chapter 8

Same Game, New Players & Different Rules

WHEN I FINALLY MADE IT TO THE AIRPORT, CINDY WAS ALREADY WAITING ON me at the front gate with Lil' Tom standing next to her like a little soldier.

"Did you enjoy your trip, boo?" she asked me as we embraced.

"Yeah, New York was the shit. I had the time of my life. Your boy Unique is a trip," I told her thinking about my last few days hanging with them.

"Yeah, I bet. I know about how he gets down. I've been around them for years," she said as we walked out of the airport.

"Bookie, you coming to the house to play with me?" Lil' Tom asked as he tugged at my pants trying get my attention. I could tell he was getting attached to me, and I didn't want to deny him a father figure, because I knew what it was like not to have a father around.

"Yeah, Lil' Tom, we can go have fun, but just for a little while okay. I gotta go and do something in a few hours."

"Oh, Unique called me and told me that you wanted to buy one of Tom's cars. I don't know what you got planned for them, but I ain't got no use for all them cars outside so if you are interested in one, just let me know."

"Yeah, I'm gonna get one from you."

"He told me to drop you off at Military Circle and call him when you get there. Is that cool with you?"

"Yeah that's cool," I told her. We agreed that I would just make payments as the money came in, that way I wouldn't be missing a big chunk of money all at one time.

On our way to the mall, I called Unique to tell him that I had made it back safely and was headed to the designated spot. He went on to tell me where the van was parked at the mall and when I got there, I needed to look under the wheel of the car and feel for a magnet key box. After explaining to me how to open the box, he gave me further instructions, "Make sure you replace the kilos with the money and park the car back in the same location, and someone would be there to pick it up … aight."

"Oh yeah, Bookie, I put two thousand CDs in the suitcase in the backseat. Sell them all over. Let them go for $5 apiece so we can get a buzz going. Don't forget to hit up the radio stations there too, so we can get our shit on the radio."

"I got you, fam … I'm on top of everything. I'll call you next week and let you know what's going on."

I hung up the phone and saw the same MPV that Unique had drove in New York. I could tell it was his by the New York tags and the BBS rims on it.

"Hey Cindy, I'm going to follow you to your house and secure the kilos in one of the cars I'm buying from you. Then I'm going to get the money from my grandparents' house and bring it back."

"Bookie, I know I can't tell you what to do, but please—please be careful. I care a lot about you, and I don't want to lose you in these streets," she said as she rubbed her hand across my cheek.

"I'm protected well … I promise," I told her as I looked sincerely into her eyes, kissed her on the cheek and got out of the car. I walked up to the van, knelt down and began to feel around underneath for the magnet box, "Got it!" I said as I grabbed the keys and headed off. While in the van, I smelled that same weird scent that was at Momma's house in New York. I guess he blessed the van before he brought it to me.

Driving on my way to Cindy's house, I called my mom to let her know that I was back in town.

"I'll see you later tonight or the next morning, after I finish taking care of some things."

"Okay Bookie, everything ran smoothly while you were gone, I made sure of it." I thanked her for everything she'd done for me and gave her my love before I hung up the phone.

Once we pulled into Cindy's driveway, she handed me the keys to the car that was covered up in front of me and then headed towards the house.

"Yo Cindy, can you do me a favor? Call up your girl Lisa and have her go with you to the airport so you can pick up my car. Just drop it off at the shop and give the keys to my mom. She'll know what to do with it."

"Aight, but you owe me for this one," she said with a devilish smile as I smacked her on the ass, before she turned to make her way into the house.

"Thanks, boo!"

I walked over to the cars and pulled the covers off; there was a BMW 325, Mazda MPV and a Lexus GS 300. *Damn, I might have to get all these from Cindy … They're clean as hell,* I thought as I looked down to see what key I was holding in my hand. I had the keys to the MPV, "Looks like you're the lucky ride," I said as I jumped in and started the van to let it run for a while to get it charged up.

The car hadn't been driven in over a month, so I knew the battery was probably low, plus in order for the stash box to work, the van had to be working properly.

While the van ran, I went back to Unique's van and grabbed the two duffle bags out of the box and transferred them to Tom's van. Once getting them secure, I covered the van back up and headed to my grandparents' house to get the money that was needed.

"Lord have mercy, where on God's earth have you been, baby?" my grandmother asked as she embraced me with all smiles. "I was so worried about you. I hadn't heard a peep from you in over a week."

"Grandma, I told you I was going on a business trip for about a week or so, why were you worried baby? You know the Lord ain't gon' let nothing happen to your favorite grandchild. He knows I gotta take care of you two," I told her as I kissed her forehead.

"That's right Bookie, trust in the Lord!" my grandfather exclaimed.

"Grandpa, may I get the keys to the closet?"

"What happened to your keys, Bookie?" Grandpa said with a skeptical look on his face.

"My friend has my car keys and the keys to the closet are on them so I'd really appreciate it if you'd let me use your keys. I just gotta get some money for a shipment I ordered and I'll bring'em right back to you." I didn't feel bad for telling them what I needed the keys for, because it was actually true. I did have a shipment I had to pay for.

I made my way upstairs and filled the duffle bags with enough stacks to equal a hundred and thirty thousand dollars. I then ran back downstairs and told them that I had to leave, but I would come back later in the afternoon. When I got into the car, I called my cousin to let him know I was back in town.

"Yo cuz, I really need you to meet me in front of the mall by the Doubletree Hotel."

"Damn Cuz, I thought you forgot about a player … I'm on my way, fam."

I quickly hung up the phone and called Unique to tell him that everything was on point and that he could have his guy pick up the van within the next hour.

"Bookie-boy, make sure you grab the bags of CDs from the backseat, playboy. I need you on top of that, fam," Unique said making sure I didn't forget about his CDs. He wanted to get them out and I wasn't going to let him down.

"I got you, playboy, I'm not going to leave you hanging dawg."

When I pulled into the parking lot, I saw my cousin already parked at the hotel with his hazard lights blinking in the fire lane.

"Yo cuz, follow me real quick," I told him as I pulled next to him and pointed to where I wanted him to head.

After parking the van, I made sure everything was in place for the pick up then I grabbed the CDs in the backseat. I locked the doors and set the alarm, surveying my surroundings to make sure no one was looking and I then placed the key box under the front wheel.

"What's up, cuz?" my cousin greeted me as we dapped each other when I got into his car.

"What up? Take me to Cindy's house, cuz. I got something I gotta handle," I told him as we pulled off.

While I was giving him directions to the house, he shouted out, "Cuz, I know you're not talking about Lil' Tom's girl!" I wondered what he was thinking because he knew we had history.

"Yeah, she's good people—she introduced me to—well I met Lil' Tom's connect at her house and they invited me to New York and I went."

"So what's up, did they hit you off? Those foreigners are major paid. I think that's who was hitting Fred off, because ever since Lil' Tom got killed, he hasn't been doing anything and the town is dry." I wondered how he figured they were foreigners, but that was a question I had to have him answer another time. After giving him the rundown of how Unique blessed me with ten kilos at a price that was so lovely I couldn't pass it up, I told him I would let him push the keys for twenty-four thousand, the same price he was getting from Fred and he would just pay me twenty thousand a piece for them.

"That's what's up, cuz! Fam, I got you. I'll move every last one of them in no time," he said, almost having a wreck in the car because he was so excited.

"Cuz listen, I know that you're excited about this whole ordeal, but you must keep in mind that this game is very serious. One false move and we could be sleeping next to Uncle Ricky," I told him, trying to bring him back to reality on how serious the shit we were dealing with really was.

"Fam, I respect those words and you got my word that I'll keep it low and quiet," he said, realizing that what we were doing could possibly put us away in prison for life or worst … get us killed.

"Don't let anybody know I'm involved in this shit cuz, I don't want anybody to know where you're getting your shit from." I didn't want my uncle to find out that I was back in the drug game. I knew that even though he was locked down, he still had ears and eyes on the street and probably 90% of them were watching me.

"Oh yeah cuz, you can't be pushing this in your car, I got a new car for you to push it in," I told him, explaining the MPV and the safe box that was inside of it.

"Damn cuz, these dudes are on some James Bond shit with these special gadgets in the vehicles," he said with a look of shock in his face. That was exactly what I thought, but I knew he wouldn't know the half of it until he actually seen what the compartments did with his own eyes.

"Nah, these players are smart at what they do and try to protect their investments. So in order for you to make moves, you'll need the box, because we're not taking any chances by just throwing the shit in the trunk. Those days are over, it's the nineties, fam, so we gotta step our game up and move with the time."

I knew my cousin understood what was going on, but I wanted to reiterate just how serious this drug game was now, and how smart and serious Unique was when it came to his money. As we pulled into the driveway, Cindy's car was already parked; she had beaten me back to her house.

"Meet me over there at the van with the cover on it, so I can show you how to work the safe box," I instructed my cousin as we got out of the car.

"Your mom got the keys to your car so whenever you're ready to pick it up, just call her and she will take care of you," Cindy said.

"Thanks boo, just give me a minute and I'll be in there," I told her. Once she went inside the house, we got in the van and I showed him how everything worked. Just as I thought, he was amazed at how everything worked, especially the three-way motion. Once the box was opened completely, I told him to go to the backseat to see what it looked like.

"Cuz this shit is hot! Man we're on now!" he said smiling from ear to ear.

"Take this van and secure the kilos. Tomorrow I need you to go and register the van in your baby's momma's name. I'll take your car to the shop tomorrow and you can pick it up there."

"Aight cuz, I'll see you tomorrow," he said as we gave each other five and went our separate ways. After he left, I walked in the house and saw Cindy sitting at the kitchen table smoking a blunt while Lil' Tom was fast asleep on the leather couch.

"Yo Cindy, I guess all the driving wore Lil' Tom out huh?"

"Yeah, his bad ass needs to rest! He's been busy all day—getting into everything!" She said, putting the blunt up to her lips and taking a long pull while looking at Lil' Tom. "Here are the titles to the vehicles so you can change everything over," she said as she signed the titles for the Beemer, the van, and the Lexus, handing them over to me.

"So what do I owe you for these vehicles?" I asked her, ready to pay her for the vehicles or at least give her something on them.

"I know you're not going to pay me what Tom paid for them, plus he put a lot of money into them cars with the rims and music, but since Unique asked me to sell them to you, I'll only ask for eighty thousand.

You pay me in installments as we had discussed earlier, I don't expect all of it up front, I just wanna use the money for Lil' Tom's college tuition."

Being the math wiz that I was, I quickly calculated the cost of each car and realized it came to about twenty-three thousand a piece. I felt like I had hit the lottery with them because they were well worth over forty thousand a piece and that wasn't even including the expensive accessories that were included.

"I'll get you the money within two weeks," I told her while grabbing the blunt out of her hand.

"Laushaun, I didn't know you smoked weed."

"There's a lot you don't know about me yet, but since I see that you're a real down to earth woman, I'm going to ride with you and your Lil' man."

"And there's a lot you need to learn about me as well," she said while grabbing the blunt out of my hand, and leaning in towards me to give me a passionate kiss.

After talking business, we ended up finishing the blunt and before I knew it, we were cuddled up on the love sofa listening to R. Kelly's, 'Down Low'. We were mellowed out from the blunt and she had my hormones jumping out of control from the way she gently rubbed my chest with her hands. We continued to listen to R. Kelly serenade us and began to let the music overtake our bodies; and before we even knew what was happening … we were touching, kissing and grinding on each other.

"Baby, I want you. I—I'm in need of you," she said, breathing heavily as she started to take her shirt off slowly.

Then she took off her silk bra and put her firm 38D breasts in my face. I smiled at their beauty, gently wrapped my hands around them, pulled them towards my mouth and encircled my tongue around her nipples and areola, teasing her breasts.

"Baby, please give it to me," she said as she caressed and stroked my manhood through my shorts.

She then grabbed me by the shirt and pulled me to her bedroom. When I walked in, I felt like I'd entered a time zone or something, because the room almost looked exactly like Unique's room, except she had a waterbed instead of a rotating bed. We laid down on the bed and the water moved in several directions as we rolled around and caressed each other's bodies. She pulled me off the bed and standing, we seductively pulled the rest of each other's clothes off. My manhood rose to its peak while I admired her sumptuous body and well-manicured kitty. While I stared her down, she strutted towards me like a model on a catwalk, our eyes locked and then she smiled at me, as she slowly knelt down and softly put her mouth over my penis. She sucked it o' so gently, but stroked it really strong. The warmth of the saliva from her mouth, going up and down my penis made my knees slightly tremble. She was really working me out. I looked down at her and watched her as she began licking off the excess saliva from my penis ... Damn, that shit drove me wild and my whole body began to tremble uncontrollably. I could no longer wait ... I needed to be inside of her, so I lifted her up and slowly put her on top of me, and slid my shaft deep inside her tight vagina. She closed her eyes and slowly swayed her hips as she grinded all nine inches of my manhood that penetrated her soaking wet cave. Faster and faster we moved, while she jolted her hips like she was riding a galloping horse.

"Oh my God, it's so big ... Please don't hurt me Laushaun!" she screamed out of control.

"Damn girl!"

The harder I pounded, the harder she thumped back. And—and—and—we both exploded. Our bodies went into convulsions while we howled like wolves, crying to the moon. When we had nothing left and our bodies became weak, she collapsed on top of me. Her juices slowly seeped out of her vagina and oozed onto my manhood, and then without warning things became weird.

Out of the blue, Cindy blurted out, "Oh my God, please hold me! I just saw Tom! I can't take this, Tom is in this room!"

I tried to embrace her and keep her calm; but what I really wanted to do was make a dash for it. The woman was losing her damn mind. What kind of shit is this? I thought while I caressed her back. After a few seconds, I tried to ask her if she was okay and called her name, but she didn't answer. She had fallen into a deep sleep and no matter what I did nothing woke her. *I must say this by far was the craziest sex I'd ever had!* I turned on my side, closed my eyes and before long, I had fallen asleep with my pouch that held the oil that Momma gave me underneath my pillow ... I hoped it worked like she said it would.

Chapter 9

On to the Next

BUSINESS ON BOTH ENDS WAS DOING GREAT; THE CAR WASH WAS STEADILY bringing in more paper and my extracurricular activity was paying off. My cousin had the market in the Norfolk and Chesapeake area on lock. Everyone was loyal to him ... especially Fred. Now that we were bringing weight into Virginia, Fred was back in the game. When he hooked up my cousin, he became one of Scoot's main customers. Now that we were supplying him, he was able to revitalize his business because he had known everyone that was buying. Of course no one knew that I had my hands tied up into the operation, because they never saw me around any of the transactions that took place. Plus, my cousin had kept his word by keeping everything on the low between us. Therefore, people just speculated that Scoot had met Lil' Tom's connect because they knew the MPV had belonged to Tom. No one ever questioned me about Tom's other cars because they saw Cindy and I together often, and probably figured she gave them to me.

Cindy and I were doing okay at the beginning, but after about six months, the relationship fell apart. I really cared for Cindy, but the girl was always 'seeing Tom', especially after we had sex. The episodes were becoming so crazy and obnoxious that I couldn't take it anymore so I had to break up with her. After cutting our relationship off, I thought she wouldn't speak to me anymore, but we actually remained friends. I was glad our friendship remained intact, because it allowed me to still have a relationship with her son. Every week or so, I would pick him up and take him, along with my daughter, to Chuck E Cheese's or the park so they could have fun with their dad. No, Lil' Tom wasn't my biological child, but because he no longer had a dad, I considered him my son.

Unique was promoting Mecca Audio heavily and was getting heavy air rotation for his hit single. It seemed like everywhere I went people was saying the slogan, 'A Yo, Aight'. We had the market and the street credibility on lock. We were the Mecca of New York and Virgina. My uncle was doing his fed bit in North Carolina at a camp facility and in the meantime, somehow my aunt got pregnant and had a little girl name Nikki. Wasn't sure on how that went down, but I was just happy Uncle Ricky never got word of my involvement in the coke game. Plus I was a very clever dude; I gave people no reason to suspect anything … I kept myself distanced from the old crowd, and my aunt and grandparents would only talk to him about the success of my business and how well I took care of them every month.

My mom started assisting me daily at the shop, and I compensated her well; all the income that came into the shop belonged to her. Giving my mom that money bothered me at times, because she was still supporting my brothers and sister. Damn, it made me sick that they were grown as hell, but refused to go out on their own and make something out of themselves. However, I was not going to let my mother's well-being suffer because of their inability to self-preserve.

Boo-Bee was not only bringing in a killing with the coke he kept flowing from Panama, but his shop was doing well too. He was bringing in well over a hundred grand a month customizing cars. It seemed all my boys were diversifying by getting their hands in to every business imaginable, from real estate to barbershops and they were making major dough.

My homeboy Monte and his crew opened an exclusive club called Pizzazz. This place was the spot and we chilled there often. One night while at Pizzazz, my cousin and I were having a great time when we ran into Tim Montgomery and two of his friends.

"I see you Playboy doing your thing," He shouted over the bumping music. "This is my man Laushaun, he owns the car wash across the the street from NSU. He's a real player and shows me much love when I come to get the whip cleaned," he said as he introduced me to his friends. One guy, Shampoo, told me he had just finished doing a five year bid and was looking to get back in the game and get his paper right. The other guy, Brian, went to Norfolk and ran track with Tim.

"Laushaun, what are you drinking? Drinks on me!" Tim yelled over the music as he made me put my money back into my pocket when the waitress came to bring me another bottle of Moet.

"Baby girl, can I get ten bottles of Cristal sweetie?" he told the waitress after counting the heads of everyone who was with us, including the guys that were part of my cousin's crew.

"Baby, do you know how much the Cristal is hitting for?" she asked, like he didn't know what he was ordering.

"If I was worried about the price, I wouldn't have made the order or wasted your time because I know you're on your grind," he confidently replied.

"Shit, I'll have this right back to you in a second," she said damn near running to get the Cristal.

"Hold on sweetie, take this and place five hundred on your tip baby girl, but don't keep us waiting because my peoples are thirsty," he said while he handed her his American Express credit card.

While the waitress hastily made her way to the bar, Shampoo kept talking about how he was trying to get his money back right. It was only obvious that he needed to meet my cousin. Plus, I didn't want anyone knowing that I had anything to do with the drug game.

"Yo cuz, this is Shampoo. Shampoo, this is Scoot. I think y'all might have common interest—you should talk." They seemed to hit it off quickly and before I knew it, my cousin was writing his number down on a napkin for him to call.

"Get at me Dog, it's all love," my cousin said as he slipped Shampoo the folded napkin. Shampoo then placed the napkin in his wallet and gave my cousin a handshake.

I was interrupted from watching them when I heard Tim's drunken ass getting loud, "Man, the Olympics is coming up and I'm practicing for that event because I'm trying to break world records."

"Playboy, just go with your intuition, anything you put your mind to it'll happen. Just don't limit yourself and you'll achieve riches, fam," I told him holding up my glass as if I was giving a speech at a wedding reception for the bride and groom.

While talking, a sexy mixed girl came over with a group of her friends hugging on Tim like he was a celebrity. They looked exotic so I wasn't sure what ethnicity they were; I just assumed they were Puerto Rican.

"What's up Tim, can we get our drink on?" they shouted out with their hands in the air.

"Damn boo, that's how you rolling. You ain't gonna give my boys a hug and kiss too?" he told them as he looked around at us.

When they introduced themselves, one girl caught a brother's attention. Her name was Stacey and she was sexy as hell. Baby had dark brown hair that was long and wavy and her complexion was so yellow, she reminded me of the sun. She looked like she was under twenty-one because she still had a baby face. However that didn't matter, because her body was so on point that it was enough to make me call home to Momma and tell her that I found the 'one.' When she smiled the whole room lit up; this girl captivated me and I had to get to know her.

She told me that she was going to Norfolk State and that she wasn't interested in getting serious with anyone because she didn't want to become distracted. Even though she told me that, I didn't believe her, because she turned around and asked me, "So what's up, are you talking to someone?" Then she said, "I'm sure you have lots of chicks after you, especially by you being so handsome and having the hottest spot in town to get your car done up."

"Nah, I'm just chilling after me and my daughter's mom broke up." After shooting the breeze to her for a few minutes and letting her know what was going on, we exchanged numbers and I told her, "Keep in touch with me, aight."

"Yeah, I think I'll do that," she said smiling and then blew me a kiss and walked off with her girls.

"Damn, playboy, I see you got Stacey's number. She's the hottest chick at NSU! Dawg, she won't even give me any play because she knows I got the girls at college on lock."

The night was coming to an end and we knew that the females hung around to see who was driving what, so we decided to head out and floss our rides in front of the club. Tim jumped into his Land Cruiser, while his boys Bryan and Shampoo rode shotgun. I hopped into my Lexus and bumped Biggie Smalls, "It's All Good." My cousin and his boys were pushing the MPV while smoking a gang of weed, hollering at every chick that left the club.

"Hey girl, you wanna go have breakfast at IHOP and then head to my house for some luvin?" they said to groups of girls as they walked by.

While everyone was worried about putting their dicks in anything that moved, I was concentrating on finding Stacey, she was the only girl worth wasting breathe on. I wasn't hollering at no female, no matter how fine that ass was. Stacey was the only girl that at the moment had my attention.

Waiting patiently for her to leave the club, I saw her with her girls walking towards a group of ballers quick on their heels. Each girl gave the men a friendly smile, but really didn't give them the time of day as they kept walking.

"Yo Stacey, make sure you drive home safely because God knows I need you in my life," I yelled at her, while she walked toward the direction my car was parked.

"I'm going to hit you tomorrow Laushaun, you drive safe as well," she said smiling as she waved and headed across the street.

Her saying that to me made my night. It didn't even matter that I didn't have anyone to bring home; I was content. I didn't trust taking any of them girls to my home, to the place where I laid my head anyway. While everyone made their ways to either IHOP for some early breakfast or to their cribs for some late sex, I decided to head home to get a good night's sleep. I got Stacey's number and that was all I needed. Besides, I had a long day tomorrow and had to get some shut-eye so I could be prepared.

Over the next few weeks, Stacey and I spent every possible waking moment together. We went jet skiing, paintball shooting, and any other activity you could think of, we did it. When she introduced me to her parents, I was surprised to find out they were Jamaican with a deep accent. Her father was a bank manager and all I could think about every time I was around him was … *Damn, this would be the perfect candidate to help get my paper deposited in the bank.* I never acted on that thought though.

I became so attached to Stacey that I made her my exclusive woman. She was a good girl who wasn't giving up the goodies for any reason; no matter what I did. And I liked that about her, but at the same time it was making me want her more. One Spring Break I decided to take her to Las Vegas. I figured a trip to 'Sin City' would be the perfect place for Stacey to get loose and free. Then she would willingly give me her love. When I told her about the trip, she agreed to go but didn't want to tell her parents because she was under twenty-one, and couldn't legally gamble.

We stayed at the MGM Grand and enjoyed our vacation either in the pool relieving ourselves from the sweltering heat, in the different amusement parks enjoying the rides, or catching the magic show of Siegfried and Roy doing amazing acts with their lions and bears. Since the casinos of Vegas were the main attraction, I knew that Stacey would probably want to go and check them out so she brought her fake ID with her. She told me she didn't want to miss out on having real 'Vegas' fun. She was a big girl and I wasn't going to keep her from doing what she wanted to do, so we headed off to the casino in our hotel. I sat at the black jack table gambling with Stacey rooting for me; things were going great until we spotted a security guard. He made eye contact with Stacey and walked over to her with this intimidating demeanor, meaning business and asked, "May I see your identification ma'am?"

Laushaun save me was the look she had on her face so I quickly jumped in. "Boo show him you're I.D.," I said calmly, but instead of pulling out the fake one that she had made, she accidently pulled out the real one.

"Ma'am, you're very beautiful and all, but you still have two more years before you're allowed to be in the casino. Please leave." I grabbed my winnings and we left the casino.

We made our way to the elevators and headed to the suite. Once we got to the room, I called room service to bring up a bottle of wine and bucket of ice. When our wine was delivered, I popped the bottle and poured our glasses. Stacey and I sipped our drinks while we enjoyed the view looking out the window at the different hotels and the beautiful lights that stretched Las Vegas strip.

"Laushaun I want to thank you for being so patient with me and not giving up on me," she said as she made her way closer to my side of the bed.

"Baby, I care for you. You mean a lot to me."

"Would you like to gimme a massage?"

"Yeah, I'll give you one." I knew then that it was time to take our relationship to the next level.

We had been in Vegas for four nights and all I've been able to do was caress her and suck on her perfect C cup tits.

"I'll be right back. I'm going to freshen up," she said after she undressed and headed to the bathroom.

While she was in the bathroom taking a shower, I prepared the Jacuzzi with bubbles from the shampoo that came with the suite. When she exited the shower completely naked, she noticed that I was sitting in the Jacuzzi sipping on a glass of wine. I reached down to where I kept her glass on chill in the bucket of ice next to the Jacuzzi and grabbed it.

"Here baby," I said handing her the glass while she slowly entered the steamy hot water and sat between my legs.

"Damn Laushaun, I see you're ready for what you've been patiently waiting for," she said as she felt the erection between my legs.

I put my glass down and as she drank her wine, I gently massaged her body. Soon she put her glass down and began to relax, her hands fell into the water and landed on my thighs and her soft ass was nestled closely to my manhood. At that very moment I knew it was time to take our party outside of the Jacuzzi, so I suggested we go to the bedroom.

"Stacey, let's go into the room so that I can finish massaging you." I took her to the bedroom and massaged her body while teasing her with an ice cube in my mouth. When the ice cube finally melted, I started with her perfectly manicured toenails and put my tongue on every inch of her body. When I reached her vagina, I slowly parted her lips and began to taste her. I could hear her breathing getting deeper as she moaned and panted. I locked my arms around her thighs and pulled her closer so that my tongue couldn't miss a spot. The more I licked her, the more she moaned and before I knew it, she was having a G-spot orgasm. She grabbed the back of my head and began to thrust her hips back and forth, until her climax had reached its end. When she let go of my head, I came up to gasp for air and then she quickly said, "Laushaun, put on your condom."

After she was fucking my face so vigorously I didn't want to put the condom on. I wanted to feel all of her, but I knew that she wouldn't do it without one. I was wrapped up in the moment of ecstasy and wanted to come inside of this girl … Damn, I wanted her to have my baby. I grabbed the condom off the dresser and bit into it to rip it open. When I put it on, I notice there was a hole from opening it up with my teeth.

"Do you have the condom all the way on Laushaun because I can't afford to get pregnant. I'm not ready for any kids."

"Baby, I have it completely pulled to the shaft," I told her while I covered the small hole in the tip of the condom.

"Baby please take it slow, it's been awhile," she said while I laid my 180-pound frame on her petite body. I slowly entered her; she was tight as a virgin, but one of the wettest women I'd ever been with.

"I promise, I won't hurt you baby," I assured her as I penetrated her with all nine inches of my loving. We got into our rhythm and I could tell that she was getting more and more into it because the faster I thrusted, the harder she grinded her hips while putting her nails deeply in my back. While our passion became more intense and every thrust became stronger, I felt the condom split in two. The sensation of her caves felt like I was in paradise. I think not having the condom on felt even better to her too because she wrapped her legs around me and I pounded harder and harder until we both reached our long awaited orgasms. Exhausted, I rolled off of her with my eyes closed and laid on my back.

"Oh my God Laushaun, your condom burst!" she cried.

"What? Oh my God, I didn't know that," I said, acting like I was surprised. She jumped out of the bed and ran into the bathroom attempting to press on her lower stomach to make the semen drip in the toilet. After trying to get the sperm out of her, she came back into the room with tears welling up in her eyes, "I hope you didn't get me pregnant, because I told you that I wasn't trying to get pregnant!" she murmured.

"Baby you're fine, don't worry yourself. If you're pregnant, I'll pay for the abortion, okay," I told her trying to ease her mind.

After assuring her that everything was fine, we both took a shower and bathed one another and got some rest before preparing for our eight-hour long flight back to Virginia.

Chapter 10

Going for the Gold

A YEAR HAD PASSED AND MY RELATIONSHIP WITH STACEY WAS STILL GOING strong. We had a very trustworthy relationship … or so I thought, until one rainy Saturday night. After several hours of paging and calling Stacey, I decided to head to her house; I was worried that something had possibly happened to her. Earlier that day, she had told me that she would be home all night so there was no reason for her not to answer her phone or my pages. The rain was pounding on my windshield and my tires sliced through the thick puddles of water on the highway as I raced to Stacey's house. When I got to her street, I quickly turned the corner; water splashed in the air and hit my windshield blurring my view. As I sped my windshield wipers up to clear my view, what I saw next astonished me. *You got be damn kidding me! Where the hell is this girl's car?* Her driveway was empty. Right then, I knew that she was still at the Rockafella studio with her girl, Tobie and her man, Bink. She had mentioned to me earlier that Tobie's boyfriend was getting his CD ready and had asked her to go with her to the studio, but she said she wasn't going to go.

Why the lies? I was so upset that she lied to me that I drove off as fast as I could, but just as I was pulling off I saw her Stanza pull around the corner. I wanted to jump out of the car so bad and drill her ass about where she had been all night and why she didn't return my calls … but a brotha's pride wouldn't let'em. My foot stayed on the gas pedal and kept rollin'. I was so angry that I began talking to myself out loud.

That girl ain't got to worry about me calling her. Shit, I didn't do nothing wrong—she gotta call me.

* * *

It became apparent after a significant amount of time had passed that Stacey wasn't calling me either, because I never heard from her. Now I can't lie and say a brotha' wasn't hurt … because I was. It bothered the hell out of me not ever really knowing why she did what she did. From time to time, when my phone would ring, I caught myself hoping it was her calling to apologize to me … but it never was. One day I woke up and decided that she wasn't worth the headache and I moved on with my life. I let go of that false hope … and changed both of my numbers to make myself stop believing that she was ever going to ring my phone again. For quite awhile I felt a void … but in no time, I began dating a schoolteacher from Maury High School and my void became filled.

Her name was Donna Bly, and she would come to get her Mazda 626 detailed on a regular basis and made sure she made it a point to speak to me every time she came. After a few months of flirting at the car wash, we finally exchanged phone numbers and it's been on ever since. Donna was cool as hell; I like her for her open-mindedness and the way she supported my business and me.

When I first laid eyes on her, I didn't find anything particularly stunning about her like I did with Stacey, but her personality was so sweet that I couldn't resist. When I would talk to her, she seemed like the sweetest woman in the world. I guess you can say she kind of grew on me. You know what's funny though? I didn't even know her name until one day Tim walked up to us and greeted her.

"What's up Donna Bly?" Tim said greeting her as he pulled me to the side.

"What's up with you and old girl Stacey?"

"Man I think she was cheating on me. I couldn't deal with it—I cut her loose."

"Man you know how these women are, but I see you haven't stopped popping game," he said as he nodded his head towards Donna.

"What do you mean, playboy?"

"Man, do you know who sister that is?"

I thought to myself, *am I supposed to know who she is?* I just knew that she was cool and we had a great vibe with each other.

"Nah, who is she?" I said like I really didn't care what he was about to tell me.

"Man her brother is Dre Bly, the football player."

"Okay … What's wrong, her brother doesn't want her hollerin' at ballers or something?" I asked Tim.

"Nah dawg, it ain't nothing like that. Her brother is cool peoples. He plays for the Tarheels—the dude is number one in college in interceptions alone. He's gonna be doing big things in the NFL one day."

"Damn, for real. That's what's up … so he's gonna be going pro soon, huh." Before Tim could even respond, Shampoo walked over to me with a grin on his face so big, I thought he hit the jackpot or something.

"What's up, Shampoo? What the hell you smiling for, dawg?" I asked him looking around hoping he wasn't trying to play a practical joke on me or something.

"Peep this, playboy; ol' girl over there, Donna, that's my home-boy's sister and she's feeling the hell outta you. I think you should go over there and holla at her. Show her what you all about."

"Yo—really?" I said trippin' out a little bit.

"Yeah really dawg, she got her own. She got a good job, a house—she got everything dawg, trust me. She's waiting on you to come over and say something to her," Shampoo said as he looked back over his shoulder to make sure she was still standing there. When I looked over at her, I saw her turn her head fast, but I could tell she was watching me.

"Oh word. So why don't she come over here and say something then? She scared to open her mouth or something?"

"She's shy. My girl doesn't know how to approach you." I understood where he was coming from. It's not everyday a woman just walks up to a man and spit game to him.

I had to head to the office to take care of some things, when I looked out the window and saw Shampoo walk over to her. I could tell they were talking about me because they kept staring my way and she even pointed towards me at one time. I stepped out of the office and looked their way.

"What's up boo? Cat got your tongue or something? Why haven't you come over here to talk to me yet?" I shouted out while standing in the front of my office door.

Walking my way, she just laughed and sassily said, "I'm a grown ass woman. I don't need anyone talking for me." Now that the ice was broken, Donna sat down with the fellas and I and talked for a while.

"Yo Shaun, we gonna head out," Tim said as him and Shampoo stood up, dapped me and gave Donna a hug.

"Aight, see y'all later." I didn't even realize it, but more than three hours had passed and the shop was actually closing up. I immediately grabbed my keys and was headed right behind them.

"Where are you going?" she asked in a slightly irritated tone.

"Oh, I'm sorry. I'm going to get something to eat—a brotha' is starving. We were so busy, I skipped lunch today."

"Am I invited?" she asked flashing me a smile.

"Girl, as sexy as you are, you can eat with me anytime," I said smiling back at her. Before we headed out, I went to find my mom to tell her I was gone for the day, but I would be back early the next morning to put in the supply order.

"Hey ma, I want you to meet my girl, Donna Bly," I told her and smiled when I saw the shocked look on Donna's face. I knew she would be mine; it was only a matter of time before we made it official. My mom gave Donna a good look over; I could tell she was approving of her by the look she had in her eyes.

"Now this looks like a real woman who deserves my baby. Not like that rest of them gold diggin' gals. But I can tell you're not like that, are you?" Mom said as she extended her hand to Donna giving her a questioning look.

"No ma'am, not at all. I got my own job; my own car and I pay my own bills. I'm very independent," Donna said with a smile on her face.

"Now that's what I'm talking about right there. See that's a real woman. Laushaun, make sure you treat her special. I can tell she's like you. She wants something out of life and she's willing to work hard to get it."

"I will Mom—we gotta go now. I love you." We told my mother goodbye, and then walked out to my car.

"Donna, I'm gonna drive my car, you mind following me?" I asked hoping she wouldn't get offended.

"Okay, that will work—I can follow you. What restaurant do you want to go to? It's my treat." I was impressed that she actually offered to pay for my meal, but being the gentleman I am, I quickly interjected.

"Nah boo, I got this. It's ladies night tonight. Dinner's on me, but thanks for the offer—it speaks volumes to me. Now, where would you like to eat?"

"I'm not picky at all. We can go to McDonald's for a burger and I'll be satisfied."

Damn, this is too good to be true. Whenever I asked most women where they wanted to go, they would shout out some 5 star restaurants that they couldn't even pronounce.

"Aight boo, I tell you what—follow me." I jumped into my car and led her to Ruby Tuesday's. I had been feening for their rib eye steak for months, but never got around to eating it. I also knew that no matter what she had a taste for; she would be able to find it on their menu.

When we got to the restaurant, I opened the door to let her walk through while I admired her curvaceous body and imagined how good her bare flesh looked as she sauntered in front of me towards our table. As the waitress seated us, I treated her like the princess that she was and pulled out her chair to seat her. Looking at her, I couldn't believe how beautiful she truly was. Her high yellow toned skin was radiant and her full pink lips appeared to be supple.

"Thank you, Laushaun. You are spoiling me," she said as she pulled her reading glasses out of her purse. Damn she's even sexier with them glasses on. I think I was falling in love. I was so in awe that I couldn't stop staring at her, which obviously made her feel uncomfortable.

"I hate wearing these damn glasses," she said as she pulled them back off after catching me stare. She then started struggling, trying to read the fine writing on the menu.

"Yo Donna, please put your glasses back on."

"I hate them, they make me look ugly," she said looking like she wanted to cry.

"Nah, they don't. I think they make you more attractive."

"You really think so? Oh—okay," she said smiling at me while she placed them back on her face. I could tell after I had told her, her confidence level was boosted.

We started talking, enjoying our meal, and enjoying each other's company. I learned that both of her parents were teachers and that she was inspired by them to become one too. Her mother taught at Ingleside Elementary and her father taught at Norview High. Even though Tim had put me up on who her brother was, she told me about him too. I listened to her and didn't let on that I already knew that her brother, Dre, was a football player on a full scholarship ride at North Carolina. The most important thing that I found out about Donna that night was that her family meant a lot to her and she would do anything for them. I liked that about her, because I felt the same way about my family … There's nothing I wouldn't do for them too.

During our conversation I was upfront about my upbringing … I told her that I was very fortunate to make it out of the struggle that I went through growing up. I explained to her that I was trying to be a better man by learning from other people's mistakes and with God's help, He would see me through to the end. We talked for hours and then she invited me to her crib.

"Well, if you'd like, you wanna come to my condo in Chesapeake? We can finish this date off with a movie, if you don't mind."

"Of course, I'm down," I said feeling relieved that she invited me over. I wasn't ready for the night to end; I was really enjoying her company. Shit, I would have gone to the moon with her if she'd asked me to.

We pulled up to her condo, and I was shocked. Damn, she must have been making some nice money as a teacher because she was staying in the nice part of Chesapeake. The community she lived in had its own security guard patrolling the area. She waved at the guard and let him know I was with her.

She pulled up on the side of me and rolled down her window, "Hey, park in the visitor's spot, since your car isn't registered here, I don't want them to tow your ride," she said as she directed me to the spot. When we entered the condo, her toy poodle ran to the door and started barking excitedly. I could tell that the dog loved her because the dog all but jumped into her arms at the first sight of her.

"Hey Kobe, how is Momma's baby? I missed you—how is Momma's good boy?" she said, talking to him like he was an actual person. After getting him situated with food and water, she told me to get comfortable as she went upstairs for a second.

Making her way upstairs, Kobe followed her every footstep, barking the whole way. Sitting down, I noticed a Playboy magazine that said 'All American' on her table. I picked up the magazine and saw a bunch of athletes on the cover. I scanned my eyes over to the left and noticed this one dude looked just like Donna. Then I realized it was her brother, number 32 of the NC Tarheels, Dre Bly. They couldn't deny that they were brother and sister … The only differences between them were their complexions. She was yellow where he was a caramel brown complexion. I read the article and was very impressed with his accomplishments. It was good to see someone like me actually make it to the top and be recognized for it.

Donna headed back downstairs and I noticed she had changed her clothes.

"Where's Kobe?" I asked although I really didn't care.

"He's upstairs. I locked him in the room so we could have some peace and quiet."

She walked over to the VCR and bent over to put a video in it, when her long white t-shirt ascended up her back, giving me a wonderful view of her beautiful yellow ass cheeks peeking out of her panties and staring me right in my face. As I gazed back at the lovely view, I imagined making love to her and then my manhood began to rise.

"Have you seen *Coming to America,* Laushaun?" she asked while walking back towards the couch to sit with me.

Snapping out of my daydream, I quickly responded, "Nah, I'm not really into watching fairy tales or nothing like that."

"What's wrong, you don't enjoy happy endings?" she asked me while lightly punching me in the arm.

"Nah, it's not that, just not my thang," I told her.

"Well, just give it a chance. I'm sure you'll like this movie," she said laughing. "Can I get you something to eat or drink? I got some Absolute Vodka, Beringer's White Zinfandel and some cokes," she asked after the movie started.

"No I'm cool, but do you mind if I smoke in your house?" I asked her. I knew some people were funny about smoking in their homes, especially if they didn't smoke and I wanted to make sure I had permission first.

"Yeah that's cool, but let me open the patio door. I don't want Kobe and I to catch a contact high," she laughed, getting up to open the door while I pulled out a blunt that I had previously started.

As I fired up the blunt, she sat next to me and cuddled on her soft sofa pillows. After getting into the movie, we started getting personal as she started telling me about her past relationships. She had dealt with a lot of drug dealers in her past and I found it very interesting that a woman of her caliber dealt with dudes like that, but I didn't question it … because truth betold, I was that dude too.

"Well I was hanging in the clubs a lot when I was younger so you know how that goes. I just kinda got wrapped up in the life. You know what I mean?"

"Yeah I feel you there."

"So are you still talking to your baby's momma?" she asked me although she didn't look me directly in the eye. I could tell she hoped to hear the right answer."

"Yeah, we talk when it's pertaining to my daughter, but that's it. I do take care of her, by paying her bills and stuff, but that's because I have to. I do it for the sake of my daughter. I mean don't get me wrong or anything, she's a great mother, but she's spoiled as hell and refuses to do anything with her life."

After soaking everything in, she surprised me by telling me that she's been checking me out for over a year, but was afraid to approach me because of all the women who appeared to be coming after me.

"I ain't trying to be someone's backup woman, you know what I mean. It's all or nothing with me," she said and I could tell she was very serious.

"I feel ya, Donna. But I'm not that type of dude. When I'm with a woman, I'm with her and no one else. I'm not like these other cats out here who are trying to get with every woman they see."

"So are you looking for a woman right now?" she asked.

"Not really—I mean, I just got out of a serious relationship a few months ago and I just don't wanna be hurt again."

"I'm not like that. I know what it feels like to be hurt by some-one. When I'm with my man, I'm with him 100%." I listened to her speak and she sounded sincere … I took her words close to heart. She made me feel secure and I knew that I could be with her. From then on, we were inseparable and I made sure everyone knew it. I even made sure Donna knew what type of lifestyle I was living; that's how serious I was about her. When I told her, she was cool... She had no problem with me being in the drug game because she was used to rollin' with heavy hitters anyway.

I made sure Donna was well taken care of, there wasn't a thing I would not do for her. I upgraded her Mazda 626 to a Lexus 400 and even bought her an Acura Integra with her own personalized license plate. I wanted her to represent her brother to the fullest so her plate said, 'UNC 32'. Her parents loved me and welcomed me into their home with opened arms. We would stop by her mom's job several times a week to bring her lunch and anything else she needed. Next to my mother and grandmother, Donna's mom was the sweetest thing in the world. The woman treated me like I was already her son in-law; I was always invited over for dinner and at-tended various family functions and activities. Donna's father was pretty quiet though, other than speaking whenever I came over, he stayed in his computer room for most of the day.

Every weekend, I treated Donna's family to Dre's games, no matter where they were, and would get new Tarheels wear for all of us. I would even invite their uncle and his wife from time to time, just to make sure that the whole family was there to support him.

One day after a game, Shampoo and I stood outside our cars in the parking lot and Dre walked over to speak.

"What's up Shampoo? What's up Laushaun? What ya'll up to?" he said approaching our cars.

"I didn't know you knew Shampoo, Dre."

"Yeah, we go way back," Shampoo said giving him a five.

"Now how the hell do ya'll know each other?" Dre asked me with a curious look. I knew he knew what Shampoo did for a living and even though his sister was aware of what was up, I didn't want him to know that I had any dealings in that lifestyle.

"Oh, we know each other through my boy, Tim Montgomery," I told him, hoping it would resolve any further questioning he had.

"Oh, okay," he said, appearing to be satisfied with my response.

***

LIFE WAS SO lovely for me. If I wasn't putting in an order for my cousin to push work, I was spending all my time with Donna. We were like a match made in heaven. I felt like she was that rib that had been missing from me. I was feeling complete. A few months into our relationship it was her birthday so I dressed her wrist with a Rolex watch. If my baby was gonna tell time, I wanted her do it with style.

Every week I would buy her a dozen roses and have them delivered to her job. And to spice up our sex life, I would spend thousands of dollars on Victoria's Secret lingerie. To reward me for my generosity, Donna would always entertain me with something new when we had sex. She would go to the Pink Bananas Adult Toy Store and buy whips, handcuffs, vibrators, dildos and many, many other toys that would be incorporated into our playtime together. She loved playing with toys, and I sure as hell didn't mind. That was a side of Donna that I knew no one knew about. My quiet little schoolteacher, who presented herself as a lady on the streets, was a massive freak behind closed doors. I knew that every time I had sex with Donna, there was gonna be a new adventure.

Aside from her toys and gadgets, Donna had an erotic fantasy that she would constantly talk about. "Baby, I have always wanted to sleep with a woman … and have threesomes," she would say. At first, I thought she was just joking, you know saying something just to get me excited, but as time went on, I could tell that she was serious.

One day I told Donna about going to Atlanta to support my boy, Tim, in the Olympics. I knew he was going to break some records and bring home the gold, and I wasn't going to miss it for nothing. She told me she was all for going because there was a club there called Magic City where she could possibly make her wildest fantasy come true.

"Yeah, I want some chick to give me a sensual lap dance," she said, looking like she was fantasizing about it. Hell, I was secure with who I was, so it didn't bother me that Donna's main reason for wanting to go to Atlanta was to tickle her fancy. So our trip was set … we were heading to the A-T-L.

As the time got closer to the Olympics, I could tell that Tim was getting even more excited. It was time for him to finally show the world who Tim Montgomery really was. When we got to Atlanta, I couldn't believe how many people were there. There were people from every country around the world … it was an amazing sight to see. Celebrities were there too, strolling in like they were on the red carpet in Hollywood instead of the Olympics. It was funny watching how each one tried to outshine the other.

On the other hand, I wasn't worried about flossing and showing off, my two concerns were Tim and Donna. I wanted Tim to know that I was there for him and not for the show and as for Donna, well since Unique turned me on to the orgie fest we had in New York, I couldn't wait to see my woman with another woman. Just thinking about it had my manhood hard.

When we got to the stadium, it was ridiculously packed that it was impossible to even see what was going on, so I did the next best thing. I decided to just watch the event at the club, Magic City itself. Entering the club, I thought I was in booty heaven as I watched all the women approach Donna and I while we made our way to the bar.

"Oh my God, Laushaun, I'm dripping so much that my thighs are starting to stick together," she whispered in my ear while she looked around the room at all the beautiful women. Just as she finished whispering in my ear, I saw a sexy caramel sister walking over to us.

"Do you wanna dance?" she asked, directing the question towards me.

"Nah sweetie, I'm cool. I just want to look at you, but check this out. It is my lady's biggest fantasy to get a dance. Can you make her dreams come true?" I asked her as I handed her a thousand dollars to make it possible.

"Oh definitely," she said as her and Donna stared each other in the eyes. Donna was smiling from ear to ear as the dancer moved towards her rocking her body to Too Short. I could tell Donna was getting more excited when the dancer gently caressed Donna's breast as she moved up and down Donna's body. When she got to the perfect level, she teased Donna by placing her breast in Donna's mouth and then slowly pulled it out. I could tell that Donna loved every minute of it because she was opening and closing her legs … She was most definitely turned on. The dancer knew Donna was feeling it too, because she got down on her knees and started licking and caressing Donna's inner thighs. She was so close to Donna's vagina that I thought she was eating it.

"Damn, your juices taste so good," the dancer said as Donna tilted her head back in ecstasy. I didn't know what she was talking about until I saw that Donna's juices were running down her leg. *Damn, she's cumming that hard,* I said to myself and lightly chuckled.

Donna held the dancer's head as she grinded deeply into her face and moaned loudly as she came multiple times. I just smiled because I knew that she was getting a pleasure that even I couldn't provide for her at that moment. As her body started going into convulsions, I knew that she had her every fantasy fulfilled with the dancer and it was well worth my money. Damn, I see why they call Atlanta the Chocolate City, I said to myself as I watched Donna come down from her sexual high. ATL was a Mecca, and anything went in the Mecca … They had no discrimination when it came down to it; the only color that mattered was that green paper.

The weekend was beautiful. Tim had won a gold and silver medal and Donna had finally fulfilled her lifelong fantasy. While we were on the plane headed back to Virginia, my phone vibrated repeatedly. I didn't even waste my time looking to see who it was because I couldn't answer it on the plane anyway, so I just had to wait until we landed on the ground. During the flight, Donna confessed her love to me. She couldn't believe that not only did I accept her sexual fantasies without looking at her differently, but also that I actually let her live them out.

"Laushaun, I love you so much. I wanna marry you—I wanna have your kids," she said and then I leaned over and passionately kissed her.

"Dang woman, you don't even give me time to speak my mind, do you?" I said laughing at her. I had been thinking about asking her for weeks, but wanted to wait until the time was right and it seemed like that time was now.

"Well, I guess there's no better time than in the friendly skies," she said and smiled at me. Even though it was not done in a traditional way, it was official. We were engaged. That made the end of a perfect weekend, however, that was short-lived. When I finally looked at my phone, I saw that my voicemail was full. I looked at the missed calls and noticed that they all came from the 718, area code, which meant it was either Unique or Boo-Bee calling me. *What the hell is going on?* I had a funny feeling that something had happened.

While I was checking my messages to see what the problem was, Boo-Bee's call interrupted.

"Yo Lo-co, where the hell you been, man? I've been trying to call you since last night!" Boo-Bee said in a frantic tone.

"What's good fam? I've been in the ATL for the Olympics. My boy, Tim, won a gold and silver medal, dawg. And you ain't gonna believe this … but guess what? A player is engaged." I didn't hear anything on the other side of a phone for a while and thought he may have hung up.

"Hello? Boo-Bee, you still there?"

"Yeah man, I'm here. But listen, business is hot as hell, man. The Feds came and raided Unique's studio and a few of his houses, man. They're looking all over for him."

"Man, what the hell happened?" I asked. I knew we were keeping it on the low, so I didn't know what was going on. He told me that Peter's baby's mother had been indicted and that Peter and Unique were going to be seized by the Feds. They are going to charge them with conspiracy to traffic drugs from New York to Virginia.

"Yo Lo-co, I'm gonna have my wife keep you posted on what's going on. We're gonna have to lie low, because I feel this is the calm before the storm. I just got a feeling this ain't the last of this. And they know shit has been movin' to Virginia …" I knew what he meant too. The Feds just don't come knocking at your front door and wait for you to answer. They bust into your crib and take you and your family until they get answers. I had to get home and prepare for the worst.

"I got you, dawg. Let me get my shit in order," I said, trying to stay calm and not let Donna know something was going on.

"Man, make sure you got your shit right, because it's time for you to protect everything you own," was the last thing he said before he hung up the phone.

Damn, right when I was feeling on top of the world, someone had to knock my ass right back down.

Chapter 11

Put Your Hands Up

Six months later, I didn't know what to do. It was as beautiful as heaven on one end but on the other, I felt like I was in a living hell. After talking to Boo-Bee's wife on a regular basis, she told me that they finally caught up with Unique, after being on the run for so long.

"Damn, for real, so what's gonna happen with his song and Mecca Audio?" I asked her. That song was a huge hit and it was sad that it would be a waste. She told me that he sold the rights of Mecca Audio and everything that went with it ...

"Have you ever heard of the rapper, Dougie Fresh?"

"Yeah, I love him."

"He's made Unique's song a huge hit. You ain't been listening to the radio. They have been playing it all over," she told me.

Knowing that there was an on-going investigation and that any day I could be implicated ... I hadn't been doing too much of *any-thing* as of lately. But I was happy to find out that Unique's song was out there where people could hear it. Of course, no one would ever know that Unique wrote it, but in his mind, he knew that it was his. Boo-Bee's wife also told me that Peter had gotten killed in Texas. The police weren't even trying to find out what happened to him because he was just considered a fugitive who was armed and dangerous. Boo-Bee flew to Florida to try to stay low key. He heard the Feds were talking to Unique and offering him a plea deal, but he wouldn't take it. Unique felt that if he paid enough people, he would get off, or get his time reduced.

I got off the phone with Boo-Bee's wife and stared at the wall in front of me. *It's just a matter of time until they trace everything to me. It's just a matter of time that they find out that I'm a part of this whole operation. I gotta tell Donna.* At that moment, I made the decision to tell Donna that the Feds may be indicting me for the business that me and my New York fam was involved in.

"Laushaun, I don't care. I still want to be with you. I want to be Mrs. Robinson and have your kids. I'm not leaving you, okay," she said crying. I knew that I had found the woman of my dreams. Most women would run for cover when trouble comes their way, but Donna was determined to be with me through thick and thin.

"We'll get through this, Laushaun, and don't worry about it, because when Dre goes pro, I promise, you will never have to do anything in the streets again. We'll be set for life!" She told me and I believed her.

Time was truly of the essence so I began to handle some things. The first thing I did was set aside a hundred thousand dollars to make sure that my grandparents were okay. Next, I had Nicole, my daughter's mother; I fixed her up to run the car wash so that as long as it was running smoothly, she wouldn't want for anything. When I told Donna about Nicole operating the car wash, she became overzealous. She felt that I was disrespecting her because she was my fiancée.

"I don't want Nicole being the sole operator of the car wash, Laushaun. I'm gonna be your wife, not her." I understood where she was coming from, but she knew what was up with Nicole from day one … and if I didn't set Nicole up with the business, my daughter's lifestyle would suffer. Therefore Ms. Bly, soon to be Mrs. Robinson, had to get over that shit—and quick.

The next person on my list was Scoot, but to my surprise, my cousin transitioned out of the drug game safely and started a legitimate business. He had nothing to worry about.

* * *

1997 WAS COMING to an end and Shampoo and Tim had reached stardom in their own rights doing business together. On the other hand, Donna and I had done a lot of traveling, because we knew that our time together was short and precious. They had finally picked up Boo-Bee in Miami and were planning on indicting me for distributing cocaine from New York to Virginia. I just didn't know when.

It was the end of December and since I was still a free man, Donna and I decided to go to Diddy's grand opening of his new restaurant, Justin's. When we pulled up to the restaurant, Diddy was there to greet his guest, so we shook each other's hand and took a picture with Donna by my side. After having a great time at the restaurant, we headed over to Times Square. I knew if we made it in time, we could still see the ball drop and celebrate the New Year in together. As twelve o'clock hit, I turned to Donna, got on one knee, and pulled the ring out of my pocket.

"What are you doing, Laushaun?" Donna said when she saw what I was doing.

"Donna, I love you more than life itself. You are the first thing I think about when I wake up in the morning and the last I think about when I rest my head. I want to be with you today, tomorrow, and forever. I know we kinda did this on the plane, but I want to do it the right way. Will you marry me and accept everything that comes with me now and what's to come?" I asked her as I grabbed the two-carat solitaire princess cut diamond band with beautiful VVS baguettes surrounding it.

"Are you serious, Laushaun? Oh my God! Yes—Yes, I will marry you," she said as she looked at the ring while I placed it on her finger. "I am the happiest woman on earth," she spoked softly with a huge smile on her face.

We ended our memorable night in Atlantic City at the Trump Towers. We made love repeatedly and hoped that we could have the love child that we both wanted so much.

January came and I finally had to face the cold destiny that awaited me. It was four in the morning, and I was lying in the bed naked while Donna was taking a shower. All of a sudden, I heard banging on the front door. BAM, BAM, BAM, BAM, BAM! Donna popped her head out the shower.

"Laushaun, who da fuck is banging on the door like that at this time of the morning?" she yelled.

"I dunno, let me go and check it out." Still naked, I grabbed my gun and ran downstairs. "Who is it?" I yelled, pissed that somebody was waking me up out of some good sleep.

"U.S. Marshall, open the door," they yelled while still continuing to knock on the door.

Shit. I ran upstairs and hid my gun. I walked into the bathroom and told Donna the Feds were here to get me. "Baby, stay upstairs and get your clothes on quick. I love you." Without me even putting clothes on, I ran back downstairs to open the door, before they rammed it in. In a matter of seconds, twenty men rushed in the house encircling me with their guns drawn.

"U.S. Marshalls, put your hands up—Willie Laushaun Robinson—we're looking for Wille Laushaun Robinson—are you him?" one man yelled.

"Yes," I replied as my heart raced rapidly. I put my hands in the air and stood like the Belgian statue, "Manneken Pis"—on display naked peeing—as I watched them search my house and questioned Donna. They searched but there was nothing to find, because I lived by the rule that Uncle Ricky taught me … Never stash your money or weight where you rest your head.

"Mr. Robinson, let's get you dressed." Two men escorted me upstairs to the room where they watched as I threw on a t-shirt, pair of jeans and sneakers. When I was done, they handcuffed me and took me into custody. At Portsmouth City Jail, I was officially indicted for being part of a five million dollar a year drug operation.

Although Donna and I had planned for a big wedding, she was still by my side. She was determined to marry me right away and be there for me through my federal sentence. Her parents had a different opinion though. Through the weeks they saw my indictment on the news, and they told Donna not to marry me so that she could protect the family's reputation. They did not want to be associated with a king pin drug lord. However, my Donna didn't listen to them, instead she followed her heart.

Our ceremony was at the Portsmouth City Jail. While we waited on the minister to announce our vows, Donna said, "Baby, I have to tell you something because you may not want to be with me after I tell you this." I suspected of what it was and I didn't care. I loved her for who she was.

"Sweetie, as long as you are faithful to me, nothing else matters."

"Yes it does. Laushaun, I'm losing my hair." I knew that's what she was going to tell me.

"Baby, that doesn't matter to me at all."

"But I'm going to be bald soon. I don't want you to be embarrassed with a woman who has to wear wigs," she said with tears welling up in her eyes.

I had known something was going on a while back, because she would never comb her hair around me. I'd never seen her wash, treat, or even touch her hair too much for that matter. Whenever I took her to the salon and tried to wait on her, she would get in defense mode and make me leave before they even put her in their chair.

"Baby, I love you for you. I don't care what you look like, as long as your heart stays forever mine then there is nothing that will keep us apart," I told her. Although I didn't care about the details, she told me that it was a hereditary thing from her father's side of the family. She said that she would be getting implants when Dre makes it to the NFL.

"Baby, I'm cool about the hair, okay."

The Chaplain made his way to the room; we said our vows and were officially connected as one. After the wedding, Donna happily changed her last name to Mrs. Donna Robinson.

Since it was my first offense, they offered me seventeen years for the federal indictment. However, it was reduced to eight to ten years with my plea bargain and accepting my role in the operation. Everyone got this deal except Unique; he took his case to trial and received life in prison. But a few years later, it was appealed and was lowered to thirty years.

When I entered the courtroom, I saw Donna in the audience. I could tell she was being strong, but I heard a sigh in her voice when they started reading off my charges. Conspiracy to distribute kilos of powdered cocaine … Money laundering and possession of a firearm while committing a felony … My lawyer petitioned the firearm charge and got it dropped … My final sentence was for seven years.

Once the judge finished reading my sentence, I looked back at my family, Donna included, and they were all holding hands. When the officers came to take me out of the courtroom, I saw the hurt and anger in my family's eyes. It pained me deeply to see them that way … I wanted to run up to my mom and Donna and just hug them, but I couldn't. So I looked at them for a moment and mouthed goodbye.

Trying to make the time less stressful, I would call the shop everyday and see how things were going. Nicole told me that everything was running smoothly and that she let Donna handle the deposit everyday, so she really didn't know what kind of money the business was bringing in. I knew the girls bumped heads a lot, but there was nothing I could do about it since I was locked up.

It took ninety days for me to actually be shipped to the federal prison. I didn't understand why the process took so long, but they took major safety precautions when it came to transporting people with federal crimes. When I got on the bus with over a hundred other inmates, I noticed that the windows were barred and the tint on the outside was so dark you couldn't even see in. From the bus, we were taken to a plane and we flew a long and uncomfortable ride to make our way to the Atlanta United States Penitentiary.

When I got to the two-man cell, I was surprised to see an extra mattress in the center of the floor. I couldn't believe I was crammed up in a tiny cell with two other people. We were locked up for twenty-three hours a day with one hour for recreation time, Monday through Friday. The cell reeked of body odor, because showers were only allowed every other day; but eventually I learned to adapt to the smell, I had no other choice but to. It wasn't like I could request to move to a bigger cell. The dudes in my cell were pretty cool. They gave me the rundown on how the federal system worked and the codes of conduct amongst inmates, including what clique was what.

A few days later at three in the morning, my cell door flung open and the guard called my name. "Mr. Robinson, pack up your linen and let's go. You're being moved to Manchester, Kentucky medium-high Federal Prison."

We loaded the bus and we began our long ride. Several hours later, I looked out the window and saw nothing but mountains. Where the hell are they taking us? There ain't nuthin' out here. The bus turned down this dirt road and began to slowly make its way up a steep mountain. I wasn't sure how long it took us, but it felt like an hour … The bus finally began to descend down this road into my home for the next several years. I looked out the window and mumbled, *Damn, I never thought it would happen to me,* but here I am.

Chapter 12

Two Years and Counting

I HAD BEEN IN PRISON FOR 2 YEARS AND MY TIME WAS GETTING STRESSFUL. Shampoo had just beaten a murder rap and thought he was clear until the federal inmates decided to testify against him on the distribution of kilos. He was skating on thin ice and it was just a matter of time before they finally stuck a charge to him. I knew that if the Feds knew about Shampoo then it wouldn't be long before Tim was tied in the mix, so I decided to give him a heads up on what was going on so he could try to get himself together. Ever since Tim invested into Shampoo's weight, they were inseparable. The word on the street was those niggas were calling themselves 'The Bird Man' and I knew that name only came from pushing kilos.

After I called Tim to let him know what was going on, I talked to Shampoo. I was surprised to find out that Shampoo had gotten married and Dre Bly was his best man. He told me that everyone joined him and his new wife in the Caribbean Islands during his honeymoon and he was really happy. After he shared his good news, I had to let him know what I heard on the inside. When I told him what was up, all Shampoo could say was, "I feel what you saying, dawg. I just gotta weigh my options before I make any final decisions." He didn't realize that the clock was ticking and if he waited too long, then his time would soon run out.

"Dawg, they could be getting more evidence on the homicide case that was just dropped in your favor," I said, trying to convey the seriousness of the matter. But all he could say was, "I feel you, dawg." I didn't know what else to say to him so I let his fate lay in his hands.

Donna was getting stressed over our situation. It seemed that society, loneliness and her family values weighed down on her constantly. One weekend while visiting me, I noticed that something was very different about her. Whenever we would talk, she avoided eye contact with me, which was something she'd never done before and she kept spitting into a napkin like she was sick or something. Although I wasn't a woman, I wasn't stupid either and knew something was up.

"Donna, I'm about to ask you something and I need you to be honest with me. Can you do that for your husband?"

"Yeah baby, what is it?" she asked, as she turned sideways to make sure I couldn't see her face.

"You aren't cheating on me, are you?" I asked her, checking out her body language more than the actual answer that came from her mouth.

"Why—why you ask that?" she said as she stiffened up and looked down to the floor. Her body language told me the answer, but I wanted to know what she had to say.

"You just ain't been acting yourself and your schedule has been crazy lately. It seems I can never get a hold of you when I need to." Whenever I would call her, she wouldn't answer the house or her cell phone, and when she did answer and I asked her of her whereabouts, she would get defensive and flip things around on me. When she was about to answer my question, a weird feeling came over me, and I knew right then what was wrong with her.

"Yo Donna, what the hell are you spittin' so much for?" I raised my voice while trying to tame the fire that was welling up from within me. I knew the signs of pregnancy and I knew nausea was one of them. She had never done this before and her face was so pale, it looked like she hadn't had a drop of sunlight in years.

"I—I just got a bad taste in my mouth, Laushaun. I ate something for breakfast and it just has me all messed up. That's all."

I could no longer control the anger and I fired back with a full barrel, "Whore, you must think I'm stupid. I know your ass is pregnant. Who the hell have you been creeping with? I knew you weren't shit. Not only did you cheat on me, but you had the nerve to get pregnant by the fool." The words came roaring out of my mouth like a lion. I was so livid that I didn't know what to do.

"Baby, I'm so sorry. I just missed you so much and I got lonely. I didn't mean for it to happen, the condom just broke," she cried as she told me about her affair with some guy named D. Shawn. After all the things she promised me, I couldn't believe she could do something like that. I didn't want to hear another word she had to say. I was hurt by my own wife.

"I don't want anything else to do with your ass. Don't ever come visit me again. In fact, I expect to see the divorce papers … I'm not going to be married to a cheating, lying whore who can't keep her damn legs closed."

"Baby, I'm so sorry. Please forgive me, it will never happen again. Just tell me what you want me to do. I don't want to lose you Laushaun," she begged as I got up and left her sitting in her misery. That was the last time I saw Donna. She tried to visit me a few times after, but I refused all her visits and finally months later, I received what I'd been waiting for … divorce papers.

Apparently, Shampoo was not worried about his safety at all because he started balling out of control and before long, he was found viciously murdered with his brain matter spilled inside of his Honda. I was devastated. I didn't know what to think or do, but I wasn't the only one hurt by his death, because just a few weeks later while watching BET, I saw a Clipse video with a tribute to Shampoo. They wore t-shirts stating, 'We love and miss you Shampoo'.

I was still distressed over Donna's deception. I learned that the guy she was pregnant by was a major drug dealer who was known for having several babies' mommas. Donna was the seventh woman to bear his child. The woman who I called my wife, and that I loved so much was now some other nigga's baby's momma. Damn, we were supposed to have a baby together, it wasn't supposed to go down like this, but because her ass couldn't do the one thing she vowed to me and to God to do … Any love I had left for her—has now completely gone away.

So much had happened in such short time that I didn't know where my world started and ended. I prayed every day for my grand-parents' safety and that my money would stay safe because every-thing else in my life had gone down the drain. Feeling that she was much more than just a detail shop owner, Nicole decided to do other things with her time, which started bringing my business down hard. My mother was there for me every step of the way and gave me en-couraging words when I needed them most. It seemed like every woman I ever gave my heart to has double-crossed me in some form or fashion.

Eventually, I learned that I had lost my business. My life was in shambles and I felt I had no one to really lean on for support. Daily I began walking the yard to clear my head and think about things. One day, I met this dude, Prince from New York, while walking around the yard. He had already been locked up for 10 years and was just counting down the next couple years to his freedom. Prince was cool peeps; from that day forward, he and I became homies and all we ever did was talk about different ways we could make money.

"Yo Shaun, since you only have a year and a half left, you should call your Panama connects so that you can reconnect when you get out," he said to me one day while we were on our usual daily walk. "Man, with Panama being right there, I know we could make a killing. I know a kilo will be less than five grand. Hell, heroine would make us rich, because that's the hot shit going right now. A kilo of that would be less than 20 thousand for sure."

I decided to take his advice and send them a Christmas card. I knew that just with me contacting them, they would know what was up and get back at me. In the card, I just left a simple message that said … "I'll see them soon." Prince and I also talked about ways to triple our money once it started coming in and I knew just the way to do it.

"Yo Prince, real estate is the hot thang right now. It's a gold mine and everyone I know who is getting into it is making money hand over fist," I told him, while thinking about the large amount of money that could be made.

"Word, I'm down," he said as he gave me dap.

If I was going to do the real estate thing, I wanted to do it right. I had my mom send me all kind of books on real estate and send me the laws of real estate in Virginia. For four months we studied hard and I knew everything there was to know about the business. I was excited about the possibilities that lay ahead for me. My plans were to jump back in the game for a minute, make some quick cheese and then get out; using real estate as my 'out'. It was the perfect business for me to clean up my dirty money and actually make a lucrative profit.

When Christmas rolled around, I couldn't believe that I'd actually gotten a card from Donna. She told me that she'd been thinking about me and had a little boy named Deshon. I tripped out when I learned his birthday was just a week from mine, August 6th. After telling me about her brother's career, she ended the card with, "I hope this year brings you home closer to the one you love the most."

What the hell? I couldn't believe she was trying to play me for a fool after all I'd done for her. Instead of dwelling on Donna's card and the past, I decided to look towards the future and not look back.

In less than 90 days, I would be a free man and could do what I longed for forever, to reconnect with the world.

Everything was in order for my release date and each day I thanked God for seeing me through for six years. I called my mom and told her to meet me at the Newport News train station. I wanted her to be the first to see me. I had a lot of catching up to do with many people, but she meant the most to me. I also told her to call my grandparents and cousin to let them know that I would be there soon. My mom was the middleman when it came to my grandparents and cousin, because I didn't want to get them involved with anything that the Feds were doing, so I kept my distance from them.

When the day finally came, I felt like I was floating on air. Before the guards dropped me off at the train station, they gave me $500 cash, an $8,000 check and my ticket and I was on my way.

"Mr. Robinson, make this the last time you enter this system. You're too smart for this," one of the guards told me as I exited the car.

"Thanks for the inspiration," I told him as I shook his hand and headed into the station.

The train ride took six hours; I thought I would never get there, but once we pulled up and I saw my mother's and brother's faces, the long trip was worth it.

"Welcome home, Bookie!" they said in unison as they hugged me. When we got to my mom's house, I didn't know what was going on. There were cars everywhere. The house was full of people. All my boys were there and showed their respects to me being home. There was so much food in the house I didn't know what to start with first. As the party got started, my crew had given me several cards with money in them that equaled well over $50,000.

"Yo, come on ya'll. We gonna finish this up at Ridley's," one of my boys said as he grabbed his girl and headed out the door.

I didn't know what I was going to wear, but to my surprise my mother had that all figured out. There were several outfits for me in her room as well as a cell phone.

"Thanks Mom, you didn't have to do all this," I said while I picked up the clothes to quickly look at what she got for me.

"Oh hush, Bookie. You know I would do anything for you," she said as I kissed her and headed out of the room. Making my way into the living room, I gave everyone my new cell phone number and told them that I would meet with them later. I wanted to just relax and spend some quality time with my mom. She was the one who made sure that I was comfortable while in prison and I wanted to thank her for that through my actions by chillin' with her for a few hours. I didn't want to disrespect her by getting stuck in the moment and run out with my friends just because I hadn't seen them in awhile.

After spending time with my mom, I took a much-needed bath; and then I made a few calls to get everything back in order. The first person I called was my cousin. I hadn't talked to him since I'd been locked up and wanted to see what was going on with him. When he answered the phone, it was like I never went away. We immediately started talking about old times. He told me that he had gotten married and had two beautiful daughters since I'd been gone. He told me things were going good at his store and life was great for him.

"So are you coming to the party that they're having for me?" I asked hoping I could see him.

"No doubt cuz, you know wifey and I will come through to show some love."

After hanging up the phone, I decided to give Tim a call. While I was away, he had moved to North Carolina and bought a mansion in Chapel Hill. I think when he saw the 757 area code, he knew it was me because he answered on the first ring.

"What's up, man? When did you get home?" he asked. I could tell he was smiling.

"I got home today, man, but enough about me. Congratulations on being the fastest man in the world," I told him. When I found out he had broke the record, I felt like I broke it too. That was my man and I knew that he was doing big things. I also congratulated him on dating track star Marion Jones as he gave me the rundown of his new life. He told me that he now had four children, one by Marion named Monty and three by another lady who lived in Virginia.

"You gotta come down and check how I'm living, dawg."

"No doubt, I will come visit you," I told him. I couldn't wait to see how he was doing and meet his lady, Marion. I just had to check with my PO and get some paperwork taken care of, but after that, I was in North Carolina.

"Alright man, I'll holla at you later."

"Wait dawg, take my numbers," he said. Before hanging up, he gave me two numbers where I could reach him.

After getting off the phone, I put the new clothes that my mom had got me on and headed to see my grandparents. When I walked inside, I was surprised … Although several years had passed, I expected them to look the same. However, that wasn't the case. Old age had crept up on them and they almost looked like different people.

"Hey Bookie, thank God you're home. We couldn't wait to see you. What took you so long to get here?" they said, turning away from the television.

"Well, I'm here now and that's all that matters," I told them as I hugged and kissed them both. After talking with them awhile, I asked about the safe.

"Is the safe still in the closet, Grandma?" I asked her, hoping nothing happened to it.

"Yeah it's still there. I was wondering when you were coming to get it. We didn't want to die and just leave it here for someone else to get your fortunes," she said. I couldn't even imagine them not around. Just thinking about it gave me a weird feeling in the pit of my stomach.

"God knows what He's doing. He ain't ready for ya'll yet. He knows my heart couldn't take it. We still got a long life ahead of us—we not gonna even talk about death."

After sitting with them for a little longer, I went upstairs to see just how much money I had saved up. As I opened the safe every dollar that I had in there was still in place. Not one penny had been touched. I recounted the money just to make sure; I smiled thinking about how far I'd came in the drug game. Feeling satisfied, I closed the safe and headed back downstairs to say goodbye to my grandparents.

"I'll see ya'll later. I gotta get out of here ... I'll talk to you soon," I told them as I headed towards the door.

"Okay baby. Just make sure you're careful out there. It's gotten so bad since you've been gone," Grandma said, concerned.

"I promise. I'm not doing anything out there in them streets. I'm just taking my time and living my life as slow as possible," I told her, bringing a smile across her face.

When I got to my mom's house, I realized my phone was ringing off the hook. When I looked at the caller ID, I saw that it was my cousin.

"What's up, cuz?"

"Man, what's up with you? What time are you gonna be at the party tonight?"

"I'm not sure, but I'll be there fa sho'."

"Well, what you drinking on tonight? I wanna get a few bottles for us to pop."

"Man, I'm ready for a celebration. Let's pop some of that Cristal. I'm ready to get pissy drunk," I told him. I couldn't wait to get the feeling of alcohol back in me. While hanging up the phone, I walked into the house and saw my mom cleaning from the party earlier.

"Hey Mom, let me help you. Knowing you, you'd be up all night long tryin' to do this by yourself," I said teasing her. "You know, I'm gonna look for a place to stay this weekend so you ain't got to worry about me being all in your space."

"Bookie, you ain't no problem."

"Momma, you know how I am. I'm a grown ass man, I gotta take care of me—that ain't your job no more. This weekend I'll have a place, okay?" I could tell she understood where I was coming from, because she smiled at me and kissed me on the forehead and continued cleaning.

Given that I was on probation for five years, I knew I had to play my cards right. If I slipped up one time, I would be in deep water. I knew I had to get a place in Norfolk so that I had somewhere to check in with my probation officer, but I decided I was going to get another place to rest my head too. In view of the fact that the Feds were in my life, I had to be two steps ahead of the game at all times. However, I was well aware that one false move would land me right back in the pen. Therefore, intelligent planning and strategizing became my crucial ingredients for me to achieve a successful comeback in the game.

Chapter 13

Welcome Back

IT WAS FINALLY TIME TO PARTY AND I COULDN'T WAIT TO MEET BACK UP WITH my boys. When I entered the club, there were so many balloons around that I could hardly see. Every table was adorned with a bottle of champagne and the music was jumpin'.

"Welcome home, Bookie!" The deejay said while he played 'All Eyes on Me' by Tupac. Before I knew it, everyone started rushing me, popping bottles left and right. After thirty minutes or so of hugging and talking people, I was on the dance floor getting my groove on when I saw my cousin walk in with his beautiful wife and two cases of Cristal.

"What's up, cuz?" I said running up on him and giving him some love. He introduced me to his wife and I gave her a hug.

"Yo, your husband, this is my family right here," I said while my cousin popped a bottle of Cristal and handed it to me.

"Welcome home, cuz." We toasted my homecoming with a bottle of Cristal each and started talking about old times again.

"Cuz, I hope you're here to stay cuz you can't be leaving me like this, fam."

"I'm home, man. I got a real legit business lined up for us now, cuz. I'm on top of my game."

"Tell you what. After you get yourself together and everything hit me up and let me know what I gotta do on my end to get the ball rolling." Talking to him for a few more minutes, he then told me that he had to leave because he had to get up early to open his store and get the kids ready for school.

"Aight then, I'll check you out later then," I told him while dapping him and then I watched him and his wife leave, before I hung with all the people who came down to show me love.

I couldn't believe all the people who showed up to the party. A few hours later into the party, it got so crowded that the Fire Marshall came to shut the place down. It was all good though, because I was tired so I headed to my brother's house to crash. I wanted to drive, but I was drunk out my ass and had a suspended license so I knew if I was to get pulled over, I was through. So my brother handled his business and drove us safely to his crib where I stayed 'til the next day.

The next morning, I got up and I had the biggest hangover known to man. Damn, I should have known better than to drink like that since I ain't had any alcohol in years. It was so bad that it felt like the room was spinning so I hurried and popped two aspirin to ease the pain. Once my head started feeling better, I remembered I had to go and check in with my PO so I asked my brother if he'd take me downtown to see him after breakfast.

We ate our breakfast and then I freshened up before we headed to the federal building to see my PO. While in driving, I told my brother about my plans to connect with some of the guys that I met in prison so that we could make some money once they were released.

"Man, tell me you ain't planning to do that shit again. Didn't you learn your lesson the first damn time? You determined to go back inside ain't you?" he said, a little disappointed in what I just told him.

"Man, I got a job to do. I can't stop until the mission is complete. If I don't finish it, the next man will take the torch and get all the money that's out there for me," I said enthusiastically hoping I would get a reaction out of him, but instead, he remained quiet until we reached our destination. When I entered the building, I felt like I was locked up all over again. Suddenly, I couldn't breathe and it felt like the life was being sucked right out of me. There were guards everywhere. There was no doubt this was a federal building, there was so much order in it that it was actually intimidating.

When I met my PO, Mr. Elliot, I thought he was really down to earth. He told me that I only had to check in with him once a month with recent check stubs and let him know if there were any changes that occurred in my life like changing jobs or moving. He also told me that he would do random check-ins at my house and that I wasn't to involve myself with other convicted felons. After giving me the rundown of what he expected of me, he asked me if I had any questions.

"Yes, actually I do. Whenever I get my money right, will I be able to move into my own house?"

"That's no problem at all, Mr. Robinson, as long as you can afford it."

Then thinking about Tim, I asked him about leaving the state. He told me that if I went more than 500 miles, I had to let him know or that was an immediate parole violation. Damn, I had to be on point with them. They wanted to know where I am, when I'm there, and how long I'm staying.

"Do you have any more questions for me, Mr. Robinson?"

"No, not at all, Mr. Elliot. Thank you."

"Well good luck, Mr. Robinson. I'll be in touch," he said while shaking my hand.

Getting back inside the car, I told my brother I needed to go to the DMV to renew my license. While we headed to the DMV,

I started thinking about my visit with Mr. Elliot. *Damn, this shit is really tight. I got no time to make any mistakes—gotta be on my A game at all times.* Quickly, another thought interrupted... *Oh shit, I have to deposit the check they gave me when I left prison. Good thing I'm going to the DMV because the bank ain't gonna let me do anything with the check without the proper ID.*

When we got to the DMV, my brother stayed in the car while I went inside. While I was walking up to the door, I was dreading having to wait in a long line, but to my surprise the place was nearly empty. In no time, I retook my driver's test, paid my fines from the suspension and got my license reinstated.

Once leaving there, I went to the credit union to open a savings account. I knew that depositing a check from the federal government was the perfect way to get a large sum of money in the bank under my name without anyone questioning me. Once that was in order, I then headed to get me a rental car until I found some wheels that I liked. At Budget Rental, I had my eyes set on a big boy Lincoln Navigator. The truck just seemed to fit me in so many ways. With plans to visit Tim, I rented the car for two weeks.

I thanked my brother for running me around and we parted ways. I started up the Navi and rolled out, while dialing Tim's number to let him know my plans.

"What's up, fam?" he said when he picked up the phone.

"What's good, dawg? I'm trying to get everything in order so I can start making this money that's out here to be had," I told him, knowing he would understand what I meant.

"So are you coming down here or what, man?" he asked me. He told me that he wanted me to meet his parents and his fiancée and see what he and his crew had been up to since I'd been gone.

"Okay, that's what's up. I'll be down there soon."

"Oh yeah, bring your girl down here too. That way she can keep Marion company while we catch up." Damn, I didn't know how to tell him I just wasn't with anyone right now.

"Aight, I can handle that. I'll call you when I'm on the road."
After hanging up the phone with him, I quickly called Dawn, an old
female friend from around the way. We kept in touch while I was
locked up and I knew she would be down to go with me. When she
found out I was married, she moved to D.C. to finish her career and
start a new life. When I called her she was on her lunch break.

"Hey sweetheart, what you gon' be doing over the next week?
I wanna to take you to North Carolina for a vacation."

"Laushaun, I would love to but I gotta work all week. I can't
afford to just up and leave."

"Don't worry about it, ma. I got you. Whatever they are paying
you, I'll pay you double." At first she was still a little hesitant about
the trip, but once I told her I was visiting Tim Montgomery and
Marion Jones, she quickly changed her mind.

"Oh—oh yeah, I can go. I think I got some vacation time built
up that I could use. When are we leaving?"

"We can leave tonight if you can make it to Virginia."

"Okay, I'll be there." And just like that, it was on.

Once I made it to my mom's house, I told her that I planned to
visit Tim and if my PO stopped by to visit, just tell him that I'm out
job hunting. She just started laughing.

"My baby refuses to sit his ass down for just a few seconds.
Okay baby. I will let him know," she told me. I then let her know
that when I made it to North Carolina, I would give her a call. I also
told her that if anyone came looking for me, just tell them that I had
to handle some business and that I would be back later that day.

"Be safe on the highway, Bookie," she said as I kissed her on the
cheek. Leaving there, I headed to my grandparents' house to pick up
some money. I couldn't be traveling broke, because you never knew
what could happen. When I got there, the smell of fresh fried catfish
and potatoes hit me so hard; it made me realize just how hungry I was.

"Hey baby. You're just in time for dinner. Come make a plate,"
my grandmother said as she blew on the hot fish. As much as I
wanted to, I was on a mission and didn't have time to stop and eat.

"Oh Grandma, I'm not hungry, I just ate two sandwiches from McDonalds," I lied, but that was exactly where I was headed when I left their house.

"So how's everything going baby? Are you staying out of trouble out there?" she asked.

"I told you Grandma … I'm not doing anything but enjoying my freedom, one day at a time."

After a few minutes of talking, I went upstairs and got a few stacks of money. Grabbing five thousand dollars, I went back downstairs and told them that I would be out of town for a few days visiting a friend.

"Don't worry about me. I will be safe okay?" Then I gave them both a kiss and ran out the door.

Pulling away from the house, Dawn called my cell phone. She told me that she was waiting on me at her parents' house in Portsmouth, VA. I told her that I was going to the mall to pick up a few things, but would be there to pick her up within the hour.

"Do you need me to get you anything while I'm out?" I asked her.

"No I'm fine. I'll just be here resting until you get here," she told me before hanging up the phone.

Finally at the mall, I picked up a few personal hygiene products. That was really all I needed because my friends and family had practically got me a whole new wardrobe. With little time to spare, I jumped in the Navi to head to Dawn's parents' house. While driving I started to think about Donna. Should I call? Well, I don't even have her number anyway. What are you thinking Lashaun? She tried to play you— Hmmm, I could call her mom, I know her number hasn't changed … and besides she always did like me. After the internal battle I had going on in my mind, I finally decided to call Donna's mother, Mrs. Gloria to see if I could get Donna's new number. To my surprise, when she picked up, she had a very excited tone in her voice.

"Hey Laushaun, I'm so happy to hear from you! How's everything going?" I told her that everything was great and since I was home, I wanted to give Donna a phone call if it was okay. She said she didn't feel comfortable giving out Donna's number, but would take my number and give it to her. After ending our conversation, I headed to pick up Dawn at her parent's house.

"Hey Dawn, I'm outside in the driveway," I said as I called her on her cell phone.

"Okay, I'm on the way out," she said as she hung up the phone.

Coming outside, she was flawless. I mean there was nothing that looked out of place on her. I was very impressed. Her hair was free flowing down her back and her skin was glowing as if it was just kissed by the sun.

Giving her a big hug and kiss, I said, "Damn Ma, you still looking as good as ever. You ain't aged a day, have you?" She lightly chuckled while I grabbed her luggage from her and put it in the car.

"You ready to head to North Carolina?"

"Yes, I've been ready," she replied and then we jumped in the car and I drove towards the highway. Driving on the highway, she told me that she was very hurt when she found out that I had gotten married. I didn't know that her feelings were so strong for me.

"I waited so long for you, Laushaun. And you didn't even notice me," she said almost in tears.

"I didn't know you felt that way about me. If I did, I would have pursued you without even giving it a second thought."

"You didn't know because you were too busy with all them other women in your face."

"Well baby, I apologize about it. But I'm single now so if you're not in a relationship, I think we can make this thing work this time. We can make this last forever. Sweetheart, I've handed in my player's card and I'm a one-woman man. I'm gonna be successful ma, and I need a good woman by my side that can be on my team. Can you handle that?" I knew I gave her a lot to chew on, but I didn't have time to play no games. After a five second pause, she straightened her back, took a deep breath and began to speak.

"Before you make that decision Laushaun, I want you to make sure I'm what you want. I got a lot going for myself, but I don't have time for nonsense. So if you gon' be with me, you gotta come correct or don't come at all." Right as I was about to respond, my phone started to ring. I looked at the caller ID and saw that it was Donna. My heart started beating a million miles a minute. I excused myself and answered the phone.

"Hey!" I said in an excited tone, not saying a name so Dawn wouldn't be suspicious.

"Hey Laushaun, how are you?" she asked.

"Cool—cool—cool," I said, preparing to cut the conversation short.

"Hey Dee, I'm on the road right now so I really can't talk, but I'll call you back later, okay?" I could tell that she knew something was going on because she got quiet.

"What's wrong? You can't do two things at once now?" she asked questioning me.

I started laughing so Dawn wouldn't think anything, "Yeah I can, but I'm actually talking to someone right now and I don't wanna be rude. Know what I mean?"

"Alright, I'll just call you back later when you're not so busy," she said as she emphasized the word 'busy' like I was doing something wrong. We weren't together so I didn't understand why she was so mad.

I hung up the phone and tried to get back into the conversation with Dawn, but it didn't go how I expected it to.

"Huh, was that your ex-wife?" she asked with her arms folded underneath her firm tits.

"Yeah, when I got locked up, a lot of my things that are valuable to me stayed in her possession. So I called her mother to tell her to give me a call … Basically, I need to meet up with her so I can get my stuff back—but that's it. There's nothing going on between us."

"Oh, okay," was all Dawn said. For the rest of the ride she just sat there and didn't say another word to me.

When we got to Chapel Hill, it was well after midnight. I called Tim to let him know we were in town. I could tell he had fallen asleep.

"I'm here, man. Now how do I get to your house?" He gave me the directions and told me to call him once I got to the front gate. When we reached our destination, I was amazed to see the huge houses that surrounded me. The houses were incredible. When we got to the front gate, I called him and he gave me the security code so I could enter. We traveled up the long driveway and came to another gate. The gate automatically opened and we entered into Tim's private paradise. Pulling up into the large driveway, I parked the Navigator and noticed the expensive cars parked. There was a Benz 600 coupe with the Benz truck, a Porsche Cayenne car with the Porsche truck, and a couple of old school Impala's wrapped around the driveway. When I got to the front door, I saw Tim walking up to let us in.

"What's up, playboy?" he said, embracing me.

"Yo fam, it's been a minute." I turned and introduced him to Dawn. They shook hands and then Dawn started yawning.

"Oooh, I'm sorry. I'm really tired from the long ride," she said so Tim took us to one of his guestrooms for us to unwind and rest up for the next day. Dawn wanted to take a shower before she went to bed so Tim took me to his movie theater so we could chop it up. Once we were inside, he handed me a bottle of Cristal and some Purple Haze marijuana. I hadn't smoked weed in so long, I hesitated to take it.

"Man, I'm on probation. I could get in trouble for this," I said then thought about it. "Fuck it! You only live once and I'm getting ready to get my smoke on."

"Now that's the OG I know. That's what I'm talking about. Here is to a welcome home and to new beginnings," he said smiling at me. After drinking the bottle of Cristal and smoking a few blunts, we were slightly faded. He then grabbed the movie, *Paid in Full,* and we watched it while talking.

"So what you got planned for yourself this time around, my man?" he asked me as we sat back and continued to smoke.

"Man, all I know is I ain't ever going back there again. I got big plans out here. A couple of my boys just got out, we all gonna re-connect and get that paper doin' real estate and import export busi-nesses. Shit, dem boys gonna have to kill me before they catch me, because I ain't going back."

"So what was the Feds like?"

"Man, I guess it's like anything else in life. It's whatever you make it," I told him.

"Right, right—so what a playa got to do to play ball? What can a hundred grand get me if I invest?" he asked me, looking to get in on the hustle.

"It'll get you two hundred, but it'll take me six months or so to get everything straight. Man, let's make this money and set our fami-lies up for life," I said, raising my glass in the air.

"Fa'sho, let me know what's up. I might have to take you up on that offer." Then we started talking about Shampoo and how things turned out so ugly for him in the end. Tim told me that Shampoo had took my advice and actually planned to turn himself in and take a 5-year plea deal right before he was killed. He was supposed to turn himself in that Friday but instead, he decided to go to the Hard Knock Life tour and never made it back.

Things became quiet between us, and then Tim pulled out some pictures, looked through them, and said, "Once he got inside I was supposed to put $30 thousand on his books so he could do his time smoothly. I was supposed to send him these pictures too."

"So do you know who killed him?" I asked Tim. Word on the street was that it was a hit out on him for stealing thirty kilos from his connect.

"Hell, he decided to enjoy his freedom instead of doing what's right and got caught slipping."

"So what happened to all that damn money he had?" I asked. I know he had money stashed away somewhere because it wasn't like him to be broke. Tim told me that Shampoo had an apartment that no one knew about. After he died, Tim paid the apartment manager a few thousand dollars to go in and get his belongings. He went straight to the closet, grabbed his safe, and took it to his car.

"So what was Sham holding?" I asked, wondering how much money he accumulated over the years.

"It was about a half a million."

"Damn. There ain't no love in the heart of the city, rest in peace Sham."

"Rest in peace, brotha," Tim said while he raised his glass in the air and then took a drink. He then told me about what was going on in his life.

"Dawg, I moved to North Carolina when things started getting hot with Shampoo." He continued telling me the Feds were questioning him almost every day about how he knew Sham and what their connection was. "Man, they wanted to know why Shampoo lived in my house and drove several of my cars. I just told the police that we were just roommates and that I didn't know anything about his personal life."

"Damn, playboy, was you scared?"

"Hell yeah man, that's why I packed my shit up, sold my house, and moved to the country." We then started talking about Dre Bly and how some people were against him since he made it to the NFL. Apparently, some folks were feeling Dre acted like he forgot where he came from and didn't even want to acknowledge their existence.

"Man, Dre fucked Shampoo over. Once you left, Shampoo was takin' care of him like he was his brother or somethin' but now that Shampoo's gone, this fool just shitted on Shampoo's wife."

"What you mean by that? What happened?" I didn't know what Dre could have done that was so bad.

"You see, Dre promised Shampoo that if anything happened to Sham that he would take care of his wife and child. But as soon as Sham died and wifey needed money, Dre threw $10,000 at her and changed his damn phone number the next damn day. Nobody has heard from him since."

I thought to myself, *that's real messed up. As long as I've known Dre, I didn't think he would do something like that.*

"Man, word on the street is that once Sham died, she got $100,000 and married his right hand man. I heard she tried to open a store with the money or something."

"Yeah, she was so afraid that dem folks were gonna question her about the money, she blew through it like it was water. She even let some of Sham's family hold some of the money for her, but they just played her ass like a thief in the night."

Damn, people are ruthless. I could do nothing but shake my head.

"So where you living at now, man?" he asked. I told him that I was staying with my mom for the time being.

"Well, this is what I want you to do. Why don't you and your girl move into this house?" He began telling me that he and Marion were building a new house for them to live in, and then he proposed a plan that I almost couldn't pass up.

"Dawg, I want you to stay in the house and I'll pay all the bills and everything for the first year." Then he offered to open whatever business I wanted and he would pay the cost. I knew he was banking, but I didn't know he was doing it like that.

"Man, I might as well, ain't nothing in Virginia for me," I told him after thinking about it for a while. "It sounds real good, but I gotta talk it over with Dawn first. I'll let you know something soon though."

"Aight fam!" he said as we gave each other a high five. "I love you dawg. You've been my OG since day one and I'm just trying to show some love in return." We stood there talking for a few minutes longer, and then he told me that he had to go to bed because he had practice early the next morning.

"Aight, we'll hook up tomorrow once you're finished with practice."

"You get some rest dawg, you home now."

When I went into the bedroom, Dawn was fast asleep. I took off my clothes, got into the bed and a minute later, Dawn rolled over and started to kiss me passionately.

"Laushaun, I want you. I've been waiting for this moment for years," she said.

"Baby, I want you too," I replied while thinking about how many years it had been since I had sex. I hoped she was ready for what I was about to give her. The night was passionate and wild; we loved each other nearly 'til the sun came up. Before we went to sleep I told her about Tim offering us the house. I continued to tell her all my plans and how I wanted us to take our relationship to the next level.

"Sweetheart, I want you to be my woman."

"Well, I dunno … Let's just see, okay. Let's take things slow."

"Slow? Baby, you're either down or not. I know what I want and right now, there's no other woman I'm seeking." Without saying any other words, I kissed her on the forehead and held her until we both fell fast asleep.

The smell of breakfast woke me up bright and early the next morning. After taking a long hot shower, I went downstairs and saw Tim's mother and father preparing a breakfast feast.

"How are you doing today, Mr. and Mrs. Montgomery?"

"How are you, Laushaun? Have you met our Monte yet?" they said as they pointed to the baby in the walker. He looked just like Tim. I began helping Mrs. Montgomery set the kitchen table while she talked about how she was very pleased to meet me and had heard very great things about me.

"My son considers you a close friend and he couldn't wait until you got home," she told me with a huge smile on her face. She was a full time nanny for her grandson while Tim and Marion traveled the world. While we were talking, Dawn had come downstairs looking fine as hell. I introduced her to the family and as she met little Monte, he had an instant attraction to her. It was almost as if she was his mother, because he wouldn't let her put him down, not even for a minute.

After breakfast, Tim's father invited me to play a round of golf with him while the women began to straighten up the house and prepare for lunch. During our time at the golf course, Tim's father talked to me about all his son's achievements. I could tell how much of a proud father he was, and rightfully so. He talked about how Tim deserved to be the fastest man in the world and all the hard work he had put in to win his medals.

"I'm so happy that all his hard work finally paid off," he said at the end of our last round before we headed back to the house.

When we got back to the house, I was still amazed at the fifteen cars that were in the driveway. When we walked into the foyer, I saw everyone sitting in the family room talking to one another like they were all best friends. Dawn looked up and greeted me as I walked towards her.

"Hey baby," I said as I kissed her on the cheek.

"Hey playboy, I want you to meet the love of my life, my beautiful fiancée, Marion." He was right she was very beautiful.

"I'm pleased to meet you, Laushaun. I've heard so many great things about you." I was surprised on how much Tim had talked about me. I thanked her and sat down with everyone else to get better acquainted. After a while of talking, Tim took me to his game room where his crew was smoking weed and playing pool. They were all rappers. The names of their groups were Lumber Jacks and Dough Boy Entertainment. While they listened to their tracks, I must say, they sounded pretty good. They were all independently distributing their music and planned to make it mainstream one day. Tim believed in them so much that he invested major paper that helped them with studio time and distribution of their CDs. My boy kept it real with his crew and each one of them dudes had mad respect for him.

While we continued to play pool and smoked weed, the women were downstairs preparing dinner. Finally we heard someone yell that it was time to eat. It was perfect timing because everyone had the munchies like crazy. We all raced downstairs and ate the delicious meal that was prepared for us. When everyone's bellies were full, we decided to go outside to the pool area and talk some more. Three or four hours later things began to wind down and people started to head home.

Once everyone had left, Tim and I went outside to the waterfall in the driveway and fired up another blunt. "Yo playboy, I'm proud of you. You have done well for yourself."

"Thanks, dawg," he said while he took a pull of the blunt and passed it back to me.

"Yo, check it playboy. I don't wanna leave, but I got to get my ass back to Virginia and make sure Dawn gets back to D.C.," I said, and then blew a big cloud of smoke in the air.

"Man I feel you and all, but why you wanna leave? Didn't you say ain't nothing in Virginia, I can get you everything you need."

"I feel you and all Tim … but right now I gotta just do me. I gotta get my life in order before I begin making moves like that. Ya feel me?"

"Yeah, I feel ya on that. Dawg, I got much love and respect for you so the door is always open for you. But listen, before you leave tomorrow, I got something for you."

"What you got?" I asked curiously.

"Im'ma write a check for you for 10 G's, aight. And if that ain't enough, I always got a hundred grand lying around at all times in case something comes up."

"That's a bet and when I get my business going, I'll let you know what's up. But let me get my household straight in Virginia first and then I will let you know."

"That's a bet," he said as we shook hands and headed back inside.

Chapter 14

The Virginia Docks

THE NEXT MORNING IT WAS TIME FOR US TO LEAVE. MARION WAS GETTING ready for practice and didn't want to see us go. When we began to say our goodbyes, Tim handed me the check. "Please don't be strangers … You're welcomed back here anytime," Marion told Dawn while they hugged and kissed each other on the cheek. We thanked both of them and headed to the truck.

On the road back home, I began to continue the conversation that Dawn and I were having the other night that we really didn't finish. "Sweetheart, I plan to be the next millionaire and I want you to be on my team. I was serious when I said that I want you to be my woman. Baby, I'm going to open my own corporation and I want someone I can trust. I'm gonna have a security division and I know with your background experience, you can lead it."

"I hear you Laushaun. Just let me know what you need me to do and I'm there for you." When we made it back to Virginia, we decided not to immediately end our time together. We stayed at a 5-star hotel for the night and had explosive sex until we fell asleep in each other's arms. When mid-morning came, she headed to the shower to get ready for the road.

"Dawn, you mind if I jump in there with you?"

"Of course not, silly. Come—on—in," she said seductively while pulling me quickly in the shower. After we bathed each other, we got dressed, checked out of the hotel and drove back to her parents' house so she could pick up her car to travel back to D.C.

On my way back to my mom's house, I stopped by a liquor store to pick up a newspaper so I could start looking for an apartment. When I got to the house and got settled in, I began thumbing through the rental section and found a few apartments that I was interested in. Later that afternoon, I headed to the bank to deposit the ten thousand dollar check that Tim gave to me, and then I quickly set out to search for the apartments that I had found in the newspaper. By the end of the day, I had secured two apartments. One was located in Ghent, a subdivision of the Norfolk area, and the other was in Chesapeake. Now that I had my spots, I needed to furnish them, so I went to Grand Furniture store and purchased everything I needed to make my house a home. The following day, I went to my PO and gave him my new address in Ghent.

Once all my living arrangements were handled, it was time for me to take the necessary steps to get my business in order. I visited an employee that handled my taxes for the car wash so we could set up my corporation. We had done great business in the past. When he saw me, he was so excited since we hadn't seen each other in several years. After telling him my plans, he drew up the necessary paperwork for me to be incorporated. After leaving his office, I went to city hall to get a business license under 'Import-Export' using my residence as my business address. After obtaining my license, I called my PO to let him know what I planned to do. That way, he couldn't harass me about finding a job since I was opening my own business.

After getting off the phone with him, I decided to pay Donna a visit at the school. I hadn't seen her since I'd come home and never returned her phone call so a visit was in order. When I had made it to the school, the bell had just rung and kids were being let out for the day. Instead of going inside, I waited in the parking lot so that I could meet her when she left the building. After sitting for ten minutes or so, I finally saw her still looking beautiful as ever. But there was something different about her. When she got closer I realize what was different, it was her hair. She had on a wig that was cut into a bob. It looked good, but it made her look years older than she really was. When she was about ten feet from my car, I got out and greeted her.

"What's up Donna Bly?" I asked her with a million dollar smile on my face, letting her check out how sexy a brotha still looked.

"Oh my God—Laushaun—what are you doing here?" she asked, stunned while dropping her briefcase.

I picked up her briefcase and said, "You know what I'm doing here … I'm here to see you, girl," I told her while I walked her to her car. She was driving a S class 430 Benz that her brother purchased for her.

"That's a really nice car," I told her, making small talk.

"Why didn't you ever return my call, Laushaun?" she asked, getting to the point.

"I was going out to visit Tim and Marion and didn't get a chance to call you back."

"So who did you go with?" she asked with that look in her eyes that said she wanted to know the truth.

"Just a long time friend," I said.

"A long time friend, huh … You know that was supposed to be me with you, not some friend," she said stressing the word 'friend'.

"Hell, how was I supposed to know what the hell you were doing? You got a child by some dude. How am I supposed to know that you're not still with him?" I asked. I couldn't believe she had the nerve to say 'she wanted to go with me'.

Moving past her trying to give me a hard time, we continued talking and she told me that she and the father were no longer together, but he tried to get back with her every chance he got. When our conversation was coming to an end, Donna asked me if I had plans for the evening and if I didn't, could she take me to dinner.

"Just give me a call," I told her as we hugged each other and I left.

Once I made it to my apartment, I called Dawn to tell her what all I'd done over the last few days and that I couldn't wait to see her that weekend. After talking for a little while, I told her I would call her back later because there was further business I needed to handle.

"Okay baby, talk to you later," she said and blew my kiss before hanging up the phone.

Shortly after I had talked to Dawn, I got a call from my boy Prince that I had connected with when I did my time in Federal Prison.

"Yo Shaun, I'm here in Virgina Beach, man—I'm living with my brother. What's up with makin' that paper?" he said with excitement.

"My boy Boo-Bee was deported back to Panama so I think now's the time for me to make moves."

"Yo, call me and let me know what's up, aight. I'm ready when you are," he said.

"Aight, just let me make some calls." I told him goodbye and hung up the phone. I called to talk to Boo-Bee to find out how soon we could get the ball rolling.

"Once you get everything together, give me a call and we can send something to you but first, make sure you find someone that works at the docks. That way I can send it on a ship that's coming into Norfolk."

I told him that I would get on top of it and would call him back when everything was right. Because I needed legal capital so my PO wouldn't question me, it was time for me to begin my Import-Export business. I got in contact with my boy, Wong, a friend that I had in prison and told him that I wanted to start shipping clothes and other products to him in Ghana so I could start making money.

"Please let me know what's in demand, and then I can start placing orders to ship out."

"Sounds good Shaun, I'll be in touch soon. Hey, do me a favor. Find out what the seafood market is like out there … maybe we can undercut some prices by sending some out your way." We gave each other a timeline to find out everything that we needed, and promised to talk within a week.

After getting all my things in order, it was finally time to meet Donna for dinner. I called her and she picked up on the first ring.

"So where is dinner tonight?" I asked her.

"At my place if that's okay with you." She told me that her son was visiting her mother for the weekend so she had the place to herself. She gave me the directions to her new house so I could make my way over there with no problems. After getting off the phone with Donna, I called Dawn. I had to make up an excuse for my whereabouts for the rest of the night because I had a strange feeling that I would probably be with Donna until the early morning. When she picked up the phone, I played like I was so tired from running around and doing errands all day.

"Heeey baby," I said while yawning. "I was just calling you back like I said I would," I told her as I yawned a second time.

"You sound hella tired hun."

"Yeah, I've just been running around doing so much today that I think I'm just gonna rest my eyes."

"Dang, you that tired," she said sounding a little disappointed. I knew she really wanted to talk, but I didn't have the time, Donna was expecting me soon.

"I'm sorry baby. I'm just so tired. That's all. I'm cranky and I just need some sleep. I'll talk to you tomorrow, okay?"

Hesitating she responded, "Oh—well—okay. Sweet dreams baby."

"Bye," I said and hung up the phone, jumped in the car and drove to Donna's. When I pulled into Donna's driveway, I was very impressed with the neighborhood she lived in. It was nice. I rang the bell and she came wearing a pair of sweat pants and a white tank top, looking sexy as ever.

"Damn Laushaun, you smell good," she said as she gave me a tight hug. "I'm so happy that you're finally home," she said, not letting me go. I quickly pulled myself away because I didn't want her to think that we were getting back together and went into the living room with her following closely behind. She had all new furniture and several pictures of her and her son on the mantle. Checking out the pictures, I noticed that he didn't look anything like her.

"He looks just like his daddy," she said as if reading my mind.

"Where is he anyway?"

"Are you talking about my son or his father?"

"I'm talking about his father, Donna." She told me that she hadn't even really seen him since she told him she was pregnant. He just up and left her. She then talked about the mental abuse he put her through and how it caused her to go into a major depression.

"So do you want a glass of wine?" she asked, quickly changing the subject.

"Yeah, that sounds good right about now." Although we weren't together anymore, I still had feelings for her, but I was doing my best to keep them mutha fucka's suppressed.

While sipping on our glasses, I told her about my relationship with Dawn. She wasn't too thrilled about it, but knew there was nothing she could do. I knew I needed to be upfront with her in order for her to understand that there was no more us. I then told her about my plans to invest in real estate and my import-export business.

"Oh really ... Well, I want to invest in it. I have a little extra cash I can dish out. How can I be down?"

I didn't even respond to her question. I just sat and ate the dinner she had prepared. I didn't know if I wanted her to be any part of my business because I didn't fully trust her. Donna saw that I was unresponsive and began to talk about her brother, Dre, and how he was a huge success playing football with the Detroit Lions.

"That's what's up," I said. We continued our conversation by talking about the good and bad old days that we'd experienced with each other.

After an hour or so of drinking wine, we started getting a little too tipsy and before I knew it, we were all over each other. We headed to the bedroom and I imagined her once again as my wife, not the woman who had cheated on me and gotten pregnant. We had wild and crazy sex. And as usual, after I sexed her, Donna wanted me to use one of her handy dandy dildos on her. The one she chose was ten inches, and she swallowed it up with her cave, enjoying every minute of it. By the time she climaxed, my manhood was standing at attention, and I was ready for another round. Donna's freaky ass was more than happy to oblige and let me thrust my manhood in and out of her mouth until I exploded all over her face.

After hours of erotic pleasure, we took a long hot shower together, laid in the bed, and dozed off to sleep. The next morning, I woke up to the smell of breakfast. I went downstairs and saw Donna cooking a hefty breakfast. I kissed her on the cheek and sat down and she served me pancakes, eggs, bacon and grits. She watched me eat my meal; I could tell that she wished everything was how it used to be, but I didn't want to make her think that we were back together.

"Yo Donna, you know what's up girl. We cool right?"

"Yeah—yeah, we had fun. We cool …" Not wanting to stay too long, I finished my meal, got dressed, left her house and started my day getting ready to make money.

Once I got home, I called Tim and told him my plans with the company and asked if he was still interested in being a partner. I planned to buy foreclosed homes and sell them for what they were worth. After we figured out how much money would be needed, I read the contract that I'd made and he quickly agreed. He said he would be in Virginia that weekend to bring the start up money for the business. I decided to take my boy Prince and show him the properties I wanted to buy.

I checked out two homes that I was interested in and had to go to the auction at City Hall to make my bids. Prince and I drove to City Hall and when we arrived I found out that the owners were behind on their property taxes and the houses were valued at $200,000 each and could be bought for as little as $20,000 each. Therefore, if everything worked out in my favor, we could profit $100,000 to $150,000 with no problem. We looked at the list of houses that were up for auction, but noticed that the two that we had just viewed weren't on the list.

"Excuse me. I'm interested in two specific houses that don't seem to be on this list. Can you tell me why?" I asked the gentleman in the courthouse. After giving him the addresses, he told me that the owners were still in the final stages of their court proceedings so the houses wouldn't be for sale for another month or so.

I didn't know what to do. Should I try to buy another house and get my business started or just wait and buy the ones that I'm interested in? After a minute or two of thinking, I decided to come back and buy the ones that I was interested in. That way, I could show Tim the houses we were investing in and make sure he was down for it.

While dropping Prince off he asked me if I could lend him some money until his paper got right. Without hesitation I gave him a thousand dollars to hold in his pocket. Driving off, I began thinking about Donna and decided to call her to see if she was available to have lunch. She was in the middle of class, but said she could leave right away to meet me at a secluded diner. Once we arrived at the diner, I told her how I was down because the auction didn't go how I expected. I thought she would give me words of encouragement, but instead she did something else. She reached inside her purse and handed me a white bank envelope.

"Here, this is for you. This should be enough money to help you get back on your feet and to get your business started. And if you need anything else, you know where to find me." I couldn't believe that she'd just give me some money.

"Thank you so much Donna. You don't know how much this means to me," I said as I kissed her on the cheek and put the envelope in my pocket, not even counting to see how much it was. We got into our conversation, and I told her that although I was in a relationship, I still wanted her to be in my life. I wanted to remain friends. I just didn't want to hurt Dawn. I knew what it felt like to be betrayed and I didn't want to do anyone the way Donna had done me. I also explained to her that I didn't want any problems with her baby's daddy. I wasn't the type of man who was with drama. I wanted to keep my life as simple as possible. She agreed and told me that I wouldn't have any problems from him and she would protect our friendship because she valued it a lot. After finishing our meals and a very chill conversation, we left the diner to finish out our days.

Right after Donna and I parted ways, Dawn called my phone.

"What's up baby? How is everything?" I asked her in an excited tone. However, I didn't get that type of response back from her. She sounded like she was very annoyed but I didn't let that get to me and continued to tell her about my day. She told me how much she'd missed me and wanted to know if it was still cool that she could come down for the weekend to visit me. I told her that it would be good for her to come because Tim and Marion were also coming down so we could all hang together. After a few more minutes of romantic talk and assuring her of my love, we hung up to kisses to each other.

The weekend had finally arrived. Tim was here with his mom, Marion, and their son. To show him that I appreciated the love and support he'd given me, I headed to the mall to buy a black length fur with matching hats for both Marion and his mother. Two hours and seven thousand dollars later, I had them a perfectly wrapped gift waiting. Leaving the mall, I headed to Tim's beach house that he had in Virginia. With box in hand, I arrived to many hugs and kisses from everyone.

A few minutes of small talk went by, and then we told the ladies we'd be back in a few hours. Tim and I walked out to the car to talk about the plans that I had going. We decided to discuss our business arrangements over lunch and a few drinks. He immediately called his team to meet us at the restaurant. After hanging up the phone, we talked about my corporation and how if everything went well, we would make a hundred grand easily. I then showed him all the paperwork for the corporation and the contracts to the houses and my plan to flip them quickly.

"I see you're on top of your grind, baby boy," he said smiling. I then told him about the people I had overseas and how I would soon be doing business internationally. We pulled up to Applebee's, and the parking lot was full of his team. Some of them I remembered from North Carolina, but about 20 or so of them, I'd never seen.

During lunch, I saw a kid I knew from back in the day from New York, his name, Black Shawn. "Yo Black, what's up kid?" I said as we greeted and then talked about old days. We exchanged numbers and then I went back to the table to join Tim and his crew.

"You know Black Shawn?" Tim asked me as I sat back down at the table.

"Yeah, that's my boy from way back. He's cool peeps." We then continued to talk and he told me about his crews' upcoming show with Juvenile. Tim was going hard for his crew; he had invested a couple more hundred of thousands of dollars into them. So I asked how I could get a piece of the pie. He told me a hundred grand would get me in and he could handle everything else.

"Bet dawg, once things start poppin' off I might have to get at you about that." Soon after we finished lunch and headed back to Tim's beach house because he had something that he wanted to show me. Once we arrived, he popped in a DVD of him and Marion promoting a new shoe called XO2 that they were sponsoring although they were still under contract with Nike. After watching the video, he showed me a demo shoe that they wanted me to market for them.

"Man, if you help me push this shoe on the east coast, I will cut you in on the deal," Tim said, hoping I would go in with him. He told me that Courtney Bellmore, one of the designers of FUBU, designed the shoe exclusively for them.

"Man, these shoes are hot as hell and with ya'll being the top athletes of the world, you can promote them like crazy in your meets and have them flying off the shelves." After telling him I was in, he said he would draw up the proper contract and let me know my role.

"Where's my girl? Is she in town or what?" Marion said looking for Dawn.

"No. She'll be here tomorrow though. We'll all hang out then." I then told Tim that I would get with him tomorrow so we could all go see a movie or something. I said my goodbye to everyone, and I drove to my home in Chesapeake.

Once arriving home, Dawn called and told me she was in town and would be at my house within the hour. I told her I would wait up for her and grabbed a bottle of wine to congratulate myself on all the accomplishments I had made thus far. When Dawn arrived, she was very impressed at how I decorated my house. While giving me compliments on the house, Dawn walked up and began teasing me by kissing me on my neck. Soon our hormones were raging and before another compliment came out of her mouth, we were on the living room floor making love for well over two hours ... without any protection.

The next day, I wanted everything to go as planned. I wanted to spend time with Dawn early in the day so that I could party with the boys later that night. Once we were dressed, we drove to a seafood restaurant to meet with Tim, Marion, and David Lee, the promoter of the XO2 shoe. When we arrived at the restaurant, we were seated at our table and immediately started talking business. Mr. Lee said he wanted to fly me to Vegas to the Magic Show that August and to Atlanta to promote the shoe ... all expenses paid. He also told me that I needed a warehouse for distribution until we could find a permanent home for the shoes. After discussing business, Mr. Lee gave me his business card with all his contact information and then we indulged in great seafood.

"Yo, I can get the bill. That's the least I can do, man," I said, reaching for the tab.

"No playboy, I got it. The bill is $3,200 anyway. We can take care of this."

"Damn, why is the bill so high?" I asked, looking at the lobster I ate. It was good but it wasn't that good."

"The wine was $1500 a pop, but it was worth it because we'll be making millions with this shoe deal," he said as he dapped me across the table and I agreed with him.

After leaving the restaurant, we headed to the mall for a movie. Before we even entered, there were fans screaming Tim and Marion's names. We just quickly walked through the crowd as they tried to take pictures and get autographs from them. I thought they would be rude, but they actually were very polite to their fans telling them that it was their personal time and that they would sign autographs another day. I decided that I would pay for the tickets.

"Good looking out, fam," Tim said, thanking me for my generous offer.

"You see baby, that's a real friend right there," Marion said as we entered the movie, *Why Did I Get Married.*

After the movie ended, we went back to his beach house and talked business while the women went upstairs to gossip. I told Tim that I would have the business up and running within a month. I also told him that I had a few guys that would help me push the business and get it going full circle. We decided to meet at the club later that night so that I could tell his crew what was going on. I then called Prince to tell him where to meet us and to let the bouncers know to escort him to VIP whenever he got there. After getting off the phone, we headed to the girls to tell them that we had business to take care of, and that we would be back shortly. Instead of grabbing clothes from his beach house, he had clothes inside of his car so we headed to my house to get dressed for the night's events.

While getting dressed, he handed me a diamond Brietling watch and a diamond Tennis necklace.

"This is for you, dawg. This is a gift to you until you get your money right."

"Damn, playboy, what's the price on these pieces?"

"About sixty grand, fam, chump change." I admired the two pieces as I placed them on and headed out the door.

"Yo Tim, I was just wondering about that shoe stuff, dawg."

"What?"

"You think it's gonna work since you and Marion's faces are synonymous with Nike?"

"Playboy, if it's gonna make me more money, hell yeah it's gonna work. Why, you worried?"

"Nah, I ain't worried. Shit, it ain't my face on the shoes; it's y'alls. I was just curious on how you feel about the whole deal. Know what I mean?"

"I'm cool ... now let's go sit up in the VIP and watch my crew perform before Juve hits the stage." We walked out of the house, got in the car and headed to the club where Tim's crew was performing. Once at the club, the line was ridiculously long. We pulled up in the Benz, and then the security led up pass the crown and into the club. Before entering, I gave the security guard a thousand dollars and told security to let my boys do the same when they got there. Once inside, I noticed that more than 50 of Tim's crew were already there waiting on us. I talked to a few people and talked about old times until the bottles of Cristal started popping. While we partied with the rest of the people, I noticed Stacey at the bar. When I asked her what she was doing, she said she worked for Pharrell and that she'd gotten pregnant by a successful rapper but had a miscarriage. While we were talking, gunshots rang out and we headed to the nearest exit.

Getting away from the danger, we got back into the Benz and fled. I thought we all made it out safely until my boy Prince called to tell me that Black Shawn, my boy from New York, didn't make it out alive. I couldn't believe my ears. I was devastated. It has to be a mistake, let me call him. I rang his phone several times and he didn't pick up. Damn, maybe it's true. When we got back to Tim's house, I went into the bedroom where Dawn was sleeping, laid next to her and fell asleep.

The next morning, everything felt like a dream. I thought that I'd had a terrible nightmare until I heard the many messages on my phone telling about Shawn's death. What made matters even worse was that people were saying that I had something to do with his death. I called Prince to tell him to get things straightened out with his New York peeps, because I couldn't be mixed up in any murder investigations.

"Yo, I got you covered. Just come down to the shop and we can get this cleared up," he said, letting me know he would arrange a meeting with his peoples. I hung up the phone and Dawn was awake.

"Baby what's wrong?" she asked out of concern. I told her there was a little misunderstanding about a situation—and left it like that.

When Dawn woke up, we headed downstairs to meet with Marion and Tim. After having breakfast and small talk, I went to the backyard with Tim to tell him what was going on.

"Dawg, they got me twisted up in this shit, and I ain't had no part of it; that was my boy. I'm going to have to straighten this all out, man, before it gets out of hand. Ya feel me?" I told him thinking about meeting up with Prince to get my name cleared.

"Do you want me to go with you?" he asked.

"Nah, I got this one, but good looking out though," I told him, appreciative that he would ride with me on this journey. We then went back into the house; I got Dawn and my things together and said goodbye to Tim and his family. When we got into the Navi, Dawn started questioning me about the rental.

"Don't you think you're spending too much money on this rental? Why don't you just buy one of your own?"

"I plan to, but I don't want my PO questioning about where I got the money for the car. It's better like this for now," I said, praying that she'd stop nagging me about the damn rental. Once we arrived to my apartment, I helped her to her car with her luggage and kissed her goodbye. When she left, I called Boo-Bee overseas to talk about the business we had.

"What do we need to get the operation started, playboy?"

"Bookie, we need 10 Gs ... Also I need you to supply me a business address," he replied.

"Okay, okay. I can handle that." I told him that I would wire him ten thousand dollars through Western Union and provided my boy's barbershop as the location to send the packages to.

"And Bookie, you need to get connect with someone at the docks; someone who has access to the containers."

"Aight, I'll handle the docks first thing in the morning. I know someone down there that owes me some favors ... I'm sure he won't mind doing some business. Ya know what I mean."

"Cool. Now listen, once the money is sent I can have the package ready for shipment. It will take five to seven days for it to get to Virginia. For security purposes, send half the money in my name and the other half to a business partner of mine, Martin," he said while I wrote down everything he was telling me. After squaring everything away with Boo-Bee, I got off the phone and decided to handle the other business at hand ... my boy, Black Shawn's death. I called Prince to tell him I was on the way to the shop.

"Come alone man and don't bring trouble with you. It was just a big misunderstanding. That's all," Prince told me, but my instincts told me otherwise so I stopped at my brother's house to pick up his 9mm and have him ride with me in case anything went down. When I got to my brother's, I explained what was going down and he was ready to ride out with me.

Before I went to Prince's shop, I had to first stop at Western Union to wire Boo-Bee the money in Panama. I had my brother wire $5,000 to 'Martin' while I wired the other $5,000 to Boo-Bee. After I had taken care of the money, I headed to the jewelry store to clear my damn name. When we pulled up, there were several cars with

New York tags in the parking lot and my gut told me something was about to go down. Before getting out of the car, I cocked the gun so that I would be ready if I had to blast on one of them and my brother followed suit.

When I got inside the shop, there was a bunch of people mourning Shawn's death. However when they looked up and saw me enter, everything became tense. I walked over to Prince while my brother stood at the front door.

"Hey dawg, I want to let you know we found out what happened with Shawn and your name has been cleared. My people are sorry for dragging your name through the dirt," he said as he gave me dap. Happy and relieved to know that I was cool, I told him that if they needed any donations for Shawn, to let me know. Then Prince and I stepped aside to a private room to dicuss the heroin shipment that I had coming in next week.

"Get your crew ready to distribute the heroin," I said in a serious tone. When it came to my paper, I didn't play.

"Yo, did you say heroin?" Prince asked in disbelief.

"No doubt, that's how we get down, playboy." I told him it was 98% pure, so each brick could be worked over twice and still be considered raw product. I went on to explain that each brick was 50 grand and that off one brick, he could double his money. When I finished telling him everything, he told me he would have everything in place within a few days. We shook hands and I left the jewelry shop.

A week later, my boy gave me a call and told me my shipment had arrived. After securing the shipment, I called Boo-Bee and told him that everything was safe. Once at my apartment, I opened the container to find my 5 kilos of heroin stuffed inside candle wax. I went to the kitchen and grabbed the biggest knife I could find and began to open each candlestick to verify how much I had. It was a little over 5000 grams of raw dope. Damn, them Panamanians are fuckin' geniuses—all this weight in candles. Shit, after I send Boo-Bee his cut and with me flipping one brick at a time, I can walk away with close to a half a million off this shipment alone. I smiled at the thought of stacking my dough up again and then called Prince to set a time to get him his dope.

"Come now. I got the hundred grand ready," he said. Without hesitation, I picked two bricks up and headed to Prince's shop.

Over the next month, business was doing well. The dope was moving faster than I could get it in my hands and the houses I had bidded on finally came through. Within a couple of weeks of getting the houses, I turned around and sold them and made a hundred thousand dollar profit.

One day while driving down the highway Stacey called me. I was happy to hear from her and asked if she would like to ever meet up with me for lunch or dinner.

"Yeah, I'd love too," she replied. However, our schedules would always conflict and we would just end up talking on the phone. Over the course of weeks we kept in touch and then finally one day we had lunch. During lunch we decided that a great business move was to bring Pharrell in to see if he would invest in me. I knew since she was close to him, she could get the ball rolling. "Laushaun, I will see what I can do," she said as I handed her one of my business cards. I knew with him I could make millions, but at the same time, a brotha wasn't holding his breath. I thought if she could make it happen … cool, but if not, there was no love lost … next.

Chapter 15

No Honor Among Thieves

EVERYTHING WAS GOING AS PLANNED. I WAS STACKING MONEY AND HAD JUST finished selling my first shipment. Although this was going good, I had to make sure my connection at the dock was all in to minimize any risk. I coordinated a meeting with him and told him I'd handsomely compensate him for his efforts in making sure my shipments were safe. That way, I could get fifty to a hundred kilos at a time, which would take shipments from monthly down to twice a year.

Life was moving at a fast rate and before I realized it my birthday had rolled around. I was so busy with making moves that I didn't even plan anything spectacular for my own special day. However, that all changed when I got a call from Donna. She had told me that she'd prepared a special meal for me and would like me to come over around 6 o'clock. When 6 o'clock arrived, I pulled into the driveway at Donna's house and noticed another car in the driveway. Damn, is she tryin' to set me up? Being cautious, instead of going to the door, I called her to ask who else was visiting her.

"See Laushaun, you are spoiling my surprise for you. I have my girlfriend over here, but since you are so paranoid, I will meet you at the door and take you to her." I didn't know what to think, but I headed to the door anyway. When I got to the door, Donna was standing completely naked and took me straight to her bedroom. As we entered the room, her girlfriend Tracy exited the bathroom. I said what's up and thought to myself; *yeah, she is the guy in the relationship with her tomboyish ways.* Except I had to admit, the girl was pretty; I could see why Donna was attracted to her. She had full lips and perky tits with toffee colored skin and long braids that went down to her nicely plumped ass.

"Boo, go sit on the couch and get ready to enjoy the ride," Donna said as she got into a kissing frenzy with her girl. Then out of nowhere, Tracy pulled a strap out with a dildo attached, strapped it on around her waist and started hitting Donna from the back while smacking her ass. After watching them for a while, Tracy guided Donna toward me on the couch while she was still doing her.

"Take—take—take—take your clothes off," she said barely able to get her words out of her mouth as she moaned and groaned. I quickly took my clothes off and Donna then opened her mouth and started sucking my manhood while Tracy kept hitting her from the back. Since Donna's mouth was full with 9 inches, Tracy told me that I wasn't allowed to penetrate either of them, but as long as I could keep my dick up, I could get all the lip service I wanted. I was okay with that … The girls continued to take turns penetrating each other while giving me head for hours, until they couldn't climax anymore. Once it was completed, I went to the shower and got myself ready to leave.

"Did you enjoy your birthday gift, Laushaun?" she asked looking like she had just jogged around the block a few times.

"No doubt, I loved it," I said as I kissed her on the cheek and walked out the door.

The next morning, I got an early call from Tim. I knew something had to be wrong because he wasn't an early morning person unless he was headed to practice.

"Hey dawg, huh—I might have to take you up on that offer, man, you proposed to me. They're trying to fuck with me, man."

"What's going on?" I asked him.

"They are messing with my paper, man—threatening me about steroids and shit." After calming him down, I told him that whatever he needed, I would take care of it for him.

"Thanks man, that's why you my boy."

"It's all love, fam, I got you," I said and then hung up the phone to start my day.

I went out to breakfast and picked up a paper to catch up on what was happening in the world. When I opened the paper, dead smack on the front page was a picture of Tim with a heading that read, 'Steroid Scandal'. The article began by saying, "NSU track star, fastest man in the world, Tim Montgomery has no where to run to …" However, the article did not stop at steroids; it mentioned Tim's association with 'Drug King Pin Shampoo'. *What the hell?* I was shocked that they would bring Shampoo up after all this time. I quickly read the rest of the article and then I called Tim back to get a better understanding of what was going down.

"Bay Area Laboratory Cooperative or BALCO is what most folks call it, is a company that Marion and I are affiliated with … and they got busted for a steroid called 'Clear'. So with the 2004 Olympics coming around, they have decided to test everyone who wants to compete for steroids. Yo, I was told the 'Clear' was supposed to be undetectable, but apparently there is a test that can find it in my system," he said; as I continued to listen to him talk I could hear the bitterness in his voice. "I got to go do these tryouts without any kind of performance enhancers. I got to do it natural. Well at least I get a hundred thousand for going, right?" He said with his voice cracking. It sounded like he was about to break down in tears. Although I didn't know what was in store for him, I wished him luck and prayed that everything would work out in his favor.

The weekend of the Olympic tryouts came and both Tim and Marion did horrible in almost every event. Marion only qualified for the relay and long jump, but Tim failed at everything. Later that night, I tried to call him to lift his spirits, but he wasn't hearing it.

"Man, they are fucking with me—it's their entire fault—everything!" he said, highly irritated. I tried to say words of encouragement, but that was the last thing on his mind. For a minute there was a pause, and then I heard Tim talking to someone in the background.

Next thing I knew, a woman's voice spoke, "Hey Laushaun, its Marion. How are you?" she said.

"I'm good. How are you?"

"Yeah, I'm good. Hey Laushaun, you know they're about to ice us so we gotta go. I'll have Tim get back with you later, okay?" she said in an upbeat tone.

"Okay, that's cool. I'll talk to y'all later. Oh and tell Tim I said for him to keep his head up."

After I hung up, Prince called me and was ready to give me the rest of the money he owed me.

"Yo Laushaun, I need some more bricks for my soldiers. How much you got left?" he said, anticipating my response. I told him I only had a stash of two ounces left until I placed an order for the next shipment. He told me that he wanted them and he would pay me once I got there. In route to his place on a two-way street, I encountered a roadblock. I knew something was going down because they had several dogs checking each car that passed. Shit, shit, shit! What the hell? I got this dope on me. Hastily, I rolled down the passenger window and started throwing the powder out so I couldn't be caught with it.

When I finally pulled up to the checkpoint, the officer asked me for my driver's license. Once I gave it to him, he asked if he could search my truck. Since I knew I was clean, I didn't have a problem with it … I just wanted to get it over with as quick as possible.

The officer guided the K-9 through my truck to search for items that were prohibited by law. Feeling confident, I relaxed as the dog searched my car. However, when the dog got to the front passenger seat, he started barking and scratching. Startled by his bark, I jumped … and then I looked over at the seat where he was to see what he was barking at. Damn, I dropped a piece of heroin when I was throwing it out the window. The officer picked up the dope and looked at me and asked, "You know what this means, don't you?" Before I could even respond he said, "Sir, you're under arrest for the possession of heroin." My bond was $4,000. I didn't want to alarm my family so I called Prince to come get me. Within the hour I was out, but I knew there was more to come. I had violated my probation so there was a stong possibility that I would need to serve the rest of my prison time. I just didn't know if it would be the full five years or if I could get it knocked down to two or three. Trying not to think about my fate, I focused on how to keep the ball rolling in my absence—and I had two days to do it.

I immediately instructed Prince on how to orchestrate the operation on his end and then connected him and Boo-Bee together so they could keep the money flowing. In appreciation for hooking him up, Prince agreed to send me twelve thousand a month to keep me straight. I wanted to tell Tim about what was going on, but I wanted to see how everything would unfold before I broke the news to him.

In the meantime, I called Dawn to tell her about my arrest and how I would most likely be sent away to prison.

"What? Oh my God, Laushaun. You're playin'—tell me you're playing'," she said.

"Nah boo, I'm not," I sadly replied and then she broke some news to me.

"Wow, I dunno what to say. I have somethin' to tell you, but now I don't know if I should."

"Baby, what is it?" I curiously asked.

"I'm two months pregnant," she blurted out.

"That's great. I'm happy Dawn—real happy," I told her while a thousand thoughts ran through my head. My life seemed to be going down the drain in a matter of minutes. Not that I didn't want to have a baby by her, but because it was happening at such an inopportune time. Although she was devastated, Dawn promised to have the baby in my absence.

"Then when you come back, we can all be a family. Right?" she said with uncertainty in her voice.

"Right baby, I got you—we gonna be a family."

Monday morning had rolled around and it was time for me to see my PO. Once I got to his office, a small voice inside me told me to just leave. *Shit, if they gonna find out, let them work to find me,* I said to myself as I started to walk away. But right when I pivoted my foot to go in the other direction, Mr. Ellis walked outside and stopped me.

"Mr. Robinson?" he said with a question in his tone. I knew I had nowhere to go so I went into his office and got straight to the point.

"Sir, I was arrested last week. It was for possession of heroin," I said feeling lower than dirt as I handed him the paperwork.

"Mr. Robinson, you were doing so well for yourself. How did you go back down the wrong road?" I told him that the truck wasn't mine, it was a rental but since it was in my name, I got the charge for it, but I didn't have any heroin on me. He told me that he didn't think a judge would buy my story, but we would find out the next morning in court.

Once leaving his office, I called Prince and told him that I was going back and he had to keep the ball rolling. When I hung up with him, I called Donna to tell her the bad news. She was upset about the situation. I told her that once I got situated, I would give her a call. Then I called Dawn to tell her to get my keys from my mom and to pick up the safe that I had for her and take it to her parents' house.

Later that evening, I met Prince and told him to keep the balance that he owed me since he was holding things down until I got back. After leaving him, I went to my mom's house to tell her what was going on. When I arrived at her house she opened the door and immediately she knew something was wrong—a mother's intuition.

"Bookie, what's wrong? Tell ya momma what's goin' on?" she asked, staring straight at me.

"I messed up, Momma—I'm goin' back," I said as I hugged her like I was a 7-year-old child again. My mom was heartbroken; she listened to me as I told her to keep my keys until Dawn comes for them later in the week.

"Momma, no matter what, you gonna be taken care of."

"Don't you worry about me—ya hear? You just take care of yourself." I hugged her again, and then we sat and drank wine all night long. Although I wanted to cry, I didn't want my mother to see any weakness in me, so I just silently counted down the hours until I had to see my PO in the morning.

The next morning I called a selected few people to tell them goodbye. However, I didn't call Tim because I knew he had enough on his mind with the Olympics and BALCO scandal so I decided to connect with him later.

My mom took me to the federal building and while driving I counted down the minutes of my freedom. Once we arrived, I gave her a final kiss goodbye because I knew once I got inside the building I wasn't coming back out a free man. When I walked inside, my PO was waiting at the door for me with an arrest warrant in his hand.

"It doesn't look like the judge is going to be sympathetic. You may be getting the full 5 years," he said as my heart skipped a few beats. I got to my holding cell and when I was given a chance, I immediately called my mom and Dawn to tell them as well. Once my phone time was up, I went back to my cell and laid on the bed staring at the ceiling.

I'm back up in this mutha fucka, I thought to myself. Then all of a sudden, just like a raindrop that falls from the heavens and hits you on the cheek … I felt a teardrop trickle down my face. *Damn, I haven't shed a tear in years.* And as soon as I thought that, the tears flooded my eyes and spilled over down my face. Wiping them off with my hands, I began to question myself. *How did I set myself up like this? Why did you let yourself get back up in here?* Then I started to think about the people I loved; my mom, Dawn … my unborn child. *I'm gonna miss my child coming into this world. I'm gonna miss …* And before I realized it, I drifted off into a deep sleep.

The next morning, I entered the courtroom with a US Marshall escorting me to the front to meet my lawyer. Walking towards the front, I caught a glimpse of the spectators and saw that my whole family had come. When I got to my lawyer he shook my hand, leaned into me and said whispering, "This judge is fed up with you and these drugs, Laushaun. We'll see if we can convince him that you had no knowledge of the drugs in the rental."

"All rise …" the bailiff announced the presiding judge and as the judge walked into the courtroom; my lawyer made eye contact with him and gave a masonry sign by pulling on his suit jacket. The bailiff told everyone to be seated and the hearing began. My lawyer fought hard for me and tried every tactic in the book, but the judge wasn't having it. Everything went just like my PO told me it would and I was sentenced to 5 years in a medium security prison in Fairton, New Jersey. Right before the US Marshall came to escort me out of the court, I took one last look at my mother and Dawn and said, "I love you."

"I love you too," they mouthed to me simultaneously and then I was taken to my holding cell to await my transport to New Jersey.

Traveling by bus for twelve hours, we finally arrived at Fairton at three in the morning. As I looked out my window, my stomach became sickened viewing the all too familiar scenery. Instantaneously, I learned my surroundings and acquainted myself with my cellmate, Rome. Rome was cool peeps; he kept to his self and associated with people who weren't looking for trouble. There was this one older gentleman in particular who'd come around and drop his wisdom on us. His name was Maurice, but most called him 'P-nut King'. When he came to talk, I would pay him his respects and listened to what he had to say. I was glad that I had some OGs around that I could learn a thing or two from.

Once I was settled in, I kept thinking about calling Tim to tell him where I was at. I wasn't sure if he got word or what ... but I wanted him to know what was up. The first opportunity I got, I called him. When he answered the phone, he sounded like he had been punched in the chest. He had pain in his voice. Did he hear the news already?

"Tim, what's wrong?" I asked out of concern.

"Marion and I—we were subpoenaed for steroid use by a Federal Grand Jury. I dunno what I'm gonna do, dawg. They're tryin' to suspend us, dawg. They're fuckin' up my career—but forget about my shit—Dawn told me about your incarceration. I feel bad I wasn't there for you. How are you doing?"

"You know ... I'm doin'. I'm'ma be aight. Ya feel me?"

"Yeah, I feel you, playboy. You know your boy has been stressin'... They messin' with my paper—my lifestyle—how am I gonna maintain my luxurious lifestyle?" he said, sounding devastated. I felt really bad for him so I told him that I was gonna hook him up with my boy, Prince, and that he could probably hook him up with everything that was going on overseas. I knew I couldn't say too much over the phone but he knew what I meant.

"Ya boy needs to do somethin', because I'm tryin' to maintain this lifestyle for the next 30 years, fam. Ya hear me?"

"Bet, then I'll be back in touch witcha. Stay strong, fam," I said and then hung up the phone.

After hanging up with Tim, I called Prince to let him know about Tim's situation and to put him on with the crew. Prince said I had called him at a perfect time, because he had an 'in' to a check scam that was going to go down and he had a way to get everyone some paper, including me. I could tell he was being careful with the words he was choosing and wanted to quickly get off the phone, so I immediately gave him Tim's number so that they could handle business. Before we hung up, Prince said he would come visit me to talk about the Panama business in person. Right after I hung up, I called Tim and told him about some business he may be interested in.

"Yo, come in visit me so I can give you the run down. My visiting days are Mondays, Tuesdays and Fridays between 9 am and 3 pm."

"Bet, I'll be there in a few days, once I'm finished with this grand jury bullshit in California," he said and then we hung up. On my way back to my cell, I saw P-nut King.

"Hey young brotha, why don't cha sit down with an old man and play some chess," he said with a smirk and gestured for me to sit down. I sat down and began to chop it up with him. Two hours into the game, I had pretty much told this man my life story and about my latest business venture ...

"Whoa young brotha—let me tell ya somethin'. You be careful what you say on these phones and what business you conduct behind these here bars ... You talkin' to a person who knows from experience—I caught a fresh thirty on top of a fifty-year sentence I already had. You hear me son?" he said, looking me straight in the eyes and then all of a sudden he said, "Check mate," and he got up and left me sitting at the table.

I went to sleep that night thinking about my conversation with P-nut and decided that after I hooked Prince and Tim up, I was out. I just couldn't afford to get caught up behind bars. It wasn't worth it. I was much appreciative that P-nut took the time to put things in perspective for me. He saved me from just thinking of dollars, and encouraged me to use my sense. Daily I would run the track, reflecting on my conversation with P-nut while I patiently waited for Tim's arrival.

It was around 11 am when I was called to the visitation room. I didn't know if it was Prince or Tim so when I got there I scanned the room looking for my visitor. While searching, I saw a few celebrities in the room. *There goes Damon Dash visiting Beanie Segal and hey, that's 50 Cent visiting his uncle Trinidad ... Aww, there's Tim.* I walked up to the table and gave Tim daps.

"What's good, playboy?" he said. I could tell that he was anxious about the information I was going to give him. I could see it in his eyes. But before I gave him the details, I felt I needed to forewarn him of the possible consequences for getting involved. I leaned into him and lowered my voice.

"Dawg, no joke, if you do not follow the rules of this game, this scheme can land you in prison for several years. Ya feel me?" Once I knew he understood the conditions, I told him everything I knew.

"There's an account that Prince knows about that holds over $100 million. If you guys play your cards right, you could easily steal a few million out of the account without being detected." I paused for a moment to let him digest what I had just said and then I continued on telling him the plan. "Prince is going to act like he is investing in one of your sporting companies with the fake check and once the check clears the bank ... y'all can split whatever the check was worth."

"So how much can the check be written for?" Tim asked, almost shaking as he heard the information.

"Yo, you write it for as much as your account can hold without it looking obvious."

I went on to tell him that he could only cash one check so he had to make it worth their while. If he cashed more, it could be detected and he would be sent to prison. I also warned him that once the company files their taxes at the beginning of the next year, it was a possibility that the IRS would come after him if it were detected.

"So what the hell do I tell them if they come knockin' at my door, man? I ain't trying to go to jail."

"Tell them that someone invested in your business and you didn't know that it was a bad check. Since everything cleared, you had no knowledge of any foul play."

"Okay."

"With Prince's false ID, y'all will get away with the money and the company will get it back since it's insured." I explained that as long as Tim's company didn't have any more scams under its belt when they investigated, they would be home free. After giving him the rundown, I told him that Prince would be calling him soon so they could hook up.

"Shit Laushaun, I'm ready … I really need this money," he said anxiously.

"Well check this … Boo-Bee is gonna be coming over on a cargo ship with 50 kilos of cocaine and heroin," I said as his eyes lit up. I told him the information that I had just provided about the weight was just a little food for thought and then I quickly changed the subject by asking him about the Olympics.

Tim went on to tell me that he didn't make the Olympics that year and he decided to take some time off. He wanted to take up culinary classes and open a restaurant and club soon. He told me that Marion, however, did make the Olympics and he planned to support her to the fullest. After a little more small talk, we said our goodbyes and Tim left as I went back to my cell.

The days were moving by fast and everything was going according to plan … or so I thought. The drugs had made it to the states without being detected and the check scandal went through with no problems. Prince told me that he had put a check aside for me in a safe place until I was released from prison. He was keeping his promise by holding a brotha down. He then told me that he'd played Tim because of Black Shawn's death.

"What? Man, what you mean by that? I thought everything was cool."

"Yeah, everything was cool with you. But we found out that Tim's people and Shawn had words before leaving the club that night."

"Man, we gotta just let Shawn rest in peace, man. We can't be going off of hearsay," I told him as we quickly changed the subject.

After saying our goodbyes, I headed back to my cell and rested for a while.

***

A FEW MONTHS later, I was called into the attorney's office but I didn't know why. My lawyer didn't tell me that he was coming to visit … and I had just talked to my family so I knew everything was cool with them. While I walked to the office, I tried to figure out why and what they wanted me for. Did something bad happen? When I got to the office and opened the door, a fat, white, bald detective told me that he was working Black Shawn's homicide and needed my help. I sat down at the table, confused to why this man needed me.

"How do you need my help?" I asked, not understanding what I could do to help him. He then pulled out pictures and to my surprise it was of Tim and his crew.

"Do you know any of these guys?" the detective asked looking at me, although I knew my facial expression gave my answer away.

"Yes, I know Tim," I told him, pointing at Tim in the picture while wondering if Prince's allegations were now true. The detective then went on to ask me how I knew Tim. I told him that I was a close friend as well as a fan of his.

"You know Mr. Robinson; your phone number was the last number in Shawn's phone the night he died," he said in an accusatory fashion.

"Yeah I know, after he was killed!" I blurted out, feeling that he was trying to either connect me to the murder some kind of way, or get me to implicate my boy and his crew. "Sir, I don't believe I can further help you," I told him while I stood up and excused myself from the room.

When I got back to the dorm, I called my attorney and told him what had just happened.

"So what do you want to do?"

"Not a damn thing. He's just fishing and I can't fish with him because I don't know anything," I told him. I was a little shaken up, but my lawyer told me not to be. I calmed myself down and thanked him for advising me. Then we said our goodbyes and I hung up the phone and decided to call Tim to give him a heads up about what was going on. When he answered, he was whispering so low, I couldn't understand him.

"Man, what the hell you whispering for?" I asked, confused. He went on to tell me that he'd cashed another check for $900,000 that had just cleared.

"Okay, so what's that gotta do with you whispering?"

"Man, I'm in here getting ready to cash one for a million and I'm keeping this one for myself."

I quickly began to connect the dots. *So this is what this beef is about ... which makes sense why there is a detective sniffing in my backyard, thinking that someone I'm associated with has something to do with Shawn's death.* I didn't know what to say to Tim, but I knew something was going to go down.

"Yo, why the hell you so quiet, man?" Tim asked, interrupting my inner dialogue. I told him about the detective coming to visit and questioning me about him and his crew. Being very concerned, he asked me about what I told the detective.

"I told him nothing, because that's what I know—nothing. Tim, he had pictures of you and your boys. I really don't think it's a wise move to play Prince and muscle this check out of him. He's a powerful player in this game now. One wrong move and you could be taken out." I reiterated to him that Prince was no one to mess with... and to take into consideration that the paper trail was only following him and no one else, so he would be the one to go down.

"Hell, I'm the one that's got your back, man. Prince told me not to even tell you about the other check we cashed." I was furious. I couldn't believe that Prince would cut me out like that. That just wasn't like him. I told Tim that I would call him back and quickly called Prince.

"What's good, playboy? Is everything going good out there?" I asked him, seeing what information he would give.

"Oh yeah, everything's good. What's going on with the check thing though? Are they still poppin' off? I've been waiting for Tim to call me all week and when I call him, he won't even answer the damn phone. What's up with that?" he said. I couldn't believe what I was hearing him say. At that point I didn't know what the fuck was going on. It seemed like everyone was playing everyone. I told Prince he probably hadn't heard from Tim because he was out of the country and the number he was dialing didn't work well abroad. Therefore, I gave him Tim's Nextel number and Prince called him on a conference call to see if we could get an answer. I sat there for about a three or four minutes waiting for Prince to click back over and when he did, I could tell that they had a quick conversation that they didn't want me to hear. When Tim got on the line, he told me that he would be back in the country by the end of the week and that everything would be taken care of then.

I could tell something shady was going on and I wanted to get to the end of it.

"Yo Prince, what's up, fam? You got some shady shit going on man. How you gon' play me like that?" I asked, interrupting whatever they were talking about.

"Man, what you talking about? I've been keeping it real with you from day one."

"So you are keeping it real, huh. Then what's up with the million that just went down?" After a few seconds of silence, he finally talked.

"Oh that. It just ain't gone through yet. That's all." I knew that it was some bullshit going down and I didn't want to be a part of it. I told him to just give my mother the money that I lent him and that I was out of everything. I wasn't down for the scandalousness that they had going on. He quickly agreed and I hung up the phone in his face.

I then called my mother to tell her that Prince would be bringing her something to hold for me. As the week went on, my mom wrote a letter telling me that Prince had brought the duffle bag over and that Dawn had a little girl named Layla Robinson. I hadn't talked to her in the past few months, because she was so depressed about being a single parent that it was making her sick. Plus, her parents were also in her ear convincing her to move on with her life; telling her that she didn't need a thug like me. I decided to distance myself from her, because I couldn't be stressed about a woman on the outside while trying to take care of myself in here.

Time went on and Dawn started visiting me with our daughter. She was getting so big. It brought me joy to see her. During one particular visit, Dawn told me about how Prince was steady prospering. She told me he would call to check on her and the baby frequently, as well as offering her free services at his new barbershop. I took everything she told me in and found it very interesting that Prince was taking a great interest in the well-being of Dawn and my child. But I guessed that's how a playa was holding a nigga down … Not.

I called Tim every other month and when he brought things up about him and Prince, I kept things neutral because I didn't want to choose sides between them. Plus, I thought the less I knew about their business dealings the better, because I had strong feeling that shit was about to blow up in their faces.

One Friday, I had received a letter from Donna stating that she'd just come from supporting her brother in the Pro Bowl in Hawaii and that she'd seen Dawn and Layla at the mall and how Layla looked so much like me. After reading the letter and looking at the pictures she sent, I decided to give her a call.

"Hey stranger, how is everything? Did you get the pictures I sent you?"

"Yes, I got them. I'm lovin' them too."

"Yeah whatever, I bet you tell Dawn that same bullshit every time you talk to her too, don't you?" she said as we both laughed. It was obvious that there was still a lot of chemistry there. She then went on to tell me that once I got out, she wanted my baby. I knew that she still cared about me, but not like that. She promised me that this time she was going to do right by me. While I listened to her,

I realized I still had love for her and wouldn't mind rekindling our relationship. We both chatted for a little while longer before I had to go. When I got off the phone I prayed to God to make the time go faster because I knew she wouldn't wait on me forever.

As time went on, the BALCO scandal was at its peak. Tim had been suspended for two years for being caught with steroids and Marion Jones' and Barry Bonds' names were popping up all over the media with allegations of steroid use. Daily I listened to the news to see what the outcome would be for my peoples.

One day when I called my mom, she told me that some local kid named Shabazz had set up Prince and the police had raided his house. Inside they found a million dollars, drugs, and guns. I couldn't believe what was happening and I wondered what was going through Prince's head about the whole thing. I knew I needed to call him … and fast.

"Mom, please call Prince's house on three-way." My mom called and Prince's son answered the phone. He told me his dad would be calling at exactly 9 pm and if I'd call back, he would put me on three-way with him.

Later that night, Prince's son kept his word and put me on three-way with his dad so I could talk about what went down.

"I'm'ma do a lot of time. Yo, they caught me with my pants down. That punk ass nigga Shabazz got caught with 9 ounces of heroin and pointed the Feds in me direction," Prince said angrily.

"What was in your crib?"

"Everything man. I had 100 lbs of weed, half of a kilo of heroin and some heat."

"Why the hell you got all that stuff in your crib?"

"I dunno, but I ain't wearin' all this shit, homeboy."

"What you mean? It was all of yours was it not?"

"Yeah, but your boy Tim is dirty. I don't like how he gets down … I'm gonna give up the check scandal. "

"So who you gonna give up?" He told me he was going to give up Tim, Marion, their coach, Riddick and his assistant. He further explained that they continued the scam without him and cut him out of 3.2 million dollars.

"They cut you out of 3.2 million, huh."

"Yeah, but before they started playin' dirty … we did 2 million together." He told me he still had half of his money, and if I had his back, he would make sure I was straight. I thought that was really funny considering how he cut me out of every other deal, but now that he needed me, he would give me some money. I told him that I wasn't getting involved in any of it and that I was keeping my hands clean.

"Yo dawg, just keep my name out of it. Ya hear me—I ain't involved."

He then said, "It's a little too late for that, playboy. I already told the Feds you knew about everything, but you never received any money. Yeah, they've traced all my calls and got Boo-Bee and his partner under surveillance." My blood was boiling, but I didn't want to show him my hand. Then he repeated to me about how he was going to take Tim down.

"Like I told you, playboy, I am not getting involved in this … That bad blood is between you and Tim. I wish you luck and hope everything works out." I was about to hang up the phone when Prince said my name.

"What, dawg?"

"This ain't about you—you good. But your boy …" Before he could finish, I interrupted and told him that the beef was between him and Tim … and I hung up the phone. After hanging up the phone, I called Tim to let him know to be on the lookout. However, Tim had already heard the news.

"Tell that faggot to keep my fuckin' name outta his mouth," Tim screamed as he answered the phone. He told me that he'd already paid Prince his half of the money and wasn't giving him anything else. After explaining to Tim that he could do some serious prison time for this, he just commented, "Let them people do what the fuck they gotta do then," and slammed the phone down.

Letting him calm down for a few minutes, I called him back. We talked about his options. I told him he could no longer play the victim because he allowed Marion, his coach and the coach's assistant to cash checks.

"The best thing for you to do is to just turn yourself and negotiate for a slap on the wrist." I could hear him breathing heavily on the other side of the phone as he was thinking.

Then abruptly he said, "Fuck it! I'll have to take my chances ... Those mutha fuckas are gon' have to catch my ass." I couldn't believe he was determined to just let them catch him when they could.

"Are you crazy? Not only is Prince bringing your name into the check scandal, but he's saying you were the mastermind of the drug operation and that you supplied the upfront money for all his drugs. If that ain't enough, he's gonna have you go down for Shawn's murder." He told him he had to rethink his strategy or he would be in prison for life or longer. He still didn't want to hear it ... and I could no longer go back and forth with him.

"Aight dawg, have it your way, but remember you're playin' checkers with chess players," I said and then we hung up the phone.

***

MONTHS LATER, EVERYONE had fallen off the map because they were trying to protect their own. Tim had changed his number and Prince had changed his son's location completely. The days, weeks and months were zooming by and I hadn't talked to anybody accept my mom. After about nine months of not talking to anyone and a year left of my sentence, I received a farewell letter from Donna. She had told me that she'd gotten married and was pregnant with her husband's child. When I finished the letter, I took a deep breath and said: Time waits for no man ... I hope she's happy.

Reading Donna's letter kind of brought me down and I started thinking about who were the people who were truly in my corner. I thought for awhile and the only person I truly knew had my back was my mother. Other than Dawn writing once a month to tell me about our daughter, my mom was all I had.

One day, while in the rec yard chillin' out with the homeboys, my cellmate came up to me and told me that it was official. "What's official?" I asked. He told me that Tim and his coach had been indicted for check fraud and they had suspicions that Marion had a part in it too. I thanked my cellie for the information and pulled my cigarettes out. I fired one up and said to myself, *Prince is at work selling his soul to the devil … and at Tim's expense.*

It was all over the news that track and field star, Tim Montgomery and his coach were involved in a 5.2 million dollars check scam and was responsible for 3.2 million dollars of the stolen money. After watching it on the news and reading it in the paper the next day, I decided to call my mom and tell her what was going on.

"Baby, I'm so glad you called. Your friend that has been all over the news has been worrying the hell out of me."

"For what?"

"He just said he really needs to speak with you and he left me his phone number to give you."

"Call him, momma, please call him now," I said, wondering what this dude was calling me about. When he answered, he screamed, "Man, these folks got me by the balls. I don't know what to do."

"I told you that you could have prevented all this shit—but look at you—you didn't want to listen. Nigga, I don't want any part of this."

"Man please, you gotta help me. This is all new for me. You know how these people work—testify on my behalf—please," he said pleading with me.

"Man, is you crazy? After how you and that fake ass dude played me, you think I'm just gonna bend over and help you out? You are out of your mind. Ya'll got $3 million and you couldn't give me a dime and you think I'm gonna risk more time with perjury to help you—oh, hell no!" After going back and forth for a while, I finally broke down.

"Yo dawg, you were the only one who truly had my back when I was released the first time. I got you." Truthfully, I really didn't want to see Tim drown in quicksand; helping him in some way was the least I could do for him. "Check it out. The phones aren't safe for us to talk on. Have your lawyer come and visit me."

Within in a few days, Tim's lawyer arranged to come and visit me. When we met, he thought that I was going to write a statement about how Tim was victimized and had no knowledge of the check scam. Instead, I provided him a written list of reasons why Tim didn't need to go to trial. My list stated all the charges that the Feds were investigating him on; if he went to trial, Tim would end up being buried underneath the jail.

"How do you know they are looking at my client for all these charges?" Tim's lawyer asked.

"Because I heard it from the horse's mouth," I replied.

"Did you make any statements against my client?"

I looked him straight in the eyes and responded, "Look, I don't have anything to do with this ordeal. Tim asked me for his assistance; therefore, if you are trying to play private eye, you might as well not. I will not go into court and lie for Tim, because if I do, everyone's ass is going to prison. Like I told your client, there is no way to escape check fraud unless you cash one check and play the victim role … Your client and associates did not do that so bottom line, Tim needs to take a plea."

His lawyer looked at me like I was crazy and said, "That is not in my client's best interest."

"The hell it is. Tim needs to take whatever they will offer him. If he does this, it will kill all other indictments." After talking to his lawyer a while, he finally agreed that it would be in Tim's best interest to take a plea.

When Tim's lawyer left, I gave him a call to update him on what was going on. "Now I need to call the head prosecutor and tell her that I have some information," I said, assuring him that I would continue to do what I could to help him not see a jail cell. Shortly after, the meeting with Tim's lawyer and the conversation I had with Tim, the Feds from New York came to pay me a visit. I was told that I would not be indicted because there was not enough evidence that proved that I received any proceeds from the scam. Once they told me that, the conversation shifted to Tim and Marion.

"So what's your relationship with Tim and Marion?" she asked sternly. I responded by telling her I had known Tim for a little over 10 years and just had met Marion a year ago when I was home. She paused for a second and tapped her pen on the table, and then asked me if I knew of Tim's involvement in the check scam or with drugs.

"I introduced Tim to Prince, so I did know about the checks."

"What about the drugs? Did he ever give you money to supply your drug operation?" she asked jolting her head forward, like a dog preparing to attack his prey.

"No," I replied. Then she asked me if I knew or had any knowledge of Marion knowingly cashing bad checks. I sat up in my chair, leaned forward and said, "Nope, just what Prince told me, which was all three of them participated in the check scheme."

"I see. Well, Tim has contacted us and he's going to take a plea and Marion, well she's denying the allegations so we're going to charge her for lying to the Grand Jury about her steroid use and for lying about the checks," she said as I sat quietly and listened to her. When she finished speaking she put her pen down, sighed and then said, "Mr. Robinson, why do I have the feeling that you are trying to protect Mr. Montgomery."

"I'm not tryin' to protect him, besides he's already pleading guilty. What more do y'all want from me?" I said being frustrated by her constant questioning and then asked, "Can I leave now?"

"Yes, you can leave Mr. Robinson, but believe you me, there's more to come." I looked at her and wondered what she meant by that.

"What do you mean more to come? I've helped you." I continued staring at her while she ignored me as she put her items in her briefcase and closed it. Next, she grabbed her briefcase and then exited the room.

Later, I called Tim to tell him about my meeting with the prosecutor. He told me that Marion and the coach bailed on him, and his lawyer was in the process of negotiating an agreement with the Feds.

"I should hear something from my lawyer within the week."

"It's all gonna work out man, just do your part and let your lawyer do his," I said and then we said goodbye.

A week had passed and I was called back to another meeting with the prosecutor. She told me that she received all of my conversations with Tim and it seemed like I had convinced him to take a plea.

"Yeah, you're right. I knew Tim had a no-win situation on his hands so I suggested he do it."

Like bullets propelling out of her mouth, her words entered the atmosphere with force and she said, "I think you know a whole lot more than what you're saying. Mr. Montgomery is listening to you. Even his lawyer is listening to you, and he's a GOOD lawyer! But you know what; it doesn't matter because I got a conviction out of this deal." She paused to take a breath and then said, "This is what you're going to do, Mr. Robinson. You are going to tell the jury that Coach Riddick knowingly cashed bad checks. " I told her that I only knew about Tim, but she countered with, "Prince informed you of his involvement, correct?

"Yes."

"Well that's good enough," she said with a smirk on her face. Before she left the meeting, she told me Marion was going to be indicted within the next month or so. I thought it was interesting that they hadn't broken Marion down yet. I thought to myself, she really must be standing up to them.

I later learned that Tim took a plea with the Federal Government and became an informant. His cooperation with them allowed him to stay out of prison; his punishment, house arrest. Tim also never had to testify against his coach because the Feds used my 'statement'. Tim's only concern was to provide the information that the Feds needed to keep himself out of jail.

During a phone conversation Tim expressed his anger to me regarding Marion.

"It's fucked up, dawg; she doesn't talk to me no more. I didn't make her ass lie."

"But dawg, she was doin' you a favor. She didn't need that money—she was following your lead."

"Whatever. It doesn't matter no more, she's moved on with her life. You know she's pregnant and about to get married?" The conversation with Tim was one-sided as I continued to listen to him vent his frustrations about the woman he once loved.

Several days later I talked to Tim again while he was in San Diego, CA dealing with the BALCO case. I was surprised that he was still dealing with BALCO; I had thought that he had worked everything out.

"You know they want to strip Marion and Barry Bonds of their world records and indict them for perjury."

"Yeah, I already knew what was up with Marion, but I've been catching everything about Barry Bonds on the news."

He started laughing and said, "Barry fuckin' Bonds. That nigga don't care about being strip of a damn world record—he's worth over a hundred million." Then he said, "Man, I've been getting' all kind a death threats and other messages through the mail. Can you believe that shit?"

"What? You gotta be kiddin' me," I said shocked that someone would go that far about some damn steroids.

"Nah, I'm serious as a heart attack. But anyways man, I'll be back in Virginia by the weekend to open my new night club." I couldn't believe with all that was happening that Tim was opening a club. Although I didn't agree with it, I congratulated him on his new business venture. That was the last time I communicated with Tim until …

Chapter 16

Emotional Pain

In life I've taken a lot of losses, mainly the separation from the ones I love the most, my family and children. Not all the money in the world could amount to me being away from them. Every night before I lay down to sleep, I mark my calendar, counting down the days until I can see them face to face without limitations.

One day I was called to the prison Chaplain's office. While I prepared myself to walk to his office, I noticed my heart began to beat rapidly and the palms of my hands began to sweat. I tried brainstorming all the possibilities of why the Chaplain would be calling me to his office. I knew that when people went to the Chaplain's office was because of a death occurred within the family and the prison had to notify you of the news. I thought to myself, exactly what and who could have gotten killed or passed because I've been in contact with Mom on a regular basis, and to my knowledge, everyone was completely well and doing fine.

I entered the Chaplain's office and he stood up to extend his hand and stated, "Mr. Robinson, please have a seat."

I then asked, "Chaplain, please tell me that you haven't called me to your office to give me some sort of disappointing news."

He looked up at me and stated, "Mr. Robinson, I'm here to tell you that your mother Ms. Robinson has called the institution about an hour ago to inform us that your grandmother has had a major heart attack and that her conditions weren't well." He then told me she was in intensive care fighting for her life.

"And there's more."

"More?"

"Your grandfather tried giving her CPR and while he was administering it, he raised his blood pressure and heart rate ... Therefore resulting in him having a major stroke, son, they are both fighting for their lives."

I immediately saw flashes of the both of them during our first and last encounters ... I could hear my grandmother's voice saying, "Baby, I'm glad you made it home in time because we didn't want to go to heaven on you because our days are numbered now." I tried holding back the pain as a huge knot welled up in my throat and started hurting. No longer able to suppress my emotions, the tears started rapidly flowing down my face and suddenly I began hyperventilating from the shocking and sudden news that I had just received. My chest began tightening and my breathing became heavy as I started to feel myself go into a faint daze. Soon everything around me started spinning ...

I could faintly hear the Chaplain asking, "Mr. Robinson, are you okay son? Would you like a glass of water?"

Those were the last words I remembered hearing before I completely fainted and was taken on a stretcher to the prison medical unit. I had awakened hours later lying in the bed with several IVs running through my arm. I tried regaining my consciousness and understand why I was in the infirmary. I recounted my memory and my last thoughts came back in a flash. I remembered speaking with the Chaplain concerning my grandparents' health. Oh my God ... my grandparents. The pain was unbearable. It felt like someone was suffocating me from the inside out.

I sat up to clear my head and the doctor walked into the room while asking to check my pulse and reading the monitor from the IVs that were in my arm. While he checked over me, the Chaplain came in the room and asked the doctor how I was coming along.

The doctor responded, "He seems to be still under a bit of emotional stress and I'd like to keep an eye on Mr. Robinson for a few days to monitor his conditions so that we can get his blood pressure back at a normal rate." He began to explain to the Chaplain and me that emotional stress is a very high risk to my health and that he wanted me to relax and to get plenty of rest.

"Mr. Robinson, please follow the doctor's order and allow the Lord to handle everything else," the Chaplain told me while patting me on the shoulder and before he exited the room, he stated that he would check back in on me daily to view my progress and would notify me if my family called with any updates on my grandparents' conditions. While lying in the bed, daily I prayed and asked God to restore my health and to please protect my grandparents. Four days had passed and my health had gotten better.

When I was released back into the general population, my first thoughts were to call my mom to get an update on my grandparents. Dialing my mother's number, I prayed to myself asking the Lord to please protect my family. I listened to the phone as it rang several times and I began to feel nervous and tensed. Finally, the operator connected my call, and my mother began speaking in a solemn tone. My heart skipped a beat … My gut was telling me there was some devastating information that she needed to tell me.

"Mom, how's everything? What's wrong? Are you crying?" I asked while I heard her sniffling as if she'd been sobbing.

She was quiet for a moment and then she replied. "Baby, your grandmother has gone home to be with the Lord. She's in a better place now."

"What? Momma no—no, not Grandma—Grandma's gone?" Not trying to portray the image that I had upheld for so many years in society and in prison, I let down my guard and immediately started shedding tears in front of everyone who was in the phone room at that time. My emotional state became overwhelming; and anger, sadness and confusion were stirring within me.

"Momma, why did God take her? What does He want from us? I don't understand—please tell me His will."

"Baby, God loves us. He wants the best for all of us. We just never know the hour that He may call us home so we gotta get it right—we gotta live our lives right."

My mom continued to console me over the phone and when she felt that my emotions had gotten under control, she then told me about my grandfather's condition. She told me that he was doing well and holding strong, but he failed to realize that the woman he had been married to for over fifty years was now deceased. She said that he continues to ask the nurses and the family where his wife is, and that he's ready to return home.

"Grandpa has Alzheimers?"

"Yes baby, he's not in the same state of mind that he previously was in before entering the hospital." The impact of the devastating news I had just received overwhelmed my emotions to the point I had to tell my mom that I would give her a call later in the week once I've gotten myself together. I hung up the phone and stared at it for a minute or two. Nothing seemed to make sense or matter to me so I quickly ran to my cell and placed the towel over the glass window to block the officers' view to inside my cell.

Again, I broke down into tears while looking at myself in the mirror asking God why he took my grandmother. *Why? Why? I prayed to you, didn't you hear me? I can't take it—I can't take this. I'm just gonna end it all—ya hear me God—I'm gonna end it now!* I felt I had no purpose in life and that I would be better off dead. Quickly, I grabbed my sheets off the bed, climbed up on the top bunk and started tying the sheets to the ceiling vent. I made a hangman's noose and slip my head through it to hang myself. Just as I was about to thrust myself off the bunk bed, the officers bum-rushed my cell screaming, "Get on the ground Mr. Robinson!" I was handcuffed and taken to the steel bed and injected with Haldol. I remained in isolation under a twenty-four hour watch for three days.

I later learned that the officers had been informed by a couple of inmates that were in the phone room during the time I received the news about my grandmother, that I appeared to be in an instable state when I had left the room. Apparently, one of these same people saw that my towel had been covering the window to my cell for quite some time and felt something seemed to be suspicious so he suggested that the officers check in on me. And that's when they busted into my cell.

Once I was in a more stable state, I was prescribed Prozac by the doctor and was told that it would help me with my suicidal thoughts. A couple of days into taking the meds, I became a complete zombie and my pain was numbed. A few weeks later, my family came to visit me to tell me that my grandfather had passed away from a massive heart attack. While they were delivering the news to me, they became very stunned by my reaction.

"Bookie, are you alright? Did you hear what I said, baby? Your grandfather—he's gone." The medication had me so numb and incoherent that I was emotionless to the shared the news.

A month had gone by and I was constantly complaining of side effects to the prison's psychologist, but he wouldn't take me off the meds. One month later during a session, I spoke up again about the medicine's effects on me.

"I just don't feel normal. I've been telling you this for the past two months."

"Okay, Mr. Robinson, I've been listening to you. Before I took you off of the medicine, I wanted to be certain that you were stable enough to function on your own. You seem to be fine so I'll take you off the meds, but if you have anymore episodes you will be put back on them, okay."

"Thank you," I said, relieved. As the weeks went on, my sessions with the psychologist were not as frequent and eventually he released me from his care.

After coming around and back into my normal routine, I had called my mother. During that call she informed me that when she had came to visit me, she wanted to give me the news about my grandparents' home.

"Bookie, it was broken into, and the burglars stole all their valuable possessions including your safe."

"What, they stole their stuff and my life savings? No." When I heard news, I felt that everything that held value to me in my life was completely gone. Immediately, I felt and knew that the greatest hurt came through emotional pain.

Chapter 17

Turning Point

AFTER ME LOSING MY GRANDPARENTS AND MY LIFE SAVINGS, I FELT LOST AND empty inside. My mail completely stopped besides the everlasting love and friendship from Fred McGray, my childhood friend and the support that my mother continued to give me. I had cut back on hanging with the homies and spent most of my time walking the track in the rec yard while I looked up into the sky and questioned God about all that's happened in my life. While I interrogated Him, I never admitted or even thought that I, myself, was my biggest enemy.

To get some understanding because I felt that I wasn't hearing from God, I began to write to Fred because he had become a Minister. I thought he would be able to give me some insight about God.

"My friend, God has a plan for you, and to fully understand your purpose in life, you'll have to do some soul searching and speak with God and ask Him the questions of your concern. Be still and patiently await His answers—He will respond." Fred wrote this in every letter and at the end, he would give me Bible scriptures to read. In one letter he told me to read the Book of Job. He said, "The story makes me think of you and some of your trials and tribulations."

I couldn't believe he wanted me to read a book. During my entire years of being incarcerated, I've never even attempted to read a book because I saw reading as being uninteresting and for nerds. However, because I was lost, felt empty and had little hope, I had nothing to lose by reading the Bible. I began to give it a deep consideration, especially since my friend said that there was a story that reminded him of me.

Before I picked up the Bible, I wondered what it was about it that influenced millions of human-beings all over the world. I closed my eyes, took a deep breath and began to thumb through the Bible to search for the Book of Job. As I began reading Job to seek out understanding, I felt a sense of relief and relaxation overcome me. While reading, there were many passages that caught my attention, which made me want to read on more. When I got to the middle of the book, I questioned myself, why would God make someone suffer such as Job? Then God encouraged me to continue reading. When I finished Job, I felt I had begun to have an understanding of how God works in our lives. Not once, did I ever view my life trapped inside of a maze that continues to get the same results because of my ignorance to follow the same path repeatedly. Having this revelation put me at peace and I finally knew that my problems with life and worshipping the all-mighty dollar were behind me. Although I realized I was at the beginning of my new journey, I was hungry to learn more and determined not to let anything stop me.

Since I had finished reading Job, I decided to write Fred a letter to ask him what exactly he meant when he said the story reminded him of me. In the letter I explained to him that I had understood that God allowed Satan to strip Job of all his wealth and possessions, because He knew that Job was faithful and no matter what adversities came up against him, he would not curse God; people tried to influence him to curse God, but he wouldn't and in the end God blessed

Job and gave him double for his trouble, because he didn't fall into Satan's trap and curse God.

Fred's reply was this:

"My friend, Job lost loved ones, his stock, home … He was essentially stripped of everything that was valuable to him and not once did Job curse God for his losses. Just like Job, you have been stripped of things that were of value to you. That's how the story reminds me of you. I pray just as Job stood strong in his faith, that you will do the same. If you can make it through this time of tribulation God can bless you too …"

I continued to read his letter and when I got to the end—like he usually did—he wrote a scripture … John 3:16. I read it and immediately I felt God in my presence. After I finished the letter, I called my mom to give her the news. My mom had started crying through the phone while saying aloud, "Thank you Jesus! Thank you Jesus!"

I didn't understand why she was reacting like she was so I asked her, "Momma, I don't understand—why are you crying and saying, thank you Jesus?"

She cleared her throat and said, "Baby, after all those years of running with the devil, God has never forsaken you. And this time when you come home, God has a plan for you that no man or woman can give or take away. You just have trust and believe in God and ask Him for your forgiveness. Try it baby—just do that for yourself."

As time went on, I read more to educate myself about a God I thought I knew, but really didn't. I knew with Him, that He wouldn't lead me astray and back into prison. I started to set my mind on more productive things that would be an asset to my future. I obtained my GED and enrolled in a Computer Basic Training course to develop my skills to prepare myself for the technological computer driven society. Even though I was aware that the odds were stacked up against me to become successful in the regular workforce, I was determined to utilize my inherent skills to become a successful entrepreneur—the right way.

P-nut King had been down close to thirty years and would always mentor me one-on-one while at the chess table. So one day while playing chess, I told him about my new journey with God that I was embarking on. He was proud of me and said that he knew it was just a matter of time before I learned the true path to riches. From then on out, he'd always invite me to speak with him during the Scared Straight Program he ran for the administration of the prison. The program provided mentorship to young teenagers from society who were either having run-ins with the law, or getting suspended from school a lot.

P-nut had a way with words and when he spoke, he spoke from experience and from the heart. He would always tell me how he saw himself within me, but the difference was, I had another chance at life sooner then he did. One day while sitting in my room reading the Bible, P-nut knocked on the door and entered my cell. He sat at the desk and asked, "What story are you reading in the Bible?" I was aware he knew what story I was reading because I had shared my thoughts with him concerning it.

I chuckled and smiled, "Yo P-nut, you know I'm reading Job again," I said as he handed me a small book with about a hundred pages.

"Shaun, I've held on to this book for almost thirty years. It's one of my favorite books." I reached for the book and he said, "I'm giving you a part of me, because I want you to make it in life and this book has a message that tells you that nothing is impossible." I read the cover of the book and its title was called "Jonathan Livingston the Seagull".

I thought to myself, *What in the hell am I going to get out of book about a damn Seagull?* Even though I was a little skeptical about the book, I thanked him for it.

"Hey, after you finish that one, I have some more inspirational literature for you up in my cell," he said and then walked out of my cell.

"Good lookin' out," I said and then said to myself; *let me see what this Seagull is about.*

I read the story and instantly caught on to its moral. The story was about a seagull that did everything the opposite from the other seagulls ... and his motto was, "I can and will!" I really appreciated the reading and the knowledge that I'd ascertained from it. Because I enjoyed the book so much, I had to call my mom to tell her about it, as well as tell her how it got into my hands. She was touched by P-nut King's gesture and wanted to read the book for herself too, so she went out and purchased two books; one for her and the other she forwarded to P-nut King to carry along for the rest of his journey.

I had discovered that after reading the story, I felt I had gained insight on how to better manage myself and my life. Even all the talks that P-nut and I were having at the chess table were making more sense than ever. Then one day, it all came together like a puzzle. I was coming from the rec yard listening to my radio and I noticed P-nut coming up the walkway with a handful of books. We greeted each other and he smiled at me and said, "Shaun, boy I'm glad to see you! Here, help me carry some of these books up to the visitation room." Without thinking, I quickly offered my assistance. When we got into the visitation room, a bunch of teenagers ran up to him.

"Mr. King, Mr. King ... How are you?" they asked in unison as they shook his hand one by one. I handed him the books, he smiled and said aloud, "Class, this is Mr. Robinson and he'll be sitting in class with us today. Maybe he'll share his story and provide some great insights to you all, as well."

"Welcome Mr. Robinson," they said as they clapped, greeting me to the Scared Straight Program. I couldn't believe it; P-nut finally got me to assist him with the program.

The program's mission: to help young people make wiser and more productive decisions. All fifteen participants were on some sort of probation and had to successfully complete the program before returning to the judge in six months. If they completed the program upon Mr. King's and their teacher's approval, then the judge would not send them to the detention center.

I began observing the class as P-nut started to go over prog-ress reports each of their teachers had written up on them. It was apparent each person was making a conscious choice to become a productive citizen. I was happy to see that they were truly seeking a different direction in life than the route they were originally taking.

The class was run in a Round Robin style, where each partici-pant would take turns to speak on how they prevented themselves from stealing, getting into fights, or any other delinquent behaviors. I was impressed with how P-nut responded to each of the participants' discussion and taught them how to be proactive instead of reactive. From time to time, I would jump in and provide feedback too.

During the session, I started reflecting back on my adolescent years. I was a lot like these here teens … Just living and not having a purpose or goals set, except what I learned from my environment … What I saw Uncle Ricky and others do. Hmm, I wonder what would have happened if I was in a program like this?

When I snapped out of my inner dialogue, I heard P-nut insist that each of them write down their short-term and long-term goals. Then he paused and looked at every last one of them and firmly said, "Don't let me down. You have a chance at life to be anybody you choose to be … besides a criminal and breaking the law."

After the class was over, we walked back to the dorm and P-nut began laughing out loud.

"Man, after all this time of trying to get you to come join me in this group, I finally got you up there. But the timing was right, because you were mentally and spiritually ready for it."

"Yeah, you got me. But you're right, I was ready and I have to admit, I enjoyed every minute of it." And from that session on, I participated in every meeting that was held once a month with P-nut and became one of the mentors of the program.

P-nut would load me up on books to sharpen my intellect and that would help me further my understanding of my purpose and direction in life. Because I still wanted to be successful and be able to support my family and give my children the opportunities that

I refused to take advantage of, I read two particular books daily. The books were by the author Stephen R. Covey, titled "First Things First," and "The Seven Habits of Highly Effective People." In "First Things First," there were several passages and quotes that I would read daily to help me along, but there were two that grasp my attention the most. The first one was, "Every breakthrough is a break with a letting go. As we work to put first things first in our lives, it may be time for us to let go of things that are holding us back, keeping us from making the contributions we could make."

And the second one was, "Life is learning from our mistakes as well as our successes. The only real mistake in life, said one, is the mistake not learned from."

Those two quotes were a constant reminder of what my sole purpose was in life.

I made a conscious choice to interact with individuals who were seeking the same out of their lives as I was. The old adage, "birds of a feather flock together" is true, whether good, bad or indifferent; and the flock I would associate with had to be those who wanted to build from their experiences, as a lesson well learned and a lesson to teach.

After hours and days of reading and spending time with P-nut, things were becoming clearer and clearer. I realized that my goal in life was to achieve all along, but only with and through God. My old days of destroying the community with the drugs I sold were over. I wanted to start giving back to the world that I once helped to destroy. My mission became to be of service and provide opportunities for others who were seeking a way out of non-conducive lifestyles.

Then one day upon waking, I had a revelation. I quickly grabbed a piece of paper and wrote it down. My purpose is to share my life experiences with others … all ages, genders and races because we all have fallen short at one point or another. However, it's the ones who know what caused them to fall, who learn from it and get back up, who will be able to make it in life. My purpose: to inspire the fallen—through my experiences—to get back up.

Chapter 18

When It Rains, It Pours

As the end was nearing, time seemed to be moving slowly, and event after event seemed to be hitting home repeatedly. Because of completely losing my life savings, my last few months in prison became extremely hard financially. I went from the saying that we used in the ghetto, "Penitentiary Rich", to a state of completely being penniless. My only means of survival and making it through was my faith in the Lord, and the job that the prison provided for inmates for thirty-five cents an hour.

One day I went to call my mother and her phone had gotten disconnected. I later found out it was from all the collect calls I had made so our only means of communication was through weekly mail. Then out of nowhere, the housing crisis hit right in my mother's front yard. Her mortgage company ordered her to pay the behind mortgage balance in full or if she didn't, her home would go into foreclosure. After reading the horrible news in the letter my mom wrote to me, I began to panic because my mom's home was my release address. Having a release address was crucial, because if I didn't have a home plan, there was a great chance that my release date would be delayed until the prison could find me one of their local shelters, known as a "Re-Entry Program." The shock of news was enough to make me fall to my knees, but I kept my composure and wondered, Lord, how much more will You bear upon me? Yet in my moment of uncertainty, God used my mom's attitude towards her circumstances as the answer to my question. Although my mom became unemployed and had no means of surviving, through her letters I noticed her faith in God never changed ... She never questioned His will. She would simply rejoice by saying, "Baby, God is working and I'm going to continue to allow Him to do His will. We are turning a new leaf. Remember the story of Job ... Be of good cheer, Bookie." Every time I read my mother's letters I was encouraged.

One day, while reading the *Virginia Pilot,* my local hometown newspaper, I noticed a front page article written in bold letters stating, "Heroin Drug Operation Indicted." As I read the article, I noticed that one of the photos of the ten men who were indicted during the round up was my cousin, Anthracite Britton; he was at the top of the lineup. The article read that the Feds were investigating him since the early nineties, but could never catch him red-handed, or to get someone to infiltrate him or his operations. I thought to myself, *my cousin who had been a part of my illegal activities for many years, who had built a prosperous and lucrative business ... Damn, after all these years of evading the penal system, my favorite cousin now has to travel down this lonely dark road until he's able to come to grips of what's done in the dark, shall surely become known. All I can do now is keep him in my prayers.*

Time was finally here for me to be released. I had two weeks before I actually walked out of those gates once again. I continued on my regular schedule in prison, which was working in the kitchen eight hours a day five days a week, working out, reading the Bible to gain spiritual faith, and reading the *Virginia Pilot* newspaper. Then one day, as I read the obituaries in the *Virginia Pilot,* I noticed the name Willie Britton with a photo underneath. Immediately my heart dropped because the photo of the individual resembled me, but an older version. While I read the obituary I saw my name with the rest of my family members. Unexpectedly, tears started to instantly flow down my face. Damn, why am I shedding tears? I had never gotten a chance to really know the man who was considered my biological father besides the memories I had as a youngster and what little my mom and family would tell me about him. Shortly after reading the obituary, I received a letter from my mom informing me that in fact, the man who helped conceive me was now deceased.

The letter read, "Dear Bookie, I'm writing you to say that I love you, but God loves you first ..." She then went on to describe the event of my father's death. "He was found dead in his apartment a week later after his neighbors noticed that he hadn't been around or coming and going daily. They had gotten suspicious when they smelled an unusual strong and unpleasant odor in the hallway." My mother told me that one particular lady decided that she would knock on the door. "As she knocked on the door she could hear the music coming from the radio and after repeatedly knocking, she turned the knob to find that the door was unlocked. When she entered the apartment, the lady noticed your father lying dead on the couch with dried up foam running from his mouth and the syringe still in place sticking directly in the center of his arm."

My mother told me the lady panicked for a minute and then regained her composure and began looking around the apartment for my father's phone to call 911; she found the phone sitting on a safe next to an open closet with a couple of hundred dollar bills scattered around a couple of bulging pillow cases sitting on the floor. She dialed 911 and as the operator took her call, she stated to my mom that something told her to open the pillowcases to see exactly what contents resembled rectangular shape like objects. My mother then said that the woman paused, because the curiosity was killing her. She stared at the pillowcases as she continued to hear the operator repeatedly ask, "Ma'am, are you there? This is the operator 911."

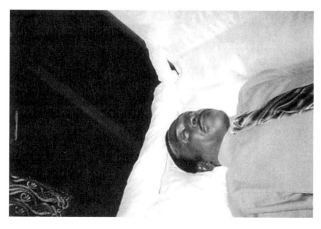

A photo I received of the final viewing of my father's body.

Chapter 19

Fear of Failure

T ODAY I WAS WATCHING THE NEWS AND THEY SAID THE STATE OF THE ECONOMY has many concerned as the jobless rate continues to climb. The news reports are predicting dire consequences for many Americans. When I picked up the newspapers, it's saying that the tough economic times could last for up to five years. The state of our nation was feeding my fear of failure and I became nervous about what was to come.

Soon my thoughts turned to my children and how I would take care of them. Then all of a sudden, my anxiety level became high as I began to anticipate my reunion with them. I began to wonder ... *What kind of father I will be? Can I even be a father after all these years of being incarcerated? I don't want to fail them. A father is supposed to lead by example, and thus far, my examples ... Is it possible I could use my downfalls to their benefit? Teach them to go down a better path than I chose? I guess teaching them my errors in life is where I can begin, and I pray that God will help guide me to show them to do better than I did.*

Chapter 20

You Can Run, But You Can't Hide

TODAY I GOT WORD THAT MY FRIEND AND BROTHER, TIM MONTGOMERY, WAS sentenced by a Federal Judge in Norfolk, Virginia to 5 years in prison for his involvement in conspiracy to distribute 100 grams of heroin. The sentence will run consecutively with the 4 years given by a Federal Judge in New York for his involvement in the 5 million dollar check cashing fraud. After Tim's sentencing hearing, my mother joined Tim's parents and his brother for dinner. My mother and Mrs. Montgomery talked about the 15-year friendship Tim and I shared, and about the special bond that we both had.

Just like the dinner conversation between our parents, Tim wrote a letter to me that expressed the friendship that he and I shared.

"Dawg, we been boys for a long time. I need you to hold me down and write me why I'm up in here," he told me while I laughed reading the sentence. I thought it was hilarious how the tables were now turned. While I was down, he talked to me via phone a few times and then cut off all his communication with me to put his attention into the streets. Although I'm on my way out soon and he has to serve his time, I thought on a much different level and decided not to treat him how he treated me. It would have been petty to do; besides my focus was on how to prosper and stay free from incarceration once I got out. Thinking about this made me realize that Tim would probably have to go through what I had before he is delivered from the life of the streets, a life that never should have been a part of his life in the first place; not with the opportunities that he was fortunate to have.

Of course, I wrote him back and told him I would honor his request and hold him down. I did so because I loved him like a brother, but also for more than that; I was going to be there for him because I knew what he was going to be dealing with. Being locked up ain't no joke.

In another letter I received from Tim, he told me that he now realizes that my intentions where he was concerned were in his best interest and that unfortunately, he failed to take heed to my warnings that the Feds were closing in on him. "I wish I listened to you, dawg," he said at the end of the letter, and then signed it, Your Friend, Tim. Tim and I's friendship began to grow back stronger. We were communicating again and I began to trust in his words and his new faith in God; funny how tragedy can bring someone close to God.

One day I received another letter from Tim about his brother Jamar Montgomery. He told me that he encouraged his brother to come visit me so that we could bond with one another before my release. He said, "Dawg, I want you to be there for my baby brother, since I can't." I was honored that he trusted me to befriend his own 'blood' brother.

When Jamar first visited me, I could see not only how his physical attributes were similar to Tim's, but how Jamar had a taste for the finer things in life because of the lifestyle his brother had introduced him to. Jamar told me that Tim's nightclub, Encore, that he was in co-ownership with Tony Gonzalez, had lost its liquor license and was being shut down because of the illegal activities that continued to repeatedly occur.

"Since Tim's indictment and the demise of Encore, I'm finding it very difficult to maintain and uphold the lifestyle I once lived because my brother was the one who helped support me," he said anxiously. He then told me that he was looking forward to me coming home and creating a new foundation ... a prosperous business that would allow him and me to build what I and his brother once had, but legally.

Tim became victim to the feeling of invincibility, which was also a part of my thought patterns. He at times felt that he was above the law, he thought he was untouchable. Case in point: After Tim was sentenced by the Federal Judge in New York to 4 years of house arrest, he turned around and shafted the Feds by involving himself in illegal drug sales. Unfortunately, Tim had no concept of the Federal authorities' reach. Unbeknownst to him, the Feds were not only watching him, but they were filming his activities. He was unaware that an infiltrator had been assigned the task of setting him up by purchasing heroine from him. He was caught with his pants down, due in part to his trust in others who only wanted to see his downfall.

Most mortal men would have laid low after being given a slap on the wrist, but not Tim, he was built up as the 'fastest man' on the planet, so his mindset was that he could literally out-run the Feds. In Tim's mind, his house arrest sentence for a five million dollar check cashing fraud was testament that he was above the law. God had blessed Tim with a light sentence for a major fraud case and he viewed this as a license to continue in his illegal endeavors.

Tim's check fraud case drew national attention from every news organization, CNN, Fox, CBS, ABC, NBC, and ESPN; his cooperation with authorities resulted in the arrest of Marion Jones' involvement in the check scam that was also publicized. The public wasn't initially told of his sentence of house arrest instead of prison.

Nevertheless, Tim still the risk taker, decided to roll the dice one more time and as a result, he crapped out and ended up copping a plea for his conspiracy to distribute 100 grams of heroin. What Tim now had lost was his freedom, access to his children as well as losing a good woman in Marion. God had put all the pieces of living a good life in Tim's hands, but the temptation of the street was more powerful. The pressure of keeping it real and don't forget where you came from, led him to the street life.

How can one explain a multimillionaire, who owns homes in Virginia Beach, VA; Charlotte, NC; as well as property in his home state of South Carolina, drives fancy cars and drinks $1500 bottles of wine, and then ends up serving time for conspiracy to sell drugs? How does one fathom that? There can only be one explanation, and that is, greed!

Tim became lost; he wanted to be in two worlds at once, the world of the elite and the underworld. However, the two didn't mix well together.

There is that simple, plain truth that can't be eluded, "We as human beings will make mistakes in our lives, but it is what we do next when we realize the error of our ways." 'God only knows', is a very popular cliché that everyone on the planet has at some point in their life used. Yet, I don't really believe that people have sat down and really taken stock of the profound meaning behind it. When we profess, 'God only knows', we need to truly start paying attention to the Word of God and let His prescription be our remedy for what ails us. How else will people be able to survive the constant attacks from the devil? We should allow His Word to be the medicine that heals our souls.

Tim has found God again and he has remorse for the crimes he committed. He tells me he has direction and is focused on the things that really and truly matter. However, the story doesn't end with this, not yet at least.

I know how wounded Tim is … Therefore, I have to be there to support him. I'll do everything I can to make his bid comfortable as can be. I'll assist him by putting the rebuilding blocks in place so that Tim has a legitimate endeavor to come home to. I pray that Tim comes out of this wiser and stronger in his faith in the Lord. I also pray for his safety and well being while inside and for all his family and friends as well; for we all need affirming words that manifest peace and harmony in our lives daily.

I hope that Tim is fortunate enough to find and maintain a relationship with another wonderful woman such as Marion Jones, and that they will know true happiness and have a long and fulfilling life together. Life sometimes comes down to one thing, how you see your situations. Tim, myself included, could be dead or we could be in prison for the rest of our lives. There is no way of determining what may befall you when you are in the life of the streets. Look at the history of others who thought that they were untouchable; some died an early death, some will die behind bars, but the point is that, when you have been given a second chance in life you need to look at your past and make a conscious decision which way you would want to live or die.

In September, Marion Jones was released from federal prison. Marion is living in Texas with her two children and husband. She has chosen to live a better life for herself and her family. Marion had mothered a son by Tim and it is unclear whether Tim will ever have a relationship with their son or not. It is my hope that Tim and Marion do not make their son suffer for the poor decisions they have made. They both are responsible for all that has happened and they both have to bear the burden of their actions, however their child needs both his mom and dad. I can understand Marion's anger towards Tim, because she willingly lied to protect him and herself, and he did not return the favor. Knowing Tim, he was probably afraid of what may become of him, so he implicated Marion in both the check fraud and the BALCO case.

Marion stood up, while Tim started to crumble under Federal pressure. Marion offered her apologies to the public and became a hero to millions of people for admitting her shortcomings in the public eye. Both Marion and Tim made great achievements, and even though they will probably be greatly remembered for their mistakes, I hope that people will remember them for their achievements and contributions to sports, for the once inspired millions around the world and right here at home. We are a society of forgiving souls, can I beg of you all to forgive Tim and Marion ... forgive Mr. Barry Bonds if he is found guilty in the BALCO case, and forgive all those who have transgressed against you and you too will be blessed. It is utterly impossible for you to achieve revenge, only God has the power of retribution, as His Son is my Savior, so shall He be my Avenger.

Chapter 21

Man in the Mirror

Money, power, and greed have fueled man throughout history; and it has revealed itself in the form of materialism in our country. What people fail to understand is that poor people want money too. They want to have nice clothes, fancy cars and luxury homes. Yet, in this competitive world, how does the poor compete? By no means am I advocating for the use of crime to acquire money, however the truth is that, while the rich get richer, the poor get poorer. Money seems to rule the world and those without it are left behind. As a result, many without monetary stability and comfort pursue diverse avenues to get it—and the avenue I chose was drugs.

Drugs have been dropped off at America's doorstep for over a hundred years, particularly at "Black America's" doorstep; and the overall result has been devastating to all the people of this country. I was once one of these young Black men who thought that selling drugs would deliver me to a life of wealth and happiness. I did not want to be a 'have not' person. I became consumed with materialism, fascinated by big expensive luxury cars and obsessed with money and getting it. My judgment had been impaired by years of taking risks and living dangerously on the edge. I was a thrill seeker, and I longed for the dollar bill and street adventure.

Growing up poor and at times hungry, made a person like me somewhat desperate at times. I am not trying to justify my actions, but instead give you a better understanding of how my vision became clouded. My environmental circumstances compelled me to take chances with my life as well as my freedom; and it was very difficult to see the wrong in my behaviors. During those times, it was a no-brainer for me; I chose the street grind, made my paper and learned to duck the law to achieve a 'better' life. I weighed the risk of my actions versus the rewards and benefits I would receive, and strongly 'believed' the rewards and benefits were worth the risks; therefore I carried on with my negative behaviors, although it never added up to anything positive or long lasting.

Sitting in prison has afforded me years of solitary thinking ... I have had flashes of my life travel through my mind a thousand times over; playing like a movie, scene by scene. With only months left to serve, my anxiety and fear levels rise as I get ready to re-enter society, but I know I will persevere. My life experiences are rich with teachings and lessons learned. I have emerged from my journey a smarter and wiser person, and am more determined to be a success, not only in my life for myself and my family, but also as a shining example for the masses in my, and all, communities.

It is now abundantly clear to me that going after the 'fast' buck will only drag one into a life of crime and misery. I know that I have to make honorable moves that will bring about positive results in my life; physically, mentally, emotionally, financially and spiritually. I have learned the value of being last. I know now that suffering builds character, and that hard work for what you want in life, has with it great benefits. I am a proud Black Man, and I have a great abundance of fortitude to stand with, and even to oppose negativity. I believe that I am a completely a new man. I have realized that God has a plan for me, something very special, very important; how else can it be explained that I have been literally pulled from the depths of hell and provided a second chance?

This book was written by me for more than one reason. Living a life of evil is inescapable, and therefore it is something that you will have to deal with under the terms of God. You have the choice, you have free-will, and the choices that we make are what transform our existence into the life we live, and your life is your master-work. So do it right!

Another reason I wrote this book is because I love you—I love myself and we are here together on this earth and we need each other. We need each other to be the best we can be, so we can make this world the best it can be. If I can contribute this work to this plight, with the hopes that it will make you re-evaluate your life, or to just think and become aware of what may lie ahead for you in your travels in life, then I have done my job.

Please remember, what may have worked out for me in the book may not work out for you. Are you willing to risk it ... your life? All the people in this book risked it, and they are now either incarcerated or just being released. This cycle of disparity will continue as long as people let greed and crime guide their ways and actions. With that said, if we all don't come back to the Lord and get our lives properly in order, we will see more of the same misery and hardship that we are facing today. This I honestly believe is only the beginning of what may very well be the benchmark for the end of days.

We were once hailed as one of the greatest nations on the face of the earth; that's because we were in the God's favor then. Now, our country, America, is in its worse shape ever in history, not merely because of the financial crisis, but because our morality has declined. I honestly believe we all can get back in God's favor by acknowledging Him and begin to display our kindness by helping others, as He would want us to do.

Ask yourselves, "What can I do to be of service?"

I say: *Be a help to your family and friends, and community by making positive contributions. Be an asset and not a liability. It really doesn't matter what it is, as long as it is something to make a positive difference. So starting today, no matter what you do, make it a good thing and do it now. Time is of the essence!*

When I am released from prison, I will repair my relationships with my children. This is my sacred duty and one that I look forward to. I also have to make amends to those whom I have hurt; this may be difficult, but with God by my side, I will make every attempt to do it.

I hope *Broken Silence of the Elite* inspires all those who read it and even those that may garner knowledge from those who speak of it. Its intent is to enlighten you, awaken you, entertain you, and to teach you very vital lessons that will reveal the path most traveled by those who don't actually want the best for humanity, while simultaneously revealing the path that is required for the same people to begin the difficult task of healing themselves spiritually, emotionally and mentally. If this book inspires just one soul to greatness, or saves one soul from the trappings of the game, or causes one man, woman, or youth to exercise proper decision-making skills, then it will have a priceless venture and be well worth my efforts.

Broken Silence of the Elite … This is my story and it was my life!

I Got to Believe

Seen many days that the sun didn't shine impossible feets to climb despair and misery crucifing my mind regret for what I can't change is the spear stuck in my side bleeding out and hope and inspiration that no longer feeds me, but feeds the ground and yet the gravity of its weight is pulling my down, where the footsteps of ants are louder, than friends of once upon a time, voice making a sound, or still being around take a journey through my life maybe you can retrieve my lost smile give it back for this frown cause I'd rather be a happy peasant than a puppet king, with thorns for a crown a macho man on the street, but in the courts just average statistical clown imprisoned by my actions, genetically inherited from Momma's family tree, internal war violence and misery, the remedy was drugs over my siblings and me it hurts to breathe, these truths I grieve yesterday I was climbing a mountain today I'm in the valley, as a fallen leaf amongst other fallen leaves telling the story of a wounded warrior defining glory that nobody believes; envy it breeds cause we're all in the same boat sailing the seas of our sinful deeds the waters deep, the fog is thick my faith is weak, all the delicacies in, which negativity feeds and, still in order to obtain the promise I must step out of the boat walk on water through the darkness and mountains are achieved so i got to believe ... I Got to believe ... I got to believe no other option is the way to succeed let the doubters and the critics all inspire my dreams set the wants aside for now and concentrate on my needs strategy before strength, against my enemies and let the God within direct my destiny it's hard to swim against a current that pessimistic when your strokes are optimistic and the way to escape, is seeing a picture beyond a picture and yet you're not creative, nor consciously artistic that be me speaking from the mirror hoping the key to emancipation is stepping outside of myself, just to see myself clearer cause inside of me, I often question who speaks the prisoner, the imprisoned, the conscious minded or the suppressed man of the past who hunger for the street ant been put totally to sleep it's hard to see the bright future when the present seems so dark and deep be inspired by a preacher, who hasn't walked the beat or felt the heat hustle to bring some comfort, to a momma's weary feet substitute the welfare cheese and honey for just a crumb of the good life and the choice cut meat, accept the belief humble and meek when I'm surrounded by the heart of wolves disguised as sheep the feast of the predators, are the bones of the weak but I got to believe, that from the dirt of the cocoon a butterfly I'm destined to because though the storms keep on raging God's grace is the air upon this tenacious will unbowed and determined in me ... so I got to believe ... I Got to believe ... I Got to believe—no other option is the way to succeed let doubters, the critic all inspire my dreams set the wants aside for now and concentrate on my needs strategy before strength against my enemies and let the God within direct my destiny.

Me on Tim Montgomery's private golf course with a bottle of Cristal that Tim had given me to celebrate my release at his mansion in North Carolina.

Tim Montgomery, his children and Marion with her and Tim's son sitting in her lap.

One of Tim Montgomery's many luxury cars, 500 Mercedes Benz (Tim is standing left-rear of car).

Encore Night Club VIP room.

Encore Night Club VIP room, equipped with bed.

ENCORE CLOSES AFTER LOSING ITS LIQUOR LICENSE

By Patrick Wilson
The Virginian-Pilot

The Virginia Alcoholic Beverage Control Board has revoked the liquor license for a club the city said was plagued by violent crime.

The Encore Lounge is closing, according to ABC documents. The building appeared deserted Friday.

The decision to revoke the club's licenses for beer and wine and mixed drinks was made at a hearing March 6.

In December, a Circuit Court judge issued a temporary injunction suspending the licenses after the city went to court to stop alcohol sales at the club at 1889 Virginia Beach Blvd.

Police said in December they were called to the club 116 times in 2008. In addition, police documented 24 instances of fights, gunshots and disorderly conduct.

Former track star Tim Montgomery had been a partner at the club. He is now serving a five-year sentence for selling heroin at Encore.

News article clipping from the *Virginia Pilot* describing the demise of Tim Montgomery's nightclub.

Tim Montgomery posing with an eager fan at his nightclub.

5-18-2009

A picture Tim Montgomery sent to me posing with other inmates in prison (Tim is on the front right side).

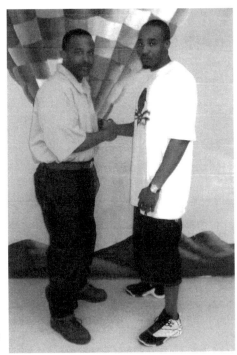

Tim's brother, Jamar Montgomery, visiting me while in prison.

What's up 1st am a 100%
and I have love for you and your
family and after going through this
shit a real friend is hard to find
and I want waste a person time
never again in life I just did a
show for HBO that will be on T.V
Nov 25 and after that the book people
will find me you know I have info
about Barry bonds, Bricks, Boy and so
many people but that's in do time
I got you and we will work
together but 1st you have to
touch 2nd I have to go with
the best agent and then put you
on after what happen to me
out there I pray 1st and think
2nd and then do 3rd So take your
time and you will be bless and
4yrs I should only have 5yrs do
to the cut and out of 5yrs I will have
to do 3yr at most and if New York come
back and help out I will be free by
aug 2009 but I will have to just

This is an excerpt from Tim Montgomery's first letter written to me from prison from the beginning of the book.

My daughter's mother and I during our youth.

241

My grandparents and me at their house.

A group of friends and me hanging out at the club (Boo-Bee is bottom right person in the plaid shirt).

Donna Bly showing off the wedding ring I gave her.

A photo Donna Bly sent to me of her chillin' in Hawaii during her stay to support her brother, Dre Bly, in the Pro Bowl.

Donna Bly in 2010, supporting my company Conscious Minds Publishing (CMP).

Long Jewelers

2817 Shore Drive   Cape Henry Plaza   Virginia Beach, VA   23451
(757) 496-9099

Property Of: Willie L. Robinson   Date: October 25, 2004

Address: 1723 Oakfield Avenue Norfolk, Virginia 23523

Jewelry Identification and Appraisal

The value(s) expressed herein is based on the appraiser's best judgment & opinion and is not a representative or warranty that the item(s) will realize that value if offered for sale at auction or otherwise. The value(s) expressed is based on current information, excluding federal, state, of local taxes, on the date indicated, and no opinion is hereby expressed as to any past of future value unless otherwise stated. I shall in no way be responsible or liable for the results of any action taken on the basis of this report.

Article(s)	Estimated Retail Replacement Cost

One stainless steel Breitling men's wristwatch. The Brietling is a Crosswind special model
from the Windrider line by Brietling. The round black face of the wristwatch is stamped
Breitling, 1884, features luminous hands with a second hand sweep, and three subdials.
The back of the case is stamped Chronographe certifie chronometer, manufacture en
Swisse entache 100 M, Breitling 1884 , A44355, 412176. The flip lock case is stamped
Registered Model, Stainless Steel, Swiss Made Breitling, Breitling 1884. The wristwatch
and bracelet have been modified and set with two hundred forty three round brilliant
diamonds. There is currently no information available to me as to if this was a special order
by Breitling or after market modification. There should be two hundred forty four diamonds,
currently one diamond is missing. The wristwatch features a diamond dial, case, and band.
The two hundred forty three round brilliant diamonds range in size from 1.8 mm, 2 mm, and
2.9 mm with a total diamond weight of 9.66 carats by formula with a clarity range of SI1 –
SI2 with G-H-I (est.) color.
The Breitling wristwatch has a total diamond weight of 9.66 carats.
Retail Replacement Value New: $21,750.00

M. Mary Henderson Gemologist (GJA)

ote: Mountings can mask important quality factors apparent only before assembly or manufacturing. Unless specifically stated that the stones were removed and graded,
ading and evaluation of mounted gems can only be done with limited testing, measurements, & observation. The stone grading is therefore base in estimates of color and
arity grades. Weight is estimated by way of formula, using the gems approximate diameter and measurements.

Unique (in the middle) celebrating in New York at Club 2000.

Unique (in the middle) celebrating the success of his hit single, "A-yo" with his entourage, Mecca Audio.

One of the first photos I took on my
first night out upon my release with
Olympic Gold Medalist, Sean Merritt.

Catching up with an old friend, Pernell Peace
(a co-defendant of Michael Vick).